T0318334

Slavery and Slaving in African History

This book is a comprehensive history of slavery in Africa from the earliest times to the end of the twentieth century, when slavery in most parts of the continent ceased to exist. It connects the emergence and consolidation of slavery to specific historical forces both internal and external to the African continent. Sean Stilwell pays special attention to the development of settled agriculture, the invention of kinship, "big men" and centralized states, the role of African economic production and exchange, the interaction of local structures of dependence with the external slave trades (transatlantic, trans-Saharan, Indian Ocean), and the impact of colonialism on slavery in the twentieth century. He also provides an introduction to the central debates that have shaped current understanding of slavery in Africa. The book examines different forms of slavery that developed over time in Africa and introduces readers to the lives, work, and struggles of slaves themselves.

Sean Stilwell is Associate Professor of African History at the University of Vermont.

New Approaches to African History

Series Editor
Martin Klein, *University of Toronto*

Editorial Advisors
William Beinart, *University of Oxford*
Mamadou Diouf, *Columbia University*
William Freund, *University of KwaZulu-Natal*
Sandra E. Greene, *Cornell University*
Ray Kea, *University of California, Riverside*
David Newbury, *Smith College*

New Approaches to African History is designed to introduce students to current findings and new ideas in African history. Although each book treats a particular case and is able to stand alone, the format allows the studies to be used as modules in general courses on African history and world history. The cases represent a wide range of topics. Each volume summarizes the state of knowledge on a particular subject for a student who is new to the field. However, the aim is not simply to present views of the literature; it is also to introduce debates on historiographical or substantive issues and may argue for a particular point of view. The aim of the series is to stimulate debate and to challenge students and general readers. The series is not committed to any particular school of thought.

Other Books in the Series:

1. *Africa since 1940* by Frederick Cooper
2. *Muslim Societies in African History* by David Robinson
3. *Reversing Sail: A History of the African Diaspora* by Michael Gomez
4. *The African City: A History* by William Freund
5. *Warfare in Independent Africa* by William Reno
6. *Warfare in African History* by Richard J. Reid
7. *Foreign Intervention in Africa* by Elizabeth Schmidt

Slavery and Slaving in African History

Sean Stilwell
University of Vermont

CAMBRIDGE
UNIVERSITY PRESS

CAMBRIDGE
UNIVERSITY PRESS

University Printing House, Cambridge CB2 8BS, United Kingdom

One Liberty Plaza, 20th Floor, New York, NY 10006, USA

477 Williamstown Road, Port Melbourne, VIC 3207, Australia

314-321, 3rd Floor, Plot 3, Splendor Forum, Jasola District Centre, New Delhi - 110025, India

79 Anson Road, #06-04/06, Singapore 079906

Cambridge University Press is part of the University of Cambridge.

It furthers the University's mission by disseminating knowledge in the pursuit of education, learning and research at the highest international levels of excellence.

www.cambridge.org
Information on this title: www.cambridge.org/9780521171885

First published 2014
Reprinted 2014

A catalogue record for this publication is available from the British Library

Library of Congress Cataloging in Publication data
Stilwell, Sean Arnold, author.
Slavery and slaving in African history / Sean Stilwell, University of Vermont.
    pages   cm. – (New approaches to African history ; 8)
Includes bibliographical references and index.
ISBN 978-1-107-00134-3 (hardback) – ISBN 978-0-521-17188-5 (pbk.)
1. Slavery – Africa – History.   2. Slaves – Africa – Social conditions – History.
3. Slavery – Political aspects – Africa – History.   4. Slavery – Economic aspects – Africa – History.   I. Title.   II. Series: New approaches to African history ; 8.
HT1321.S75   2014
306.3'62096–dc23   2014002449

ISBN 978-1-107-00134-3 Hardback
ISBN 978-0-521-17188-5 Paperback

Contents

Figures

Preface

Slavery and Slaving in African History is a synthetic and interpretive history of slavery in Africa from its earliest manifestations through to the early twentieth century, when slavery in most parts of the continent had ceased to exist. It reconstructs the processes that led to the consolidation of slavery with the broader goal of understanding – as best we can – the lived experience of slaves. Throughout the book, I integrate an analysis of the personal and relational aspect of slavery (between master and slave) into a broader examination of slavery as an institution. I focus especially on the way slavery emerged and changed over time. Mythologies about Africa have often made the study of slavery difficult. In popular imagination, the African past before the twentieth century is often portrayed as fundamentally rural, isolated, unspoiled, simple, and egalitarian. Slavery was rare, while slaves were not exploited as slaves but rather became part of African families. In other cases, Africa is portrayed as little more than the home to unknowable, savage "tribes" gleefully waging war only to sacrifice or sell their victims. An important purpose of *Slavery and Slaving in African History* is to present Africa, Africans, and slavery in a more realistic and accurate way. Africa was historically diverse; indeed, Africans would not have thought of themselves as "African" until quite recently. Before the twentieth century, the most important local allegiances were to kinship groups, religious orders, occupational groups, villages, cities, or states (among many other possibilities). Africans created cities, armies, polities, and religions over the course of centuries. Although African economies are commonly portrayed as subsistence orientated or fundamentally concerned with the redistribution of goods and resources, over time parts of the continent were increasingly orientated toward production and market exchange. People in some regions used currencies in the form of cowrie shells, for example, while groups of merchants sought actively to profit via the exchange of goods. Craft production, international trade, mining, and economic specialization were common. Thus, many different forms of political and economic complexity emerged throughout the African past. Some Africans lived in small-scale – but complex – decentralized communities. Other Africans built coercive and centralized states. In nearly all places, hierarchies developed that were based on who belonged (us) and who did not (them).

In the end, *Slavery and Slaving in African History* demonstrates that Africans used slaves in numbers that rivaled those of the Americas, Ancient Rome, and the Islamic Middle East. By the nineteenth century, many millions of Africans were held in bondage as slaves. Some Africans used slaves to grab new positions of power in decentralized societies. Others used slaves to consolidate state-based political power in response to resistance from other elites or commoners. Yet others used slaves to produce goods that they could not force or convince free people to produce. In places, slavery became a central – or foundational – institution on which African societies and states depended. But there were many kinds of slavery in Africa. I have, therefore, highlighted the ways that similarities *and* differences in African slaveries were tied to specific historical processes, including statecraft, lineage politics, and trade. Slavery was an absolutely critical element of the African past. The impact of slavery was constructive for some (for those who used slaves to build legitimate states, for example), and for others, slavery was profoundly destructive (for those communities pillaged for slaves, for example).

The following chapters examine these themes and transitions. Chapter 1 explores the broad concept of slavery in Africa. It seeks to understand and define the meaning of slavery in both theory and practice. Chapter 2 places those definitions within history. It examines the chronology of slavery from roughly 10,000 years before the Common Era through to the end of slavery at the beginning of the twentieth century. The following four chapters then examine specific themes and moments in the history of slavery in Africa. Chapter 3 aims to understand the dynamics of slavery in decentralized (or horizontal) societies. Chapter 4 explores the important role of slavery in African state formation and consolidation. Chapter 5 turns to the economic history of high-density slavery, including the various external slave trades. Finally, Chapter 6 recounts the reasons for the gradual end of slavery in Africa.

Given the broad nature of the narrative, I have inevitably focused on some places more than on others. I have left some things out. I have used a wide continental lens as well as a narrower one that focuses on specific regions and societies. I have tried to do justice to the specialist knowledge in each region and period and to develop a productive tension between a perspective that places historical change at its center while also exploring the political, economic, and social structures of slavery.

This book first took shape in a bus somewhere between Accra and Cotonou in 2007. During that trip, Marty Klein and I – in the company of many other scholars – first discussed what a new history of slavery in Africa might look like. Although I continued to travel to Nigeria to work on the history of epidemics in colonial Nigeria, the slavery project soon took over; the possibility of writing a book that (hopefully) appeals to both scholars and students, specialists and generalists, and that is broadly interpretive, became simply too exciting for me to ignore. In writing this kind of book, I have incurred a great many formal and informal debts. I owe the many and varied scholars of slavery in (and beyond) Africa a lot. I have used, and sometimes twisted, their work for my own purposes. Some people read the manuscript in draft, others contributed ideas, yet others simply wrote something exciting that I found valuable or intriguing. I thank especially Trevor Getz, Jonathon Glassman, Martin Klein, Murray Last, Paul E. Lovejoy, Patrick Manning, Suzanne Miers, John Edward Philips, and Ehud Toledano. I found Joseph C. Miller's treatment of slaving as a political strategy compelling, although I explored that concept very differently than he no doubt imagined. In this regard I sought especially to highlight the central role of slaves themselves. Given the more general appeal of this book, I made an effort to limit my citations, although I have also tried to make it clear when I owe someone a specific scholarly debt. The editorial board of the *New Approaches to African History* series and two anonymous referees saved me from many mistakes and offered thoughtful suggestions. Likewise, Will Hammell and Sarika Narula at Cambridge University Press were absolutely wonderful. Sarika especially answered my occasionally obsessive questions with good humor. Bhavani Ganesh Kumar at Newgen Knowledge Works expertly guided the manuscript through the production process. Joe LeMonnier did a great job on the maps. The librarians at UVM's Bailey-Howe library helped me in many large and small ways. I am especially lucky to work in the Department of History at the University of Vermont, where I have colleagues who are both supportive and challenging. Here I especially thank Bogac Ergene, a fierce critic; Jon Huener, an occasional pub buddy; and Steve Zdatny, my hockey teammate. Students in my Comparative Slavery seminar at UVM have been the recipients of some of my ideas – which they sometimes critiqued – and for this I thank them. Finally, I have dedicated this book to the late Philip James Shea. To those who knew Phil, my choice might seem odd. Phil lived in and wrote about Northern Nigeria, especially Kano. He was intensely dedicated to his craft and to Hausa history. I think Phil would have no doubt preferred that I finished my work on Nigeria before taking on this project. Yet Phil was also a dedicated teacher and a believer that for history to matter it needed to be read. And he was a supportive and generous colleague. I regret that I am unable to share this finally finished book with him, but I will always be grateful for the many kindnesses, incisive criticism, and warm friendship that he shared with me over the years in Kano.

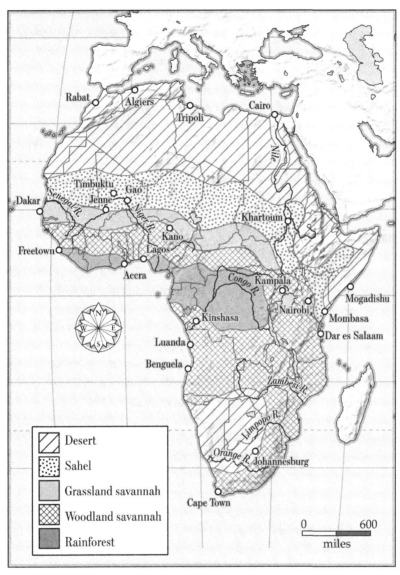

FIGURE 1. Physical map of Africa.

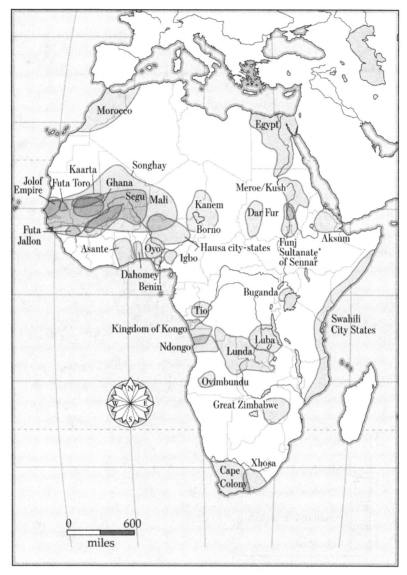

FIGURE 2. Selected African states before 1800 that are mentioned in text.
Note: The borders of these states varied over time.

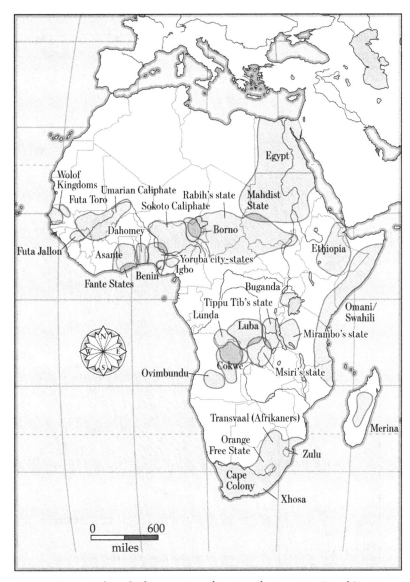

FIGURE 3. Selected African states after 1800 that are mentioned in text.

Note: The borders of these states varied over time.

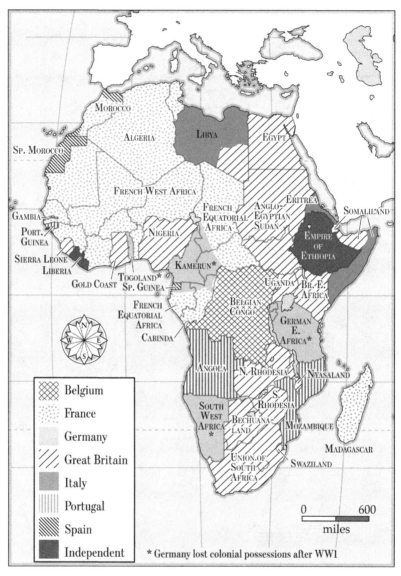

FIGURE 4. Colonial Africa in 1914.

CHAPTER 1

Defining Slavery, Defining Freedom

Introduction

In 1819, Barka became *dan rimi*, a powerful, titled, and official position specifically for slaves in the government of Kano (a major city in the nineteenth-century Sokoto Caliphate – now northern Nigeria). In his capacity as *dan rimi* and over the course of roughly thirty years, Barka advised two emirs – Ibrahim Dabo and Usman – on matters of war, state, and politics. Barka had numerous wives and children all of whom occupied a special section of the palace; wore expensive and ornate robes of state; owned many horses; commanded soldiers; supervised tax collection; and became an absolute force in affairs of state. After his death, a number of Barka's children became *dan rimi* and worked alongside numerous emirs at the highest levels of authority and power. He is well remembered today by his descendants in Kano, Nigeria.[1]

* * *

Msatulwa Mwachitete grew up in Chitete, located in central East Africa, to the west of Lake Malawai, in the house of his father, who had twelve wives. Their home was attacked numerous times by Mkoma of the Inamwanga, who regularly carried off women and children into slavery after setting fire to surrounding villages. During one such

---

[1] Sean Stilwell, *Paradoxes of Power: The Kano Mamluks and Male Royal Slavery in the Sokoto Caliphate* (Portsmouth, NH: Heinemann, 2004), chapter 2.

attack, Msatulwa was captured, along with his mother and brother. He was taken some distance from his home and given as a slave to Mitano. Msatulwa was forced to grind corn, cut firewood, cook, hoe fields, and fetch water, but was eventually given to another person, who treated him better. In the end, Msatulwa found his way home after running away.[2]

* * *

In South Africa, Floris, the slave of Francois Jacobus Roos, gave testimony in front of the assistant protector of slaves in Stellenbosch regarding what he termed an illegal beating given to him by his master. Floris explained that he had been very sick for a number of days, and that he had been sent to his master's father-in-law's farm for a light day's work. He returned home after dark and sat beside the hearth. Another slave entered the room and told Floris that their master was calling for him. Floris then entered the master's house, saluted him, and was asked by his master whether he remembered that his job was to wash his master's feet. Floris said yes, but that he only just learned that he was being asked to do so. Floris then stated that his master beat him over and over again with a stick until it broke. After the beating, he washed his master's feet, and then was beaten again, with a second stick. Roos explained his actions to the assistant protector of slaves by stating that Floris was insolent, had failed to offer the appropriate deference to him, and had not used the appropriate terms of sir or master.[3]

* * *

Chisi was born in roughly 1870 in Nanwanga, now Tanzania. As a child she embarked on a journey with her brother to see her older sister. While she was staying with her sister, she was captured in a raid carried out by the Bemba. All the men of the village were killed and had their heads cut off to be later displayed to the Bemba chief. Chisi was seized along with her sister. Her sister was enslaved and eventually made into a wife by the man who captured both girls. Chisi became a slave of the chief. She stayed as a slave for three years. At the age

---

[2] Marcia Wright, *Strategies of Slaves and Women: Life Stories from East/Central Africa* (New York: Lilian Barber Press, 1993), 59–80.

[3] John Edwin Mason, *Social Death and Resurrection: Slavery and Emancipation in South Africa* (Charlottesville: University Press of Virginia, 2003), 83–84.

of eleven she was sold to four merchants from the coast. In time she escaped and lived with a family headed by Ndeye, who eventually married her. She was mistreated by Ndeye's other wives to such an extent that she did not follow the family when they sought protection with a nearby chief, but in so doing she also had to abandon her children, whom she later managed to recover.[4]

★ ★ ★

Rosine Opo was born in 1832 in Akropong (now located in Ghana) and was the daughter of a slave woman and Kwaw Kutanku. In 1844, Rosine was handed over to Kawku Sae as a wife. Kawku Sae did not purchase her, but instead provided a smaller amount of "head money" to her father. Although Kawku had sexual access to Rosine, she was still a slave that belonged to her father's family because she had not been fully purchased. Rosine grew to hate her domestic situation, and she made trouble for her husband, who ultimately sent her away. In the meantime, Rosine had fallen in love with Charles Irinkeye, a pawn (a free loaned person) of Kwaku Sae's. Charles paid Rosine twelve pounds in order to make her his official wife, but Rosine never paid her first husband Kwaku Sae to end the marriage (by making up the cost of what he initially paid in head money), nor did she or Charles pay her father the head price. Thus, Rosine remained a slave of Kwaw Kutanku, who still had rights over her and her children. Because she and Charles failed to pay her first husband back the head price, Kwaku Sae and his family also had claims over Rosine's children. She eventually turned to Christian missionaries, who she hoped could offer her a way out of these conflicting claims on her person. Eventually, Rosine was snatched from her second husband by her paternal family and given to another headman as a wife. Her six children were divided among family members.[5]

★ ★ ★

Barka, Msatulwa, Floris, Chisi, and Rosine were all slaves in Africa. Yet, each experienced slavery differently. For Barka, slavery provided a route to power and brought him closer to assimilating into the free elite. Over the course of his career as a slave official he grew both

---

[4] Wright, *Strategies of Slaves and Women*, 81–91.
[5] Peter Haenger, *Slaves and Slave Holders on the Gold Coast* (Basel: P. Schlettwein Publishing, 2000), 32–48.

rich and influential. Msatulwa's experience of slavery was defined by powerlessness and violence. He was enslaved through war and was subjected to brutal treatment in the context of an increasingly disordered political situation in nineteenth-century Eastern Africa. Floris experienced humiliation and subordination within slavery. He was not only forced to wash his master's feet, but also severely punished for not acting respectfully, although his master had to defend his actions in front of the protector of slaves. Chisi experienced slavery as a woman and found herself attached to powerful households through marriage in ways that offered opportunities, yet she still suffered from all the uncertainties that came with her status as both a woman and a slave. Finally, Rosine negotiated complex and overlapping networks of dependency as a slave, client, wife, and mother. Her status as wife, daughter, and slave often overlapped. She experienced claims on her person, labor, wealth, and children as a result, yet she did her best to improve and stabilize her social and economic position by using those multiple identities to her advantage.

These different experiences demonstrate just how difficult it is to discuss slavery across a continent as large and complex as Africa. Yet, it is possible. Slavery in Africa was diverse: slaves occupied a wide range of roles and positions in African states and societies. The statuses and treatment of slaves varied dramatically as well. Some found that slavery offered them an opportunity to achieve prominence and power. For others, slavery became the means through which they – although most usually their children – developed ties of belonging as members of kin or other corporate social groups. For yet others, slavery was defined by being bought and sold and then forced to work at tasks ranging from household labor to difficult work on African versions of plantations. Slavery in Africa was not simply a benign path toward greater inclusion, nor was it always defined by violence and hard agricultural labor. Yet, in all cases, slavery in Africa was powerfully conditioned by the ways in which African individuals and corporate groups valued people. It is now axiomatic that in Africa, possession of – or control over – people meant power. Power over people provided access to labor, to the reproductive capacity of female slaves, and to political agents or functionaries who then bolstered the power of elites and other big men. Thus, to understand slavery in Africa, and to appreciate why slaves were often regarded as the ultimate form of wealth in people, we must understand the nature of African ideas about human capital, about value, and more broadly, about belonging.

What Is Slavery?

Slavery and freedom are slippery concepts. For most, slavery conjures images of men on cotton plantations working under the sun and subject to the constant threat of the whip. The key to understanding slavery in Africa is to understand that slavery cannot be defined by the ways slaves were treated or by the jobs they performed. Although plantation slavery existed across parts of the world as varied as Brazil, the American South, West Africa, and ancient Rome, it by no means existed everywhere, nor was it the most common form of slavery. Many slaves labored in non-plantation skilled and unskilled occupations. In Africa, male and female slaves performed a wide variety of jobs – from skilled labor to domestic work to farming to soldiering to tax collection. Additionally, men were not the most commonly used slaves; in many places, including large parts of the African continent, women were more numerous and were the most valuable slaves. Finally, violence is certainly a common theme in all places slavery existed, but violence was not always necessary for slavers and was often the least effective means for getting slaves to do what was needed. Once we remove type of work and type of treatment as the defining features of slavery, what is left? Perhaps the best way to understand slavery is to think of it as being composed of a bundle of traits.[6] The various traits in the bundle that made up slavery varied over time and place. Slavery was not static or changeless. Historical forces altered the nature of slavery. Slavery was a dynamic product of history and of the often accidental choices made by people in history. Sometimes slavery could be largely economic, at other times mainly political, and in yet other circumstances largely social. Most kinds of slavery in Africa would have contained elements from all three categories, stressing one or another depending on historical circumstances.[7]

Clearly, however, we must better develop the key features of the bundle of characteristics that define slavery. Definitions of slavery usually focus on at least one of the following three traits: slaves as kinless outsiders, slaves as property, and/or slaves as violently dominated

---

[6] Suzanne Miers and Igor Kopytoff (eds.), *Slavery in Africa: Historical and Anthropological Perspectives* (Madison: University of Wisconsin Press, 1977), 5.

[7] Also an argument made by Claude Meillassoux (ed.), *L'esclavage en Afrique précoloniale* (Paris: Maspero, 1975), 22–23.

or powerless.[8] In Africa, slavery was composed of a varying degree of all three characteristics, which often overlapped. In virtually all times and places, slaves were outsiders. In other words, they did not belong in any way to the dominant slaveholding society except in relation to their status as slaves. This often meant that slaves had no ties to kinship systems. They were, in effect, anti-kin: outsiders who did not belong and had no families or social ties except those moderated through their master. As Orlando Patterson noted, "Not only was the slave denied all claims on, and obligations to, his parents and living blood relations but, by extension, all such claims and obligations on his more remote ancestors and on his descendants."[9] Scholars have debated the extent to which slaves remained permanent outsiders and the extent to which slaves were gradually absorbed into kinship systems. Suzanne Miers and Igor Kopytoff, for example, argue that the marginality of slaves was gradually reduced as they were incorporated into broader kinship systems, whereas Claude Meillassoux sees slaves as permanently and completely kinless – fundamentally different from all other dependents.[10] In all cases of slavery in Africa, slave status was hereditary. Even when slaves were frequently manumitted or incorporated, the hereditary element of slavery existed initially, and could only be removed by granting the slave a status closer to that of an insider. In many cases – usually in societies with well-developed market systems – slaves were also salable. Turning human beings into property made them exploitable as outsiders and helped maintain their dependent status. Thus, masters gained and maintained control over slaves by virtue of their ability to both buy and sell them, which also ensured that slaves remained outside kinship systems. Obviously, the importance of the chattel/property component depended on the nature of the society in which slaves were used. Finally, violence was a characteristic of slavery in Africa. Slaves were often – albeit not always – produced through violence, usually war or kidnapping. Acts (or threats) of violence reinforced slave status and emphasized the powerlessness of the slave. Slaves were not always subject to violence, but the potential

---

[8] Martin Klein (ed.), *Breaking the Chains: Slavery, Bondage, and Emancipation in Modern Africa and Asia* (Madison: University of Wisconsin Press, 1993), 4.

[9] Orlando Patterson, *Slavery and Social Death: A Comparative Study* (Cambridge, MA: Harvard University Press, 1982), 5 as quoted in Klein, *Breaking the Chains*, 4.

[10] In general, see Miers and Kopytoff, *Slavery in Africa* and Claude Meillassoux, *The Anthropology of Slavery: The Womb of Iron and Gold* (Chicago: University of Chicago Press, 1992).

for violence and the powerlessness of slaves were unique to slavery. This is especially true because slaves tended not to reproduce themselves. Some died and others were manumitted or incorporated. This meant slave populations needed to be continually replaced by new slaves through war or other – most often violent – means.

Although scholars of African slavery generally agree that these characteristics are related to slave status, they also often disagree on which ones to emphasize. Most especially, scholars have debated the extent to which slavery was part of a continuum of dependent statuses that involved claims of rights over persons. The idea is that African societies were organized in ways that sought to make claims on people as kin, as children, as wives, and as slaves. The key question is: can slaves be placed along a continuum of statuses that included kin (those who belonged) by conceptualizing slavery as one institution among many that offered control over rights in persons? Slavery would then be at the most extreme end of dependency, whereas marriage and parentage would be at the least extreme. Slavery was, the argument goes, not the opposite of freedom or kinship but similar to other institutions that emphasized dependency and that served to incorporate Africans into broader corporate groups.[11] Other scholars have pushed back to argue that the incorporative view of African slavery erases the exploitation and struggle central to the institution; indeed, for these scholars, the dependency of slaves was something both unique and special.[12] Slaves were persons who occupied a substantively different status than did those who belonged. In the words of Meillassoux, slavery was the antithesis of kinship. Because slaves were not part of a continuum that included non-slave dependents, incorporation was much more fraught, contested, and problematic. Overall, this debate is about the extent to which we can accept binary definitions of slavery and freedom or of slave/non-slave status in Africa. The usual thinking is that an absolute opposition between slavery and freedom is problematic because it involves the imposition of modern notions about labor, freedom, and individuality on a unique African historical context. While it is indeed imperative to contextualize slavery and freedom within African ideas and histories, this book argues that Africans in most times and places did indeed see slavery and freedom as oppositional. However, African ideas about slavery and freedom were intimately connected to

[11] This view is most commonly associated with the work of Miers and Kopytoff.
[12] Lovejoy and Meillassoux are the main proponents of this position.

conceptions about belonging and not belonging. Africans drew profound distinctions between those who morally, politically, and socially
belonged and those who did not, which were in turn mapped onto
broader social distinctions between slaves and non-slaves.

On Freedom and Belonging: Insiders, Outsiders, and Slavery

Freedom is usually understood as the opposite of slavery. In most
cases, freedom is described in the context of individual or personal
freedom (to do what one pleases) and civic freedom (to be able to
influence and participate in how one is governed).[13] Thus, freedom
conventionally refers to the absence of obligations, dependence, or
other ties that restrict or narrow an individual's right and ability to
make decisions and act autonomously. In many African contexts, freedom might better be defined as the ability or right to belong. In most
African social systems, belonging mattered. Africans could belong
to numerous institutions or corporate groups – some were religious
(Islamic brotherhoods), others occupational (a herder or blacksmith),
and still others political (a state, city, or neighborhood). But in general, to belong meant that one was enmeshed – as an insider – within
reciprocal systems of mutual obligation and patronage organized
around kinship and descent.[14] It meant that one was socially, morally,
and politically a member of the community, which offered broader
opportunities to belong to a variety of institutions within that society,
and which in turn meant one could make claims on the individual
members of those groups. Thus, those who belonged to households,
lineages, and/or states had both obligations and privileges governed by
a wide variety of social norms that were broadly acknowledged.

Not everyone who belonged was equal. Many African corporate
structures were exploitative. Those closest to the center of power
or the highest of statuses, sometimes defined by age, gender, birth,
or wealth, gained the most protections and privileges. Others were

---

[13] Patterson's *Freedom in the Making of Western Culture* is a good introduction to these
concepts. See Patterson, *Freedom in the Making of Western Culture* (New York: Basic
Books, 1991).

[14] In general, see Joseph C. Miller, "Introduction: Women as Slaves and Owners of
Slaves: Experiences from Africa, The Indian Ocean World, and the Early Atlantic"
in Gwyn Campbell, Suzanne Miers, and Joseph C. Miller (eds.), *Women and Slavery,
vol. I: Africa, The Indian Ocean World, and the Medieval North Atlantic* (Athens: Ohio
University Press, 2007), 26.

profoundly dependent on those more powerful and more senior. But the exploitation of dependents was often limited by virtue of the fact that they were insiders. Social subordination was not the equivalent of slavery. Belonging offered protection *and* potential for higher status. Even the least powerful members of a group gained by virtue of their positions as insiders. The benefits of belonging might not have been as substantial for a low-status person as they were for a higher-status individual, but the ability to claim status as an insider was nonetheless valuable, for it was through belonging that one could claim socially sanctioned rights to marry, practice religion, farm, build homes, inherit, have socially recognized children, claim the labor of those children, and many other privileges. These rights were not simply defined by dependence; they offered those who could rightfully claim them autonomy – in the sense that one could exercise rights that provided opportunities, choices, and control, dependent of course on one's social position. Slaves could acquire some of the privileges enjoyed by those who belonged, but these privileges were not normally grounded in their membership within the broader community of the free; instead, they were granted at the prerogative of the master. Even when slaves secured privileges that were more broadly grounded, they were still a product of their specific status as slaves and could be revoked.

Thus, slavery in Africa was based on the distinction between people defined as insiders – those who belonged to and in local and regional social, religious, and political systems – and slaves, who were outsiders. However, slaves in Africa were not just outsiders; they were also understood as kinless. They lacked the social ties to ancestors and progeny that made one an insider and provided webs of patrons and clients on which people could draw for social meaning and for political and economic support. This in turn made slaves especially useful – as workers, political agents, soldiers, or dependents – because their special vulnerability meant that their owners could use them as they saw fit. Slaves could act as high-ranking generals or as lowly farm laborers because they were genealogically isolated and had no or weak claims to social or political capital and support. Contrastingly, the free could access a wide variety of relationships and experience a variety of claims upon their persons. This provided the free with choices and protections, along with the possibility of balancing claims and obligations across different social networks and individuals, often composed of kin. Slaves had only one avenue through which they could access the world of the free: the master. In Buganda, for example,

the opposite of slave was known as a *musenza* or "client/freeman."[15]
The latter could change patrons of their own accord, whereas slaves
could not. They were dependent on their masters and could be used
in whatever way their masters wanted. Nothing better embodies the
position of slaves in this regard than the Swahili proverb: "Slaves have
no words of their own."[16]

Africans usually wanted to acquire slaves who had been transported
far from their homes rather than slaves acquired closer to home.
Mungo Park, who traveled throughout the Senegambian region in the
1790s, noted: "The value of a slave in the eye of an African purchaser
increases in proportion to his distance from his native Kingdom."[17]
Why? Slaves acquired in this way were initially regarded as absolute
outsiders. These slaves had no rights or social identity except as medi-
ated through their master. This made them valuable and especially
useful because they were fully exploitable objects. Likewise, in the
Nkanu region of Igboland (now southeastern Nigeria), even though
slaves were theoretically conceptualized as inferior kin and thereby
brought within the domain of kinship relations, in practice these slaves
suffered profound disabilities that could only be imposed on kinless
outsiders of slave status. They could, for example, be sold or sacrificed,
whereas kin could not be subject to such violence. In addition, while
Igbo masters granted some of their slaves the right to form families,
they were not created or protected in the same way as free families.
In contrast to marriages between free persons, the slave husband did
not pay bridewealth (a payment in goods or service) to his future
father-in-law. Instead, the master of the slave literally purchased a
slave wife for his slave. This meant that, in practice, the master effectively owned the children produced within such a marriage because
the master owned the husband and the wife, their labor power, their
bodies, and whatever their bodies produced. The master could therefore do what he wished with the children produced by these unions,
which included sacrificing them at funerals, selling them, or taking

---

[15] Henri Médard, "Introduction" in Henri Médard and Shane Doyle (eds.), *Slavery in the Great Lakes Region of East Africa* (Athens: Ohio University Press, 2007), 16.

[16] Cited by Jonathon Glassman, *Feasts and Riot: Revelry, Rebellion, and Popular Consciousness on the Swahili Coast. 1856–1888* (Portsmouth, NH: Heinemann, 1995), 79.

[17] Mungo Park, *Travels in the Interior Districts of Africa … in the Years 1795, 1796, and 1797* (London, 1800), 430 cited in James F. Searing, *West African Slavery and Atlantic Commerce: The Senegal River Valley, 1700–1900* (Cambridge: Cambridge University Press, 1993), 54.

them from their families to be used in his own household as domestic labor.[18] It was impossible for the children of free unions to be treated in this manner because they belonged and they possessed rights as well as obligations as a result of their status.

Likewise, in the grassfields of what is now Cameroon, a series of increasingly violent and coercive states emerged over the course of the eighteenth and nineteenth centuries. Political elites accumulated power through their control over people – the labor power of young men and women – via organizations of extended lineages over which they presided. Elder men extracted labor from young men, who in turn looked toward the time when they might take a wife with the help and support of an elder man and assume an elite position. Over time, the demands on younger generations grew; at the same time, it became harder to acquire a wife and achieve any kind of upward mobility. Many young men voted with their feet and left their lineages to begin life in another region under another set of elites, who might adopt them as junior kin and offer them some upward mobility in return for their loyalty and labor. This floating population represented a political threat to those in power. They were viewed as a source of rebellion, and their mobility actually undermined the elite's control over people. Upward mobility was restricted everywhere by limited resources, which in turn caused elite-commoner conflict and further migration that perpetuated the basic social and economic contradiction between accumulation and the demands and expectations of kinship. The ideology of kinship meant that "fathers" were supposed to offer patronage to their "sons," but they were no longer able to do so in addition to accumulating people and resources themselves. Gradually, the most vulnerable among the most disaffected of the mobile population became subject to enslavement. Thus, vulnerable, adopted junior kin who had moved from their original homes in search of upward mobility were made into slaves and sold by traders to other polities in need of labor. Why? These people were now slaves, who could not make claims of belonging and thus could be used by political elites as the ultimate resource: humans who could make no claims based on an ideology of lineage, kinship, or belonging.[19]

---

[18] Carolyn Brown, "Testing the Boundaries of Marginality: Twentieth Century Slavery and Emancipation Struggles in Nkanu, Northern Igboland, 1920–29" in *Journal of African History* 37, 1 (1996), 58.

[19] See Nicolas Argenti, *The Intestines of the State: Youth, Violence and Belated Histories in the Cameroon Grassfields* (Chicago: University of Chicago Press, 2007), 45–56. This

In general we are on strong ground to argue that slaves in Africa were usually produced through violence, were often the objects of a property-like relationship, and initially had the status of kinless outsiders within their host societies. While variations in slavery were common, and it was possible to transcend slave status in some times and places, as an institution, slavery in Africa provided the most efficient and complete means for some human beings to exploit other human beings. Kings valued slaves for different reasons than, for example, merchants, but slaves were valuable to both because they were outsiders and thus were open to more profound exploitation than those who belonged – or the free. As Claire Robertson and Martin Klein argued, slaves were "involuntarily servile," occupied marginal positions with their society, and were "subject to the control of another."[20] This status was hereditary unless the slave was manumitted. To reiterate: slavery in Africa – as in the rest of the world – was fundamentally about economic, sexual, social, or political exploitation.

On Honor and the Master-Slave Relationship

If slaves were usually viewed as persons who did not belong, that status was often represented by their lack of honor. This is not to suggest that slaves could not honor each other, but rather that a central component of a slave's initial status was that he or she was deprived of honor in the eyes of dominant society. Obviously, honor is a historical category – the content of which changed – but the important point is that slaves were initially excluded from whatever it meant to *be honorable* and were thereby excluded from a "right to respect."[21] Slaves were, in short, dishonored as well as kinless outsiders, as Edward Steinhart notes: "The status of slaves as distinct from other forms of dependent labour in pre-colonial society was

process also led to a broader long-distance trade (both into the Atlantic trade and northward into the Islamic Savanna) in slaves, which gave elites access to prestige goods via the exchange.

[20] Claire Robertson and Martin Klein (eds.), *Women and Slavery in Africa* (Portsmouth, NH: Heinemann, 1997), 3.

[21] See John Iliffe, *Honour in African History* (Cambridge: Cambridge University Press, 2005), 4. Iliffe points out that "[H]onour exists both subjectively and objectively. It exists subjectively in the sense that individuals believe they are entitled to respect. But it exists objectively only if others treat them with respect and if individuals can if necessary enforce respect."

far more a matter of the alienation of honour rather than the alienation of labour."[22] It was this "alienation of honor" along with their
initial kinlessness that made the alienation of a slave's labor – and
personhood – possible. The forms this dishonor took in practice varied. Some slaves were made to go naked, given pejorative names or
nicknames, not buried after death, branded, ritually humiliated, or
compared to animals.

To label slaves dishonored outsiders is only one-half of the story,
however. Honor was a contested category. Slaves sought honor within
their own communities and in relation to dominant society. Slaves
often struggled to build religious connections, political alliances,
patron-client ties, and other kinds of relationships that brought privi-
lege and membership within the slaveholding society rather than
struggling to gain an abstract and individualized freedom. In some
times and places, slaves either succeeded in forcing this recognition,
or masters found it in their best interests to recognize the honor of
individual slaves (as distinct from slaves as a broad status category).
This is what makes charting the socio-legal boundaries of slavery so
complex: the statuses and relationship between insiders and outsiders changed over time, as did the relationship between masters and
slaves. During times of great upheaval, the free often found themselves subject to more profound kinds of exploitation, which in some
cases led insiders to being used in ways that looked like slavery (or,
most often, social and political turmoil led to the enslavement of those
formerly deemed insiders). This could create a blurry distinction
between slaves and other kinds of dependents. In other cases, struggles emerged between masters and slaves over the practice of slavery
itself. The nature of slavery was partially determined by the push and
pull – and the social and psychological relationship – between master and slave. The slave sought acknowledgment, status, and position, which masters offered out of affection, necessity, or self-interest,
which was in turn sometimes recognized by the dominant society. In
other cases, slaves fought to preserve their customary rights and to
reduce new obligations, while their masters looked to reduce their
slave's customary rights and to expand their control over their slaves.
This is what Cooper has called the "continual testing" of the terms of

---

[22] Edward Steinhart, "Slavery and Other Forms of Social Oppression in Ankole, 1890–
1940" in Henri Médard and Shane Doyle (eds.), *Slavery in the Great Lakes Region of
East Africa* (Athens: Ohio University Press, 2007), 198.

servitude by all the parties involved, which could dramatically impact how slavery worked.[23]

Slavery and Other Forms of Dependence in Africa

This leads to a key question of how to sort through the relationship and differences between slavery and other forms of dependency in Africa. It is the argument of this book that slavery was fundamentally different from other institutions – such as marriage – that granted rights over people. By comparing slavery to institutions that seem much closer to slavery, such as debt bondage or pawnship, we can learn a lot about the nature of slavery.

In some parts of Africa, if a person desired a loan or access to goods, the creditor providing those goods might ask for and receive a human being – known as a pawn – from the debtor's family or kin group as security for the debt. The creditor retained the pawn and access to his or her labor until the debt was paid off or satisfied. Thus, pawnship was used to both secure debts and to gain access to people. As far as we know, a majority of pawns were female. Both slavery and pawnship indicate the high value Africans placed on the control over *people* as *dependents*. In some places, pawnship was a marginal institution until the era of the transatlantic slave trade, when increasing commercialization prompted some Africans to use a precious resource – people – to gain access to another, European credit.[24]

Most production in Africa occurred at the household level through the mobilization of client and family labor. Free labor (meaning the labor of free persons) was, therefore, by definition household labor, which tended to be restricted to local, domestic economies. Free labor existed, but the problem was that free laborers were often harder to exploit and were simply not as dependable as slaves. This is why people were so valuable. Without extensive access to reliable wage laborers, Africans acquired more labor by expanding their households through birth or attachment. Pawns offered access to people – the ultimate resource – while also serving as a means to secure credit where

---

[23] See Frederick Cooper, *Plantation Slavery on the East Coast of Africa* (Portsmouth, NH: Heinemann, 1997), 155.

[24] On pawnship in general, see Toyin Falola and Paul E. Lovejoy, *Pawnship in Africa: Debt Bondage in Historical Perspective* (Boulder, CO: Westview Press, 1994).

other forms of credit did not exist. Persons who acquired pawns could thereby mobilize the dependent labor of people who were "more" than slaves but "less" than free.

Pawns were not, however, being sold into slavery. Instead, they remained morally and socially connected to their kin and descent group. They were not supposed to be treated as slaves. Children of a female pawn, for example, did not belong to the owner of the pawn but to the woman's original kin group. Pawning was very different from the practice of seizing people who had failed to pay their debts. Those persons were effectively being enslaved. Although raids, war, and kidnapping were the most common mechanisms to supply slaves in Africa, a portion of slaves originated as debtors. Once enslaved for their debt, they were subject to all the disabilities associated with slave status – including the possibility of being transferred to other owners through sale. Pawns, on the other hand, were not supposed to be bought and sold and were not hereditarily bound to their master. In a sense, they could only be pawned *because* they were kin, and they were, therefore, protected by that status. In times of stress and change, pawns could be and were converted *into* slaves, but this was generally regarded as a violation of the terms of pawnship. Indeed, pawns could not be used *as slaves* until the terms of pawnship were violated, thereby making them into slaves. Thus, pawns had protections that derived from their status as free persons who had kin and belonged, as well as disabilities as persons who were – in effect – being loaned out as lesser dependents. Pawnship was deeply embedded in unequal power relations, but the limitations placed on their exploitation helps explain why slaves were so useful and valuable (in that they had no such protections). To better understand the value placed on people as slaves, we will now turn to a closer examination of household production, African reproductive economies, and the concept of "wealth in people."

Human Capital, Wealth in People, and African Reproductive Economies

In virtually every part of Africa, household-based production was important. In the words of Meillassoux, self-sufficient domestic economies in Africa developed "knowledge of agriculture and craft techniques to run a farm system productively" and used "human labor as the prime energy source."[25] Households composed of extended families and clients were the primary producers, but these households were often incorporated into broader lineages. Lineages were composed of a group of people related by affinity and blood who thought of themselves as historical, political, economic, and social units, and through whom kinship, descent, and inheritance would be shared in a variety of ways. They were often run by elder men, who were sometimes drawn from specific households or in other cases were the most successful individuals within the lineage. In some places, lineages remained the largest political, social, and economic units. In others, lineages were incorporated into broader hierarchical state systems that sought to impose monarchical control over people – often made up of lineages and households – through (for example) coercion or taxation in order to appropriate for the state at least some of what was produced by the domestic economy.

These African political economies often valued wealth in the form of people rather than wealth in nonhuman forms of capital. People and material goods were in a sense not separate categories of capital, but were intimately linked together. Nonhuman forms of capital – such as commodities or luxury goods – were used to acquire people rather than being sought after for their own inherent value. Why did Africans tend to focus on the social value or economic benefits of the control over people? Attracting and keeping followers was a central problem for most political elites in Africa. In situations where land was readily available for use, or when other political, descent, or religious groupings might be competing for allegiance, the ability to attract and retain a wealth in people was a necessity. Africans gained access to material goods by acquiring rights to or control over the producers who actually made the goods rather than just through exchange or trade. They emphasized the importance of "people as the sources of productivity."[26]

Thus, control over people was a means to accumulate wealth, power, and social status. But it was even more complex than that. In places where households dominated production, Africans sought not to produce material objects for sale, but aimed to secure the physical

[25] As cited by Boubacar Barry, *Senegambia and the Atlantic Slave Trade* (Cambridge: Cambridge University Press, 1988), 30.

[26] Joseph C. Miller, *Way of Death: Merchant Capitalism and the Angolan Slave Trade* 1730–1830 (Madison: University of Wisconsin Press, 1988), 42.

and social reproduction of their communities via control over people in order to gain access to their ability to produce (farm, fish, tend cattle) and physically reproduce (children whose labor power could then be secured). Political elites secured their interests in both the productive and reproductive capacity of people for the future by attaching them and their progeny in dependent and hierarchical relationships. Joseph C. Miller has described this process as "aggregating human dependents."[27] In many parts of Africa, populations suffered from high mortality rates, and were subject to crop failures and fluctuations among other uncertainties, so the key was to acquire not just control over dependents directly, but to place claims on the future labor of as many people as possible by making claims on their descendants – which in effect created an African reproductive economy.[28] This attachment was accomplished in a variety of ways, sometimes by attracting followers, or through the ideology of kinship and descent (where junior members owe something to senior members and who eventually reproduce themselves and thus continue the senior-junior cycle), pawnship, marriage, or – and most important for our purposes – slavery.

Slavery was one of the best ways to claim the actual labor of people as well as to secure control over their future labor. Unlike clients or kin, slaves depended singularly on their master. Slaves were divorced from both the product of their labor and from the product of their fertility. The Bobangi described the relationship between slaves and their masters perfectly: "If I buy a slave, am his father, I am his mother." In other words, a slave *and* his or her progeny had no bonds of kinship or set of relationships beyond the control and power of the master.[29] Thus, the raw capacity of the master to control the slave – the ultimate form of human capital – was not just different in degree from the free, but also in kind. They were kinless. They were outsiders. They were subject to control and violence in a way that was uniquely informed by their powerlessness. Because slave status was inheritable, the master could enforce his sole claim to effective ownership and power over the progeny of his slave dependents, theoretically, in perpetuity. This control over *future* human capital through slavery secured the survival

---

[27] Miller, *Way of Death*, 43

[28] See also Joseph C. Miller, "The Significance of Drought, Disease and Famine in African History" in *Journal of African History* 23, 1 (1982), 17–61.

[29] Robert Harms, "Slave Systems in Africa" in *History in Africa* 5 (1978), 332.

FIGURE 5. Human sacrifice in Dahomey. In Frederick E. Forbes, *Dahomey and the Dahomans: being the journals of two missions to the king of Dahomey, and residence at his capital, in the years 1849 and 1850* (London, 1851; reprinted in 1966), vol. 2, facing page 44. Courtesy of the UVM Bailey-Howe Library.

of households, the domestic reproductive economy, and the wealth-generating capabilities of that economy.

Slaves also had important social uses. In some less stratified, sub-sistence-oriented societies, the role of slaves in production – as well as the ability of masters to extract any surplus from slave labor – was limited. Masters and free people did essentially the same work as their slaves. Slaves were desired instead for their social purpose: as objects of prestige, as objects that could be exchanged for goods in times of shortage, as objects that could be used as a reward, as a follower, as a gift to an ally, or as members of a chief's entourage. Even in complex, highly stratified societies, slaves could sometimes serve an essentially social purpose. In the Kingdoms of Dahomey and Benin, both located in West Africa, slaves were ritually sacrificed as a direct representa-tion of the temporal and spiritual power of their kings, which often occurred at the funerals of important political leaders at ritualized ceremonies throughout the year (Figure 5).[30] In most places, then, slaves were not simply valued for their role in production.

---

[30] See Robin Law, "Human Sacrifice in Pre-Colonial West Africa" in *African Affairs* **84**, 334 (1985), 53–87.

Until now we have referred to reoccurring processes focused mainly at the level of the household and lineage. The lineage ideal did not exist everywhere, nor was that ideal the same across time and space. In some places, other forms of capital – land, cattle, gold mines, or canoes – complicate our picture of people- and household-based production. In other cases, the subsistence-oriented household economies produced surpluses that drove regional and long-distance trade, which later developed into export-oriented economic sectors specializing in the production of goods via the wide-scale use of slave labor. In these societies, local, regional, and long-distance trade represented vital economic activities, and the production and exchange of commodities was a central goal. Coercive states also emerged in places, the leaders of which secured their own economic and political security through the use of slaves in politics, the military, and as producers of goods. As with lineages, political elites of these kinds of African states – ranging from Dahomey to Oyo to the Kingdom of Kongo, for example – looked to secure their social and physical reproduction by amassing and using slaves. Although the scale of this kind of slave use was very different from smaller-scale political units, slaves played a parallel role in large, state-oriented societies: their status as outsiders permitted their exploitation in a manner that was unique and that secured the productive and reproductive capacity of their owners and the political/economic/social systems of which they were a part. The benefits of controlling people – and the role of slaves in that process – was a common theme across the African continent, from small-scale lineage-based societies in the Congo Basin in 1500 to the large-scale, plantation-based economies of the Sokoto Caliphate in 1850. We will now take a closer look at the broader relationship between slavery and different economic and political structures in the African past.

High- and Low-Density Slavery in Africa

Slavery cannot be understood by simply exploring the relationship between master and slave within an ahistorical vacuum. The economic and political structures of the societies that held slaves mattered. Moreover, slavery, the nature of enslavement, and the shape of slaveholding societies changed over time, as did African ideas about freedom and belonging. One way to get at larger patterns of change is to focus on the ways slaves were held, the roles they performed, and

their location in economic, social, and political life. Scholarship on
slavery in Africa has conventionally focused on the fundamental distinction between high- and low-density slavery.[31] Some slaveholding
societies in Africa were high-density slave systems. In these systems,
slaves made up a significant proportion of the population, their use
was economically rationalized, and they were usually important factors in production (often producing commodities for external sale or
internal use). They tended to work in larger, slave-dominated units
rather than within their master's household. Social incorporation
occurred more rarely and when it happened it took more time, was
more precarious, and was usually a product of formal manumission
process that literally made a slave into a free person. In short, slaves
were valued as economic objects and were property. We can charac-
terize huge parts of the Islamic Savanna in West Africa from the sixteenth through the nineteenth centuries, parts of the Swahili coast in
the nineteenth century, Dahomey in the nineteenth century, Asante in
the eighteenth through nineteenth century, the Cape Colony in South
Africa between the eighteenth and nineteenth centuries, and even the
Kingdom of Kongo in central Africa as high-density slave systems. In
low-density slave systems, slaves made up a smaller proportion of the
population. Their role was not solely centered on production, but they
often had important social or political uses, most often related to the
desire of masters to expand their retinues, lineages, or households.
Slaves worked in these lower-density situations, but they did so alongside their masters. They also slept within the same general household
and ate out of the same pot as their masters. Social incorporation
occurred more often and was often a product of gradual assimilation rather than a formal manumission process; furthermore, their
incorporation was in normal circumstances less precarious, although
a social stigma would often persist for a number of generations.

Over time, and sometimes related to the burgeoning transatlantic, trans-Saharan and Indian Ocean slave trades, numerous African
states developed high-density slave systems that relied on the productive labor of a large slave population. However, slavery in Africa
was seldom simply an economic question. Slavery could be a central

---

[31] Moses Finley used the terms "slave societies" and "societies with slaves" for high-
and low-density slave systems; see Chapter 2 and Moses Finley, *Ancient Slavery and
Modern Ideology* (Princeton, NJ: Markus Weiner, 1998). See also James Watson (ed.),
Asian and African Systems of Slavery (Berkeley: University of California Press, 1980).

institution in both low- and high-density slavery. The value of slaves cannot simply be measured by their role in production or productive processes. Slaves were vitally important for the reproduction of kinship and lineage units as well as for the political elites and institutions that composed the basic fabric of many African societies. Slavery could thus be an absolutely central institution in low-density slave societies, in that slaves ensured the social and political reproduction of the society without necessarily engaging in productive labor. The key is to determine the extent to which slavery was institutionalized. Societies that occasionally acquired slaves were very different from societies in which slavery was common and their capture/acquisition/ use was institutionalized through wars, markets, or other means, such as debt.

Open and Closed Slave Systems

There was a relationship between high- and low-density slavery and the social mobility of slaves. Some African slave systems were open. They allowed significant status mobility and opportunities for social incorporation. Others were closed systems that offered little opportunity for movement out of slavery. The more slaves were used in purely economic roles, and the higher the density of slavery, the more likely it was that a closed slave system would predominate. These societies tended to be commercialized and market oriented, and most often viewed slaves as property. Low-density slavery tended to be more open. This was because low-density slavery offered more opportunities for slaves to move toward the center of power and belonging. Slaves in these systems often performed a wide range of occupations that were not simply focused on production. This provided a path to belonging that laboring in the field, isolated from the master's house, simply could not bring. The social and political use of slaves in households often led to gradual incorporation. As slaves adopted local ways, they came to be viewed as something other than complete outsiders. Often women had the best opportunities to make this transition in their capacity as slave wives and as the producers of children who could then be claimed and incorporated. These societies also tended to be less commercialized and connected to markets. The property component of slave status was, as a result, less important. However, low-density slavery was not necessarily less exploitative or benign.

The kinship idiom into which slaves might be incorporated was often a thin veil for profound exploitation, as a Lele man from Kasai in Central Africa stated:

> A slave is a man who will do as he is told. If you send him to draw palm wine in the rain, he goes. You call him brother, age-mate, put your arm around his neck, give him palm wine and meat, so that he is happy. He thinks you love him. Then, when your mother's brother dies, you kill him.[32]

Open and closed slavery are ideal types. They represent two extremes along a much broader continuum. In most cases, the African societies that used slaves were neither completely open nor completely closed, but fell somewhere along the continuum between the two. It was also possible for slaves who worked in one particular sector to operate within a closed system, while those who worked in other sectors in the same society could operate within an open system. But in general the position of slaves as absolute outsiders in high- and low-density slavery was often reduced by offering slaves opportunities to develop ties to the dominant society that moved them closer toward belonging. Slavery in Africa was similar to slavery throughout the globe. Along with the necessity of making people into outsiders, it was often useful for masters to recognize the humanity of slaves and their desire to belong and establish a social identity. To do so enhanced the master's own ability to exploit their slaves by offering slaves a reason to cooperate that did not involve simple violence and naked force. In Africa, one of the key dynamics of this process involved the different statuses of first generation, captured slaves, and those born into slavery in subsequent generations. In Senegambia, the *jaam sayoor* or slaves exposed for sale who survived years of slavery and who were both lucky and trusted by their masters, might be given the chance to form a family and produce offspring. The children of these slave unions – *jaam juddu* ("born slaves") – still worked as slaves, but were given protections and privileges (their own plots of land, wives, release from slavery after marriage) that were a product of their status being closer to "insiders" than captured outsiders.[33] This pattern of providing second- or third-generation slaves with advantages and privileges that resulted from their birth *within* the societies that held their parents in bondage

---

[32] Iliffe, *Honour in African History*, 120, citing Mary Douglas, *The Lele of the Kasai* (London, 1963), 36.

[33] See Searing, *West African Slavery and Atlantic Commerce*, 48–49.

was common throughout Africa, even in high-density slavery. In the Western Sudan, now mainly modern Senegal and Mali, these slaves were often known as "slaves born in the house" of their master. They spoke the languages of the slaveholding societies and were believed to be closer to the status of insider. Yet they were still subject to the power of their master. Although in theory they were not supposed to be sold, in practice they could be sold or abused until they had been formally manumitted and thereby incorporated. In lower-density slavery, where slaves generally were held by kinship/lineage/households and where they were either less directly involved in production or worked alongside the master's family, a distinction was also made between first-generation captured slaves and those born in the house of the master. In low-density slavery, however, social mobility via incorporation for first-generation slaves was far more common than in higher-density slavery.

Open systems of slavery were *not* simply products of uniquely incorporative African social systems, but were rather a product of the fundamental struggle between master and slave. Slaves struggled to have their humanity and social identity acknowledged. To do so, slaves sought to belong, and thus claim as many of an insider's privileges as possible. In some times and places these actions were resisted or denied by masters; in others masters were more willing to accept these kinds of claims. For example, Elizabeth McMahon has shown that on the Swahili coast slaves and masters struggled over inheritance and property rights. McMahon demonstrates that slaves and ex-slaves experienced real disabilities related to their specific statuses, which affirm that slave status was not something transitory or easily shed upon manumission. If a master manumitted a slave, that same slave would continue to be bound to his former master as a client, which was viewed as being similar to a blood relationship. Yet, that social tie – and claims of a blood relationship – did not allow a former slave to claim any property of his master should the former master die. At the same time, the continuing relationship permitted the former master and his heirs to claim the estates of their former slaves, in some cases depriving the former slaves' heirs of all their inheritance.[34] While

---

[34] See Elisabeth McMahon, "'A solitary tree builds not': *Heshima*, community and shifting identity in post-emancipation Pemba Island" in *International Journal of African Historical Studies* **39**, 2 (2006), 197–219 and Elisabeth McMahon, "Slave Wills Along the Swahili Coast" in Alice Bellagamba, Sandra E. Greene, and Martin Klein (eds.), *African Voices on Slavery and the Slave Trade* (Cambridge: Cambridge University Press, 2013), 511–520.

this occurred in the context of colonial rule, and the justification for these claims on the land of former slaves was that slaves had been freed by the colonial state, and thus were in the eyes of Islamic law still slaves, it is clear that distinctions between slaves and those who belonged were immensely important. The need to provide an avenue to incorporate the outsider/slave and the struggle over how close they could come to full belonging were common wherever slaves were used. The contradiction between the status of slaves as outsiders and the fact that over time slaves or their progeny came to look, speak, act, and worship in same manner as insiders became in many places difficult to sustain.

Women, Gender, and Slavery

The majority of slaves in Africa were women. Female slaves contributed to and secured African reproductive economies both as producers and reproducers. Female slaves offered important advantages to African slave owners. As with male slaves, female slaves worked. They hoed fields, prepared food, and hauled firewood, among the many countless labor-intensive tasks some Africans performed on a daily basis. Women were acquired and highly valued for these roles. The owners or users of female slaves might be free women, whose own labor burden could be reduced through the use of female slaves in their household. Yet female slaves also reproduced. They could potentially have children. These children in turn added people to the master's household or lineage. Thus, female slaves were also valued for their role in biological reproduction. If Africans tended to value people, and if many Africans desired control over people as a means to gain access to wealth, productive potential, and status, female slaves could guarantee that masters would have access to a new, initially subservient generation of people via the children of slaves. Female slaves also offered male owners the possibility of sexual access. Females were valued for both their physical and biological roles, but these women could be forced into sexually subservient relationship with their masters. In the Sokoto Caliphate in 1850, the price of female slaves varied depending on the shape and size of the slave's breasts. While "young girls" were valued at 30,000–40,000 cowries and women whose breasts had sagged were worth 20,000 cowries, girls whose breasts had formed were worth 40,000 to 100,000 cowries and women with full breasts

could command 80,000 cowries.[35] Finally, women were often socialized to be more submissive than males. This may have aided in their
gradual incorporation into systems of belonging in the same way that
their role as reproducers – often of the masters' children – might
encourage gradual incorporation in a manner much different than was
possible for male slaves. It is vital to note that this incorporation was
not simple, without limits, or uncontested, but only that the special
roles available to women rather than men might make some kinds of
incorporation more likely – or possible – in certain situations. Indeed,
female slaves might find themselves brought within the structures of
belonging, only to find themselves in extremely subservient roles as a
result of the social status of their owner (i.e., a chief vs. a low-status
farmer) or because of the preexisting gendered and sexual division
of labor that relied on the physical labor of women more than that of
men. Moreover, the children of female slaves often bore a stigma that
emanated from their slave origins, which could limit incorporation or
extend it over a series of generations.

Meillassoux has argued that female slaves were used mainly for
production and were essentially economic objects tied to productive
tasks.[36] While women performed a great deal of agricultural labor,
they were not simply used in this capacity. They were also concubines,
domestics, prostitutes, soldiers, traders, tax collectors, bakers, and
brewers (among many others). Furthermore, Meillassoux argued that
slaves did not reproduce themselves biologically, given the harshness
of slavery and its focus on production. While one must agree that the
overall growth rate of most slave populations could not have been sustained by the biological reproduction of female slaves alone – hence
the continued need to acquire new slaves – this does not mean that
female slaves were not valued for their reproductive potential. Nor
does it mean that masters did not gain from this reproduction or that
slaves did not develop slave unions that resulted in the birth children.
In low-density slavery, women would have been valued primarily for
their roles in the household, and as potential reproducers who in turn
could add dependents and therefore increase the political influence of
her master. In this context they also could have been used as gifts to

---

[35] Paul E. Lovejoy, "Concubinage in the Sokoto Caliphate, 1804–1903" in *Slavery and Abolition* **11**, 2 (1990), 159–189.
[36] See Claude Meillassoux, "Female Slavery" in Klein and Roberston (eds.), *Women and Slavery in Africa*, 50–52.

cement political and social alliances with others. In high-density slavery, women would no doubt have been valued as much for their productive as their reproductive potential, although this too would very much depend on the physical and intellectual attributes of the female slave and the overall aims of her master.

Conclusion: The Dynamics of Slavery in Africa

The life stories of Barka, Msatulwa, Floris, Chisi, and Rosine presented at the beginning of this chapter exemplified the wide range of statuses, occupations, and life experiences of slaves in Africa. Some slaves were bought and sold numerous times and lived out their lives farming for their masters in the company of other slaves; others became powerful politicians and officials and married multiple wives who produced numerous children; still others were acquired as concubines and eventually married free men and made the transition from outsider to insider. Despite the differences in treatment, occupation, and status, slaves in Africa *initially* shared much in common: they were usually produced through violence, were regarded as kinless outsiders, were often treated as property, and were believed to lack honor. Slaves were the ultimate form of human capital in Africa because they were a special kind of dependent: they were moral and social outsiders and therefore uniquely vulnerable and exploitable.

Defining the characteristics of the bundle of traits that made up slavery in Africa tells us little about the actual dynamics of slavery, however. Given the nature of African economies and societies, control over people often translated into power. Africans valued people for their labor power, sexuality, and reproductive potential. From the perspective of the powerful, with use rights over land often available, followers/supporters/dependents were difficult to attract and keep. Elites (whether small-scale household heads or kings) had to walk a fine line between extracting enough wealth or labor from their dependents to ensure their own reproduction and extracting so much that they drove those dependents away or encouraged them to rebel. Slavery emerged as perhaps the most useful means of attaching dependents to households, lineages, and states. Slaves could not make the same claims or expect the same protections as could those who belonged. Attachment through slavery resolved some of the central contradictions faced by African polities, corporate groups, political elites, and big men; namely, it provided a means to better attach *and* better exploit dependents and followers. Slavery reduced the risk that dependents would flee, successfully rebel, or challenge authority. This is not to argue that slaves were well-behaved blank slates. Rather, slaves resisted by claiming rights within slavery, by attempting to develop ties of belonging to the dominant society, or by exploiting their *slave status* to rebel or undermine their masters.

If the use of slaves was the product of strategies designed to acquire people, we still need to understand how slavery operated and was transformed in different political, economic, and social contexts. Slavery was transformed at the level of both the individual (by the variable relationship between master and slave) and the collective (by the nature of states/economies/religion). Individual slaves and masters struggled over the definitions of slavery. Sometimes masters won. Sometimes slaves won. Sometimes masters and slaves came to agreements that benefited them both. The negotiations between slave and master could dramatically alter the practice of slavery as the terms of bondage were negotiated and changed; hence, slaves gained power, families, land, wives, husbands, free status, or horses (among many other things). Slaves might find their roles or status as slaves dramatically transformed within their own lifetimes. On a broader structural level, in some parts of the continent slavers in large hierarchical, market-oriented state systems came to use slaves in large numbers to enhance their ability to extract wealth from their dependents. We have called slavery that was large-scale, economically rationalized, intensively exploitative, and market-oriented high-density slavery. Whereas in situations where commodities, production, and trade were less central, slaves were used in smaller numbers, often in noneconomic roles, which we have termed low-density slavery. While both kinds of slavery valued people, slaves were treated differently, used differently, and incorporated differently. In the cases of both low- and high-density slavery, however, slavery could be an absolutely central institution on which the reproduction (or continuation) of the society depended.

Another way to understand slavery is to focus on the role or use of slaves. In some parts of Africa, political slavery emerged (the use of slave in government/military), in others productive slavery (use of slaves in production), and in others domestic slavery (the use of slaves within households). In some places slaves played all three roles. That slaves could be used in such different tasks demonstrates just how flexible they were given their status. The different uses of slaves impacted in very profound ways the dynamics of slavery in Africa. The use of slaves as soldiers led to a different kind of institution than the use of slaves as domestic help in households, for example. Finally, in all cases where slavery was a centrally important institution, the dynamics of slavery led to the continual need to acquire new slaves. Over time slaves died, were freed, or incorporated. The children of slaves might gain protections and rights that reduced the power of masters to fully exploit them as they moved from complete outsider toward insider. The reproduction of slavery itself depended on the continual acquisition of slaves. Thus, the key to understanding slavery is to ask historical questions about the institution, which we will explore in the following chapter.

CHAPTER 2

Slavery in African History

Introduction

During times of famine, if a father wanted to sell a child in order to buy food, he would first scatter a little millet on the ground and tell the children to gather it up. He would then tell the slave merchant, with whom he had already negotiated a price, to choose the one he wanted. The victim would then be tied up and taken away. In this way, children were sold just like chickens. With the proceeds gained, food could be purchased to sustain the family.[1]

★ ★ ★

Long ago the people up the river were very hungry, and I took some food in my canoe and went to visit them. For this food I bought two little boys, and then returned to my house. When the boys had grown fat and strong, I bought them a gun and gave them spears. Then we went up the river, and the gun frightened the people. They ran away, but we caught three and brought them down with us. I made them build a house for me, and soon I had a town all my own, and my name was feared. So when I went up the river the third time, I easily took more slaves and in this way I became very rich and great.[2]

---

[1] Quoted by Andrew Hubbel, "A View of the Slave Trade from the Margin: Souroudougou in the Late Nineteenth-Century Slave Trade of the Niger Bend" in *The Journal of African History* **42**, 1 (2001), 40.

[2] Quoted by Robert Harms, *River of Wealth, River of Sorrow: The Central Zaire Basin in the Era of the Slave and Ivory Trade,* 1500–1891 (New Haven, CT: Yale University Press, 1981), 36.

* * *

There are heads of clans, male and female, because everywhere each clan has its chief. Within the clan there are two groups, one of free persons, the other of those who have become slaves or 'children of the village.' Those who were there first are the free, those who have been purchased are the slaves. When the free men marry they do not marry each other but marry slaves; however, their children are called slaves, whereas the children of free women are called free. The children of male members of the clan do not inherit membership in it, only the children of free women, who are then also free.[3]

* * *

The slaves cut straw to make huts; a single marabout superintends the slaves of the whole family, or several of his friends; and he assembles them all, sometimes to the number of forty or fifty under the same hut. Every marabout sends as many slaves as he can spare ... the slaves fill their leather bags with water every morning, and furnished with a great forked stick, they traverse the fields in search of gum; as the gum bearing trees are all thorny, this stick is used to knock off from high branches the lumps of gum which could be reached by hand. As they pick it up they put it in their leather bags; and thus they spend the day, without anything but a little water to refresh them ... the superintending marabout receives a portion of the gum; the slaves work for five days for their master, and the sixth for the superintendent, who thus comes in for the greater part of the produce.[4]

* * *

If developing the definitions of slavery and freedom explored in the previous chapter is vital to understanding the history of slavery, so too is placing those definitions within the dynamics of African history. Slavery often coalesced during moments of change, contradiction, and tension. For numerous Africans, slavery became *the* central method to mobilize labor, acquire status, govern states, and/or ensure household-level reproduction. Slavery was a common response to the need for people to work longer, harder, or in innovative ways as

---

[3] Quoted by Wyatt MacGaffey, "Indigenous Slavery and the Atlantic Trade: Kongo Texts" in Jay Spaulding and Stephanie Beswick (eds.), *African Systems of Slavery* (Trenton, NJ: Africa World Press, 2010), 184.

[4] Quoted by Paul E. Lovejoy, *Transformations in Slavery: A History of Slavery in Africa* (Cambridge: Cambridge University Press, 2000), 216–217.

Africans developed new social structures, permanent settled communities, militarized states, or new kinds of economies. Over the *longue durée*, slavery became more important and widespread. But what is the best way to understand and interpret this change? Moses Finley – followed by many other scholars – tried to understand slavery by labeling some societies as "societies with slaves" and others as "slave societies." For these scholars, "slave societies" were exceedingly rare and *only* existed when a large number of slaves became central to economic production.[5] Although the distinction between a slave society and a society with slaves is a useful one, I have chosen to broaden my use of those terms. In parts of Africa slavery became a central economic institution. But it is impossible to measure the centrality of slavery by a purely economic rationale. Slavery in Africa often facilitated *reproduction* without being tied directly to *production*. That is, slaves were regularly acquired for noneconomic reasons, most often for their reproductive capacity. Societies that relied on slaves extensively in noneconomic roles could indeed be "slave societies," although the nature of slavery in those societies often differed. In addition, I aim not just to distinguish between "societies with slaves" and "slave societies," but instead to focus on questions of slavery and historical processes in Africa: how, when, and why did some societies in Africa use slavery to reproduce their governments, institutions, households, economies, and kin groups? How did slavery change as a result? What were the goals of African slaving strategies and why were they employed in particular times and places? The rest of this chapter seeks to answer these questions using a chronological framework.

African Slaving Strategies: An Overview

There was not a singular "African slavery," because African slaving strategies produced a variety of outcomes. We have already observed just how important the general concepts of insider and outsider were to slavery in Africa. African *insiders* aimed to acquire *outsiders* as slaves to better compete with other *insiders* for power, status, or wealth. According to Miller: "The historical issue between the enslavers and the enslaved was appropriating outsiders' energies in

---

[5] Finley, *Ancient Slavery and Modern Ideology* and see Ira Berlin, *Many Thousands Gone: The First Two Centuries of Slavery in North America* (Cambridge, MA: Harvard University Press, 2000), 7–9.

support of insiders' strategies."[6] The goals and strategies of insiders varied. Early on, most Africans lived within collectivities tied together through kinship. These societies were generally small in scale, had few formal political institutions, and were weakly tied to markets. When it existed, low-density slavery was most common. Over the course of centuries, commercial and political revolutions transformed parts of Africa. Insiders sought slaves for new reasons and used them in new ways, which sometimes led to the emergence and consolidation of high-density slavery. The enlargement of scale – sometimes made possible by slavery – produced new forms of hierarchy, social stratification, coercive state-building, and production for markets. Africans responded by increasing the scale of slaveholding and broadening slave use. New slaveries did not simply displace older forms of enslavement; indeed, they were often (but not always!) an adaptation of older forms of dependence.

This process took a particular chronological shape, although regional variations were common. The foundations for the emergence of slavery were laid between 10000 BCE and 500 CE. The agricultural and iron revolutions led to new settled communities, which had new uses for people in politics and production. In this foundational period, new contradictions *and* opportunities emerged that eventually encouraged the expansion of slavery, although few societies in this period actually used slaves in substantial numbers. Between roughly 500 CE and 1600 CE, parts of Africa experienced major technological, economic, and political changes. Ambitious or clever Africans enhanced their own power by using slaves to exploit new opportunities. In this period, high-density slavery became key to state consolidation and integration, as well as to the continued production of goods that sustained state institutions. Between 1600 and 1800, European commerce and credit influenced slavery in Africa. In West and West Central Africa a major external force, the transatlantic slave trade, affected slavery, which led to a further commercialization and militarization of the African continent. Access to European commercial credit and the greater external demand for slaves drove the further expansion of high-density slavery. Slaves were used more widely in production and were increasingly viewed as property. In this period, new elites and states emerged (or old states expanded) with the expressed

---

[6] Joseph C. Miller, *The Problem of Slavery as History: A Global Approach* (New Haven, CT: Yale University Press, 2012), 31.

purpose of taking advantage of the growth of the slave trade and slavery. Although high-density slavery spread to new areas, slavery was not completely transformed. Low-density slavery continued to dominate many areas of the continent. In other places, no slaves were used at all. Finally, between 1800–1900, internal and external forces coalesced to make slavery central to many African economies and societies, tied mainly to the abolition of the transatlantic slave trade, Islamic revolutions in West Africa, and the Omani economy of the East African coast and Indian Ocean. In this period, slaves worked throughout Africa to produce goods for expansive commercial networks within and beyond the continent. After 1900, slavery gradually died out in most of Africa. The end of slavery came about as a result of major changes brought by colonialism. Slaves and former slaves moved into wage labor. A series of political changes brought an end to slave raiding and gradually reduced the power of masters over their slaves through law.

Cattle, Crops, and Iron: Laying the Foundations for Slavery in Early Africa, 10000 BCE–500 CE

Human beings create societies. Between 10000 BCE and 500 CE, Africans built new political, social, and economic structures. They created new political institutions, made decisions about food production, and organized labor in new ways. Sometimes, these decisions either led to the use of slaves or laid the foundation for their future use. Although there is much we do not know about early Africa, there is much we do know as a result of recent research. This research is not without its problems. The linguistic and archeological evidence often do not agree. Linguists have reconstructed root words from ancestral languages that suggest a very early origin for agriculture and iron-working that is not reflected in the archeological record.[7] Moreover, the archeological record alone is usually not enough to tell us whether slavery existed. Nonetheless, historians have used linguistics and archeology to reconstruct a series of broad processes that led to the emergence and spread of African populations as well as new subsistence strategies, technological innovations, and social or political structures.

---

[7] For an excellent introduction to the use of linguistics and history, see Karin Klieman, 'The Pygmies Were Our Compass': Bantu and Batwa in the History of West Central Africa, early times to c. 1900 (Portsmouth, NH: Heinemann, 2003).

Often these changes were propelled by human adaptions to historical variations in African climate. Between 16000 and 9000 BCE, four
ancestral language families began to coalesce in specific parts of the
continent. Over time the climate of the regions these people occupied changed. The period between 16000 and roughly 12000 BCE
was quite dry. Hunting and foraging were the dominant modes of
subsistence. Wild grass collection and fishing were practiced in areas
that were well watered (especially the Nile Valley region). Between
approximately 12000/9000–6500 BCE and 5500–3500 BCE, the climate entered a much wetter period (with an intervening dry period
between 6500 and 5500 BCE). Parts of what is now the Sahara Desert
became well watered. New grasslands came to dominate formerly dry
regions, and lakes emerged or expanded along the southern edge of
the Sahara:

> By 8000 B.C., the Sahara had been transformed into a mosaic of shal-
> low lakes and marshes linked by permanent streams.... Mediterranean
> vegetation, which at present is confined to coastal North Africa, grew
> in the Saharan highland regions of Hoggar and Tibesti. Elephant,
> giraffe, rhinoceros, and crocodile were widespread. Lake Chad, fed by
> streams emanating from the Saharan highlands, rose more than 40 m
> to cover an area many times its present size; this larger lake is known
> as Megachad. To the south of the present Sahara, the dunes that had
> formed in the preceding dry phase were deeply weathered and covered
> with woodland. The forest at that time may have extended as far north
> as 13N latitude.[8]

Early Africans gradually adapted their subsistence strategies to this
wetter environment. Africans first responded by repopulating the
Sahara. Although many of these early Saharans remained highly mobile
and practiced hunting, by c. 8000–7000 BCE, an increasing number
specialized in fishing or pastoralism. Permanent communities eventually developed, some of which experimented with collecting wild
grasses for food. Mobility nonetheless remained an important subsistence strategy, especially for herders. These innovations did not – at
least initially – displace older forms of subsistence. By at least 7000
BCE, wild grass collection had spread widely throughout the green

---

[8] Susan Keech McIntosh and Roderick J. McIntosh, "West African Prehistory:
Archeological Studies in the Recent Decades Have Illuminated the Prehistory of This
Vast Region, Revealing Unexpected Complexity in Its Development from 10, 000
B.C. to A.D. 1000" in *American Scientist* 69, 6 (1981), 604.

Sahara. Wild grass collection developed into the domestication of indigenous African crops, which took place in a series of independent African agricultural revolutions between roughly 7000–6000 BCE and 2500 BCE, with early dates coming from linguistic evidence and later dates from archeology. For linguists, the key stimulus may have been the 1,000-year dry period (6500–5500 BCE), when conditions favored agriculture more than fishing. Beginning in these years, agro-pastoralism displaced fishing as the dominant subsistence strategy in parts of the Sahara. Centers of agricultural innovation also emerged in the Ethiopian highlands and along the West African coastal planting zone. When wet conditions started to return around 5500 BCE, these innovations spread more widely. Eventually, settled populations grew, farming became a central subsistence strategy for some, new crops emerged, and the languages and cultures of farmers spread over a wider area, intertwining in places, while the southern third of Africa remained largely committed to hunting and foraging. Archeologists place these changes at a later date. They point to the fact that African climate entered into a prolonged dry period around roughly 3500 BCE (with the timing being regionally variable), when Saharan – and other wet regions in affected areas – began to desiccate. Early Africans therefore migrated in search of wetter environments, which eventually led to the invention and diffusion of agriculture; indeed, as Roderick McIntosh and Susan Keech McIntosh argue, "The drastic climatic oscillations of c. 4500–2500 BP may have detonated a virtual explosion of experimentation, reinforcement to change and communication about successful innovations."[9] We have good archeological evidence for the domestication of crops from this period, including sorghum and various kinds of millet. Whatever the dates, linguists and archeologist agree that major changes occurred between 9000 and 2000 BCE that transformed the ways Africans lived, although wild grass collection, hunting, and fishing remained important for some populations for a long period of time.

These changes were reinforced by the invention of ironworking. First concentrated in a few specific regions, by 500 CE ironworking spread throughout the continent. Iron tools and weapons further aided agriculture and state-building. Finally, between roughly 3500

[9] Roderick J. McIntosh and Susan Keech McIntosh, "From Siecles Obscurs to Revolutionary Centuries on the Middle Niger" in *World Archaeology* 20, 1 (1988), 146.

BCE and 500 CE, new groups of Africans expanded into and settled the continent south of the equator in what some call the Bantu
Migrations. Africans who eventually came to speak a group of related
Bantu languages migrated into equatorial, eastern, and southern
Africa, bringing with them the subsistence strategies they had earlier developed and inventing new ones along the way. Thus, by 500
CE, African populations consolidated, adopted new technologies, and
developed differing – although often interrelated – subsistence strategies as well as foundational cultural, linguistic, and political traditions
and structures.

The consolidation of early African societies led Africans to experiment with slavery between roughly 3000 BCE and 500 CE. Although
outsiders were no doubt acquired early in the African past, they were
most often killed or absorbed into collectivities as full members.
Killing captives no doubt helped solidify the boundaries between "us"
(insiders) and "them" (outsiders). But as Africans more fully engaged
in settled agriculture, the question of what to do with prisoners of war
and other captives took on a new meaning. People in these societies
had to make the decision about whether to kill, absorb, or exploit captives. Early African slavery emerged because some captors decided
it was more useful to exploit captives. New subsistence strategies,
social structures, and technologies produced a greater demand – and
wider range of uses – for people. At this point, early Africans sought to
expand their access to the reproductive potential of dependents, especially wives, children, junior clients, and slaves. This opened new economic and political opportunities for some, but also created tensions
between insiders and outsiders, as well as between insiders themselves.
Insiders (or people who wanted to become insiders) gained control
over people as political resources, which they leveraged to claim more
central roles within the community itself.[10] Slaves were of course also
useful because they worked in environments that were challenging and
sometimes perilous for all Africans. But they were not used to produce
commodities for the market. Slaves were often incorporated gradually
via marriage, childbirth, and intergenerational mobility. Slavery was
but one reproductive strategy that some early Africans pursued; slavery was seldom a central institution. These were in the main societies
with slaves and not slave societies.

---

[10] Specifically, slave owners used their control over people to make claims to more
authority, status, land, or crops.

But this era was not dominated only by small-scale societies. Along the Nile Valley, in parts of West Africa and the Ethiopian highlands, Africans built states. This political consolidation was driven by numerous forces, including improved agricultural production, favorable environmental conditions, and the expansion of commerce and trading networks. Along the lower Nile Valley, for example, Egypt emerged as one of the great powers of the ancient world between roughly 2600 and 2100 BCE. Slaves were used in a wide range of occupations, from production to politics, as part of a highly centralized and stratified state. Further south along the Upper Nile, Meroe also emerged as a powerful state between 600 and 300 BCE. Although Meroe was highly urbanized, it relied on rural workers who lived outside the urban core. Meroe city became a center of iron production and trade, including cloth, textiles, gold, and ivory. Slaves were likely to have been widely used as laborers in both skilled and unskilled occupations. In the Ethiopian highlands, the state of Axum, which emerged around 100 CE, was part of a commercial network that linked it to the regions surrounding the Red Sea (and beyond). The rulers of Axum used slaves as government officials and probably more widely as laborers as well. In West Africa, political and economic complexity was well established in parts of the savanna zone long before 500 CE. New kinds of sedentary polities emerged that were tied to the intensification of agriculture and growing commercialization of trade. The Karkarichinkat cluster (in the Tilemsi Valley) and Dhar Tichit (southeastern Mauritania), for example, were focal points for sedentarization, pastoralism, and agriculture (although in all likelihood there was significant seasonal mobility by herders as well as extensive reliance on hunting and fishing) as the Sahara began to desiccate. By 300 BCE, widespread urban clusters emerged along the inland Niger Delta, with the best evidence coming from Jenne-Jeno, where there was extensive occupational specialization and trade but no centralized state. Some of these societies were likely to have used slaves. Archeologists have explored the funeral tumuli and megalithic monuments scattered throughout Senegambia and the Niger bend, which provide evidence for increasing social stratification, kingship, and complex funeral rituals and human sacrifice at least during the first millennium CE. Such evidence suggests that slavery may have been common, but it is also important to note that finding solid evidence of slavery in the historical record is difficult in this period.

For most Africans between 10000 BCE and 500 CE, the use of slaves was not an optimal political or economic strategy. But in some places, Africans came to see the value of slavery. In the large parts of the continent where Africans lived in relatively decentralized and small-scale communities, some big men used slavery to grab power to get around broader governing ideas about reciprocity and kinship, but were still bound by those ideas to some degree. In other parts of the continent early political centralization and commercialization led to the expanded use of slaves as soldiers, officials, and workers. Unlike smaller-scale societies, slaves in complex polities had specific and well-defined roles outside the structures of kinship. Many worked longer and harder in economic or productive roles, but in all cases they remained slaves for a much longer and well-defined period of time. Although the use of slaves was quite limited even by 500 CE, by learning to exploit new technologies and environments in the face of low population densities and environmental challenges, the "colonizing societies" of early Africa also lay the foundations for the consolidation and expansion of slavery in Africa between 500 and 1600 CE, when the political and commercial revolutions that had been limited to small parts of the continent dramatically expanded.[11] This led to a further divergence in African slaveries. In some places large numbers of slaves became central to new economic and political structures, whereas in others slavery remained minimally important and played a largely reproductive role in decentralized societies.

The Early Militarization and Commercialization of Slavery in Africa, 500–1600 CE

After 500 CE, slavery became increasingly common in the more populous and well-watered parts of Africa, which relied on sedentary hoe and mixed agriculture. In large (and drier) parts of the continent, low population densities and population mobility mitigated (at least initially) against the widespread use of slaves. But in general, the scale of slavery dramatically expanded between 500 and 1600 CE. This expansion was tied to the economic, military, and political revolutions that reshaped Africa. Although many Africans, as Christopher Ehret notes,

---

[11] The phrase "colonizing societies" is John Iliffe's, see: *Africans: The History of a Continent* (Cambridge: Cambridge University Press, 1995).

"stood apart from these trends" by "maintaining or refashioning ... the smaller scale world of their forbears," large parts of the continent experienced increasing political consolidation, social stratification, and commercialization.[12] The West African Savanna and Sahel was probably most affected by these changes. Increasingly powerful warlords built new kinds of polities that relied on trade, raids, horses, and slavery. But even further south in the West African forest, slaves were used to clear forests, mine for gold, or simply as palace retainers and servants. Beyond West Africa, in this period the East African coast was integrated into new commercial networks via the Indian Ocean, which brought Islam and international trade to the coast. Although slavery existed long before this trade, the development of a coastal urbanized, commercial system along the coast led to an expansion of slavery and the slave trade. Finally, big men in the Central African forests and in the African Great Lakes region used slaves to achieve their goals, but for the most part they were much less integrated into international networks and commerce and slaves tended not be used very widely in production. Yet, the expansion of slavery in those places demonstrates that decentralized and small-scale societies were both dynamic and could generate a strong demand for slaves.

Between roughly 500 and 1600 CE in the West African Savanna and Sahel, trans-Saharan commerce brought new kinds of trade, ideas, commodities, and credit to the region, which some Africans sought to control. Emergent African rulers – who began as warlords – took advantage of these new forces to build innovative, coercive, and hierarchical states. They created new political structures partially to protect and enhance their access to the booming trade and production of the region. Miller thoughtfully describes this process as transition from war camps to courts.[13] A series of progressively larger and more powerful (and increasingly Islamic) polities emerged in this region, the best known of which were Ghana, Mali, Songhay, and Kanem. Warriors became (and remained) rulers by using horses and slaves to achieve their political goals (state centralization, expansion of kingly power, territorial control) as well as their economic goals (control over the production of commodities and agricultural products). The use

---

[12] Christopher Ehret, *The Civilizations of Africa* (Charlottesville: University of Virginia Press, 2002), 238.

[13] Joseph Miller, "Africa" in Paul Finkelman and Joseph C. Miller (eds.), *The Encyclopedia of World Slavery* (New York: Macmillan, 1998), volume I, 31.

FIGURE 6. Body guard of the King of Borno. In Dixon Denham, *Narrative of Travels and Discoveries in Northern and Central Africa, in the years 1822, 1823, and 1824* (London, 1826), facing p. 64. Courtesy of the UVM Bailey-Howe Library.

of cavalry became central to waging war – and to smaller-scale raiding. Horses – like tanks in the modern era – revolutionized the nature of the battlefield and offered military advantages to those who used them (Figure 6). Slaves, on the other hand, were used to produce goods for the rulers and their households as well as soldiers and government officials. Finally, slaves were also sold into the trans-Saharan trade as a means to acquire horses on which the military depended.

But why did emerging rulers turn to slavery in the first place? States like Mali and Songhay were far more powerful than any state in the African past up to 1600 CE (with the exception of Egypt), but their rulers faced many uncertainties. Most rulers were weakened by competition with other aristocrats, especially over the relative power of kingship and questions of succession. Rulers used slaves to control these aristocrats. The use of slaves as soldiers or as officials often proved to be a better option than relying on ambitious kin who had their eyes on the throne. Likewise, these states sought to incorporate occupational groups, warriors, Muslims, and farmers (for example) into the state, but often lacked the ability to fully compel these populations to obey. Slaves were used as labor to do what free farmers or miners would not. Slaves were, for example, widely used by the fifteenth century as laborers to produce rice, cereal crops, and salt. They were also used as muscle to force people to provide tribute and taxes. Slavery became a solution to the inherent problems of state building. In the swirling, complex, and personalized politics of the West African Savanna, ambitious insiders became *and remained* kings and aristocrats by using outsiders as slaves in pursuit of their broader political and economic strategies. This pattern was not just confined to the West African Savanna. Numerous rulers along the Nile Valley in Sennar, or across the Sahara in Morocco developed parallel slaving strategies.

The choices made by generations of African rulers and merchants reshaped slavery. Slaves were used in larger numbers in a wider variety of roles. As rulers and merchants adopted Islam, they (as slave owners) could point to an Islamic religious and moral justification of slavery. Islam both legitimized the use of slaves and provided a legal framework that regularized how slaves ought to be acquired and treated. Islam certainly offered protection for slaves, but masters often ignored those protections. Slaves were increasingly marketed and exchanged as property. Slave status meant longer-term bondage and offered fewer routes toward incorporation – although that happened as well, of course. How? Women no doubt made up a large proportion of slaves in this region and they were more readily incorporated via marriage, concubinage, and childbearing. In elite households, slavery became a way to produce loyal dependents. For men, some positions within slavery offered routes to power. Slaves were widely used as officials and soldiers. The privileges that came along with slavery meant that some slaves actually sought to remain slaves. Indeed, Songhay collapsed in 1591 after losing a war against a Moroccan army made up of 4,000 slaves armed with guns. These Moroccan slave soldiers – like those of Songhay – gained so much from their dependent status that they had little interest in rebellion or freedom. In general, then, slavery in the West African Sahel and Savanna by 1600 was large in scale, commercialized, and centered on both politics and production.

A somewhat parallel process emerged on the East African Swahili Coast between 800 and 1600 CE. For centuries, African colonized the varied terrain of Eastern Africa. By 700–800 CE, iron-using farmers, craftsmen, and fisherman populated parts of the Swahili Coast. The earliest towns were built by the end of the eighth century CE. Although they were initially small, the inhabitants of some early towns, like Shanga, were already trading with merchants from the Persian Gulf.[14] Over time, Swahili states arose along the coast, each with its own government, generally composed of wealthy and connected merchant families. Islam became increasingly important. The construction of mosques – as well as gorgeous coral and stone houses – took off in the wealthiest enclaves of the towns. Every Swahili city of note was tied to Indian Ocean commerce and trade. Swahili merchants exported ivory, timber, slaves, iron and copper work, beads, and textiles. Swahili societies along the coast became increasingly wealthy, socially stratified, commercially oriented, and economically diverse. John Middleton has argued that the Swahili were a society of middlemen, who brokered trade between the "world of the sea and the productive one of the interior":

> Like precapitalist port cities everywhere, Swahili towns were polyglot, multiethnic frontiers, composed of Arab merchants and ship owners; Indian financiers; Swahili middlemen, traders, ship builders, sailors, iron and leather workers, weavers, furniture makers, and fishermen; slave laborers; and neighboring farmers, herders, hunters, and traders. Each town had its own particular economic resources, specializations, and exchange systems within the overall ecology of the coast. Market relations were based on personal trust and kinship; kings were merchant princes; lineages acted as corporate trading houses; social identity was forged in intense competition; and status rested on shifting foundations of wealth, exchange, honor, and prestige.[15]

The history of the Swahili coast offers remarkable similarities and differences to the West African Savanna and Sahel. In both cases, Africans were tied to an international commercial world (either across the desert or the ocean) that led to an expansion of economic activity,

---

[14] See, for example, Mark Horton, *Shanga: The Archeology of a Muslim Trading Community of the Coast of East Africa* (London: The British Institute in Eastern Africa, 1996).

[15] Thomas Spear, "Early Swahili Society Reconsidered" in *The International Journal of African Historical Studies* **33**, 2 (2000), 276 and John Middleton, *The World of the Swahili: An African Mercantile Civilization* (New Haven, CT: Yale University Press, 1992), 38–45.

social differentiation, occupational specialization, and increased local production. Unlike West Africa, along the coast, merchants prevailed over warriors. No large state emerged to dominate the region in the same way that Ghana, Mali, and Songhay dominated the West African Savanna. Instead, the Swahili coast remained the home of independent city-states, often ruled by merchants, who were tied together by cultural, family, and commercial relationships. Slaves were widely used along the Swahili coast as laborers, retainers, domestic servants, and concubines. Slaves were also exported in the Indian Ocean slave trade. Wealthy merchants and rulers in large towns, such as Pate and Kilwa, held the largest number of slaves. Although the populations of the coastal towns were tied to trade and the Indian Ocean, until the nineteenth century many Swahili worked small plots of land as farmers. Unfortunately, we really have no idea how many slaves were held in the countryside until the nineteenth century, when a true plantation-style economy emerged.

In Central Africa between 500 and 1600 CE, multiple cultural and political traditions gradually intermingled. Although fewer large states existed – and the entire region was much farther removed from the commercial revolutions that were reshaping West Africa – here too economic and political changes led to slavery. As early Africans colonized large parts of Central Africa, populations were widely dispersed and land remained widely available. Over time, more land was put under production as food cultivators expanded into new regions formerly occupied by foragers. Initially, tropical farmers created societies that were highly assimilative, flexible, and relatively egalitarian. The reciprocal distribution of resources – as well as a communal ethos – shaped social and political relations. As the settlement frontier closed off after 500 CE, it became harder to found new settlements or to dispose of unwanted people simply by having them leave one settlement for another. The invention and spread of metallurgy in forests – and the addition of cereal crop production and pastoralism south of the forests – were also important.[16] Some societies became increasingly stratified, and competed over resources. The structures of kinship and descent became not just a vehicle for identity formation and social cohesion, but also became a means to gain and enforce control over

---

[16] The classic account of these processes in Jan Vansina, *Paths in the Rainforest: Towards a History of Political Tradition in Equatorial Africa* (Madison: University of Wisconsin Press, 1990).

people. We previously observed that these trends were apparent before 500 CE, but they really took off between 500 and 1600 CE. Slaves were used by large numbers of ambitious big men to increase their own political authority in the context of growing competition between and within households and lineages.

Thus, accumulation, stratification, and economic exchange created new opportunities that led to the acquisition of slaves. As much as slavery was an important institution in parts of the Central African forests, they were not used widely in production, nor were they used as officials or soldiers in the same way they were in parts of West Africa. Slaves were generally used to increase the reputation and political power of those who used them.[17] For many men, slavery meant the difference between becoming a big man, acquiring wealth, power, and people, and remaining a dependent, subject to the control of another. On the one hand, big men became powerful because they were good leaders and speakers, but on the other hand, they needed to be able to attract – and dispose of – people (wives, slaves, clients) and control wealth (domestic animals, copper ingots, iron hoes). In this regard, Jan Vansina noted that a key a route to political power "was to acquire slaves, especially women slaves. They belonged to the matrilineage of their captor as did their children, while at the same time they could be given in marriage to attract a client or keep a restless bachelor in the house. Slaves before 1700 were acquired in war, or as payment of fines or blood debts rather than by purchase and most were probably female."[18]

The political structures of Central Africa were not uniformly decentralized. In the Savanna zones to the south of the Central African rain forest (especially in the Congo Basin and Upemba depression), some local big men challenged prevailing political norms by using slaves to create new forms of chiefship. Slavery helped fuel a political revolution that led to the consolidation of states. Big men gained control over the distribution of resources and over people. They often used violence to achieve their ends. John Yoder argues that this new authority was not based on family or tradition but instead on the

---

[17] Miller notes that Central African domestic economies "tended to emphasize reproduction, continuation of the community – rather than production of material surpluses as commodities for sale – and thus sought reproductive females through slaving." Miller, "Introduction" in *Women and Slavery, vol I.*, 2.

[18] Jan Vansina, "Government in Kasai Before the Lunda" in *The International Journal of African Historical Studies* 31, 1 (1998), 8.

"ability to exercise military power, generate wealth, and gain external support."[19] The pace of these changes only increased after 1600 with the expansion of credit and commerce brought by the transatlantic slave trade, although local trade and raids mattered most in the early period. Early chiefs did not just manipulate ideas of dependency, kinship, clientage, and slavery, but also sought to control the regional production and burgeoning trade of iron, copper, salt, and fish. State consolidation was, then, not simply a product of slaving by incipient chiefs, rulers, and kings, but was deeply tied to political strategies designed to centralize power, acquire dependents and clients, monopolize force, and control key resources. Between 1400 and 1700, the Luba and Rund kingdoms, the Lunda Commonwealth, as well as the kingdoms of Kongo, Tio, and Ndongo further toward the Western Coast emerged. Although most of these states did not *initially* rely heavily on slave labor, slavery nonetheless stimulated broader processes that lay at the foundations of chiefship and kingship. Over time the courts of kings stood at the center of vast systems of authority and tribute taking, where slaves advertised a ruler's power and prestige, protected rulers, and helped produce goods for the palace and the ruling elite. The Kingdom of Kongo, for example, acquired slaves through war or trade. They placed those slaves in concentrated settlements close to major Kongolese cities (mainly São Salvador and Mbanza Nsoyo), where they produced agricultural products for the cities and courts. Although the Kingdom of Kongo was unique because it was tied to Portuguese commercial networks and the transatlantic slave trade so early, slavery solved a basic internal problem that predated the Portuguese: the need to sustain a large nonproductive population of aristocrats and their households. This in turn reshaped the nature of slavery itself. Working on an aristocrat's slave farm in the Kongo in the 1500s was a very different experience than that of a female slave working in a decentralized community in Central Africa. The farm slaves had fewer options for incorporation and worked longer, more regimented hours in an economically important sector, compared to a female slave who worked at domestic tasks within the confines of a household, who might marry her master or produce children who might eventually become part of a big man's household and lineage.

---

[19] John Yoder, *The Kanyok of Zaire: An Institutional and Ideological History to 1895* (Cambridge: Cambridge University Press, 1992), 35.

In the interior of Eastern Africa, parallel processes led to slavery. In the Great Lakes region, for example, big men gained control over territory and successfully integrated followers.[20] As people accumulated surpluses, inequality emerged. Some people sought to gain preferential access to land and followers as the open frontier closed. By 1600, access to cattle and banana gardens also became important routes for accumulation. In words of David Schoenbrun, "Rights in persons, the object of ancient Great Lakes and Western Lakes units of social organization now revolved around discriminating and limiting access to productive property. People continued to be the supreme measure of wealth, but the objects of their labor now changed form to include croplands, cattle herds and banana gardens."[21] Ambitious, successful, or well-connected men sought access to productive resources and the people to work those resources. They were in competition with other ambitious, successful, or well-connected men. Slavery became a means to recruit and control marginalized, socially excluded dependents. Some big men eventually became chiefs, and some chiefs eventually became kings, who parleyed their control over bananas, cattle, or people (or all three) into political power. Numerous states rose and fell in the region, including Buganda. These states were largely focused on war and plunder as well the control of salt, iron, hides, skins, and agricultural produce.

The involuntary transfer of persons was an old practice, although this did not occur via markets until quite late. Thus, most slaves were acquired as prisoners of war or were exchanged through nonmarket mechanisms. Much of our understanding of slavery in the early history of the Great Lakes region comes from historical linguistics. The word for captivity in this region is at least 2,500–3,000 years old and specifically referred to violent raiding for property (including persons).[22] Between 1200 and 1600, historical linguistics also tells us the words for "slave" and "slavery" became more common and widespread. People developed the words for slavery from preexisting words that articulated distinctions between kin and vulnerable outsiders. For example,

---

[20] David Lee Schoenbrun, *A Green Place, A Good Place: Agrarian Change, Gender and Social Identity in the Great Lakes Region to the 15th Century* (Portsmouth, NH: Heinemann, 1998), 105.

[21] Schoenbrun, *A Green Place, a Good Place*, 139.

[22] David Schoenbrun, "Violence, Marginality, Scorn and Honour: Language Evidence of Slavery to the Eighteenth Century" in Médard and Doyle (eds.), *Slavery in the Great Lakes Region of East Africa*, 43.

#mwiru, which meant male client, dependent, or servant, emerged around 1200 CE, while #-zaana meant female servant or slave developed sometime in the 1500s, and, finally, the term *muja was widely distributed in the region and meant dependent, servant, or slave. All of these words evolved from preexisting ideas about the dependence and vulnerability of newcomers: "When people argued that slaves were newcomers ... they put established principles of acceptable status and authority to work in marginalizing slaves.... The distinctive power and sting of such marginalization revolved around notions of honour and the force of scornful speech."[23] Slaves were certainly used as laborers, but most often served in the courts of rulers as servants or as wives to the elite. In both cases, favored slaves might be able to eventually achieve some kind of social integration over time. Although the scope and scale of militarism increased after 1600, slavery had local origins and emerged as Africans sought to gain control over new resources, technologies, and organizations.

Between 500 and 1600 CE, innovative militarized states and commercial networks led to the further consolidation of slavery in Africa. The creation of political and institutional hierarchies – as well as economic opportunities brought by technological change and the expansion of trade – led to the use of slaves in new roles. Slavery became essential in both politics and production in some places. These changes were probably most dramatic and revolutionary in the Savanna and Sahel zones of West Africa, although the roles of slaves also expanded along the Swahili coast and in parts of Central and West Central Africa. Some societies in the forest zone of West Africa used slaves for economic purposes (mining for gold, clearance of forests for farmland among the Akan of modern Ghana) or in politics and the military (in the state of Benin, in what is now Nigeria). Throughout huge parts of the continent, however, slavery simply did not exist. Labor was mobilized through kinship networks, or via the communal labor of free people. Finally, in other places slavery functioned within the structures of kinship. Slavery could still be exploitative, but slaves were used for purposes other than production within collectivities. Between 1600 and 1800, new opportunities for trade and state-building led many more Africans in many more regions to pursue slaving, to which we will now turn.

[23] Schoenbrun, "Violence, Marginality, Scorn and Honour," 46.

Slavery in the Era of Atlantic Commerce, 1600–1800

In the 1960s, Walter Rodney argued that slavery did not exist before
the arrival of Europeans.[24] Scholars subsequently modified Rodney's
conclusions by acknowledging that slavery existed before European
demand. African ideas about slavery – as well has African decision
making – are now acknowledged as central a part of the transatlantic
slave trade as European traders, forts, and New World plantations. In
the West African Savanna and parts of Eastern and Central Africa,
Africans leveraged slavery to take advantage of new opportunities.
The growth of the transatlantic slave trade provided similar opportunities for ambitious rulers or merchants to build new political and
economic structures. This process began before 1600 in Senegambia
and really took off after 1600 with the consolidation of Oyo, Asante,
and Dahomey.

Africans were part of international trade networks long before 1600.
African traders and goods flowed across the Sahara and the Indian
Ocean. Commodities were widely exchanged within the African continent as well. But by the end of the fifteenth century, European trade
became increasingly attractive for Africans who lived on the West and
West Central African coasts. Africans provided commodities, including human beings and gold, first to Portuguese traders and in later
centuries to traders from France, Holland, Denmark, and Great
Britain. For a price Africans also provided food and other essentials
to Europeans who took up longer-term residence in coastal forts
and towns. Until the nineteenth century, Africans generally had the
upper hand (with the exception perhaps of the Kingdom of Kongo).
Europeans were militarily weak, remained vulnerable to tropical dis-
eases, and were always at risk of having their food supplies cut off by
angry Africans. Africans also demanded rent for the small parcels of
land that Europeans occupied. Africans were in a commanding position to negotiate good terms of trade for commodities, and the prices
of slaves rose accordingly.

Between 1600 and 1800, European demand for slaves dramatically increased. This insatiable demand was generated by the labor
requirements of New World plantations, focused especially in Brazil,

---

[24] See Walter Rodney, "African Slavery and Other Forms of Social Oppression on the
Upper Guinea Coast in the Context of the Trans-Atlantic Slave Trade" in *The Journal
of African History* **8**, 3 (1966), 431–443.

the Caribbean, and North America. How did Africans respond to the growing international demand for human beings? Some African rulers and merchants specialized in the production or trade of slaves. Slavery existed long before Europeans set foot on the coast. So did the mechanisms to supply slaves via war, judicial punishment, and market exchange. The transatlantic slave trade gave Africans an opportunity to use a preexisting institution – slavery – to acquire valuable and rare commodities. Some imported goods – like guns – had important military uses. But others, like textiles, metals, or cowrie shells (a currency in parts of West Africa) were used by Africans to attract and retain followers. By exchanging acquired outsiders for imported commodities, African insiders increased their ability to wage war and the numbers of people they controlled, which in turn increased their political power and prestige. Over time, these same people retained some of the slaves they bought or captured, most often women, and used them as local laborers, concubines, and servants.

> The pattern of African imports reveals two contradictory dimensions of the export slave trade: its elite and mass characteristics. On the one hand, the slave trade served the interests of an elite. The slave-trading elite grasped the best clothes and liquor, the most prestigious luxury goods, and most of the firearms. These imported goods served to reflect and to reinforce the dominant positions of monarchs, big men, and great merchants. On the other hand, the slave trade involved all levels of society. The plainer textiles and much of the tobacco and alcoholic beverages passed into the hands of the common people. Some of these commoners had sold one or two slaves themselves; some purchased imports with income they gained otherwise.[25]

The slave trade made African big men that much bigger. Between 1600 and 1800, human beings became the most important commodity in the Atlantic exchange. Africans sold more than 7.4 million slaves into the transatlantic slave trade in these years, concentrated in regions along the coast of West and West Central Africa. The total number of slaves sold during the entire period of the trade approached 11–12 million.[26] Many millions of slaves were retained for local use by

---

[25] Patrick Manning, *Slavery and African Life: Occidental, Oriental, and African Slave Trades* (Cambridge: Cambridge University Press, 1990), 100.

[26] For the debate on the numbers, see, for example Paul E. Lovejoy, "The Volume of the Atlantic Slave Trade: A Synthesis" in *Journal of African History* **23**, 4 (1982), 473–501 and David Eltis, "The Volume and Structure of the Trans-Atlantic Slave Trade: A Reassessment" in *The William and Mary Quarterly* **58**, 1 (2001), 17–46.

Africans. Although it is important not to reduce the entire history of
this region to the history of the slave trade – there was much that happened that was unrelated to Afro-European trade – new, more centralized and militarized states emerged in Atlantic Africa that were
primarily tied to the production and trade of slaves.[27] These states
reproduced themselves through slavery and slaving. Participation in
the trade did not simply lead to the consolidation of states, but to the
fragmentation of them as well. Sometimes local political structures
proved unable to manage the new forces unleashed by the trade. In
other cases, ambitious big men used the slave trade to destroy older
states that failed to adapt successfully. Moreover, decentralized societies, which have often been portrayed solely as victims of predatory,
centralized states, effectively defended themselves from slave raids.
Some preserved their independence by raiding for and trading in slaves
themselves. Igbo traders in West Africa and Bobangi trading firms in
West Central Africa, for example, provided slaves efficiently independent of state involvement; indeed, as Walter Hawthorne argues,
"One of the cruel ironies of the Atlantic slave trade was that, in des-
perate times, individuals living on the frontiers of powerful regional
states might one day have feared being swept up in an attack by a
large army but on the next day might have used the power that they
wielded locally to participate in the kidnapping of a stranger for sale
abroad."[28] Many decentralized societies also retained slaves to use as
labor, although they mostly preferred women who became wives or
children who might eventually be incorporated.

Predatory States and Slavery in Atlantic Africa

In Senegambia, the slave trade began quite early. The rulers of the
Jolof Empire waged wars against their neighbors – using cavalry – and
acquired slaves. They traded slaves to the Portuguese and continued
to send them into Saharan networks in exchange for horses. Although
this initially enhanced the wealth and power of the Jolof Empire, slave

---

[27] On this issue, see John Thornton, "Cannibals, Witches, and Slave Traders in the
Atlantic World" in *The William and Mary Quarterly* **60**, 2 (2003), 277.
[28] Walter Hawthorne, *Planting Rice and Harvesting Slaves: Transformations along the
Guinea-Bissau Coast, 1400–1900* (Portsmouth, NH: Heinemann, 2003), 12. See also
Martin A. Klein, "The Slave Trade and Decentralized Societies" in *The Journal of
African History* **42**, 1 (2001), 49–65.

raiding also increased political instability.[29] Instead of being preyed upon by the Jolof, surrounding peoples (including the Sereer) sold slaves to acquire horses that they used to challenge Jolof power. Instability even occurred within the Jolof Empire. Members of the Jolof political elite acquired horses and slaves and then challenged the power of the king. This led to the creation of new states (like Kaabu) and to the disintegration of the Jolof Empire into independent kingdoms in the sixteenth century: "The weakness brought about by competing power interests bolstered by the Atlantic trade had precipitated a decisive shift in political organisation in Senegambia. Kingdoms like Cajor and Siin had new access to horses and could free themselves from the old Jolof heartland."[30] Thus, participation in the Atlantic trade drew on a preexisting slave trade and led to both political fragmentation and consolidation.

Predatory, slaving states became more common in West Africa between 1600 and 1800. Oyo, Dahomey, and Asante, for example, emerged during this period. These states were deeply involved in the transatlantic slave trade and became increasingly militarized. Their rulers acquired slaves by launching regular wars, raids, and by trading for them. They then used the generated wealth to centralize executive and state power. They became dependent on the slave trade politically and economically. The impact of the trade, however, was not uniform or all encompassing.[31] Rulers and states often pursued policies that were unrelated to the trade in slaves; indeed, the choices rulers made were often produced by internal factors. *Asantehene* (or King) Osei Bonsu of Asante proclaimed that he did not "make war to catch slaves in a bush, like a thief.... But if I fight a King, and kill him when he is insolent, then certainly ... his gold, and his slaves, and the people are mine too.... I did not make war for slaves, but because [the King] sent me an arrogant message and killed my people."[32]

The expanding trade – and local use of slaves – fueled economic growth. It also initiated and perpetuated a cycle of militarization,

---

[29] See Boubacar Barry, *Senegambia and the Atlantic Slave Trade* (Cambridge: Cambridge University Press, 1997).

[30] Toby Green, *The Rise of the Trans-Atlantic Slave Trade in Western Africa, 1300–1589* (New York: Cambridge University Press, 2012), 91.

[31] See Green, 93.

[32] Joseph Dupuis, *Journal of a Residence in Ashantee* (London: H. Colburn, 1824), 163–164 as cited by Trevor R. Getz, *Slavery and Reform in West Africa: Toward Emancipation in Nineteenth-Century Senegal and Gold Coast* (Athens: Ohio University Press, 2004), 11.

political fragmentation, and violence. Security and prosperity generally increased within the borders of the slaving states themselves. The
areas subject to slave raids faced increasing insecurity. In the case of
Asante, Rebecca Shumway notes: "When the Asantes waged war ...
they not only built a new state ... they also killed people, enslaved people, destabilized societies by removing political authorities, and established obligatory tribute payments that the conquered people were
obliged to pay, in part, by enslaving more people."[33] Not all slaving
states were successful. Oyo expanded to become an empire and generated a large number of slaves, but was unable to contain the impact
of the trade. By the 1790s Oyo descended into a civil war and in 1835
it collapsed. Oyo was replaced by a number of smaller Yoruba city-
states. Dahomey, on the other hand, became a powerful militarized
state, but was remarkably dependent on the slavery and slave trade.
Asante pursued more of a middle course. Its rulers traded in slaves
but also sought other economic options and pursued many imperial
goals that were unrelated to the trade.

Outside West Africa, vast regions of West Central and Central
Africa exported millions of slaves into the transatlantic slave trade;
during the eighteenth century alone, 2,331,800 were exported from the
coast of West Central Africa. The Lozi, Lunda, and Luba of Central
Africa became increasingly focused not just on imperial expansion but
also on capturing slaves who were transported by Ovimbundu caravans to the West Central African coast and then across the Atlantic
on European ships. Violence and disorder was as much a product of
the trade as political consolidation and expansion. By the seventeenth
century, for example, predatory Imbangala warlords (with reputations
as cannibals) ravaged large parts of the region. The slaves they captured were exchanged for weapons and other goods or (if male and
young enough) initiated into the Imbangala war bands as future soldiers. They also kept women to work, for sacrifice, or for marriage.
The Imbangala lived, as John Thornton notes, "by pillage and plunder" and as a "suggestive sample of their attitude, Imbangala soldiers
would cut down palm trees to obtain the sap rather than simply tap-
ping them as was the normal custom; theirs was a wasteful practice
that devastated the economies of the regions they traversed in search
of more palm groves to destroy."[34]

[33] Rebecca Shumway, *The Fante and the Transatlantic Slave Trade* (Rochester, NY:
University of Rochester Press, 2011), 57.
[34] Thornton, "Cannibals, Witches and Slave Traders," 289.

How did these changes impact slavery? First, the expansion of slave-trading networks meant that more slaves were acquired than ever before. African rulers and merchants retained a large number of slaves between 1600 and 1800. Although population statistics are very unreliable for this period in African history, it is likely that 15–30 percent of the population of core slaving regions were of slave status. Many of these slaves were women.[35] Second, slaves continued to be used in a variety of ways. But by 1800, many more slaves were used as laborers, producing food for palaces as well as commodities for exchange. Slavery became a central institution in Atlantic Africa because more slaves were used in production; they had a central economic role not just as objects of exchange but also as labor. Third, retained slaves were widely used as soldiers who captured the slaves to be used for labor or sent into the transatlantic slave trade. Slavery became important for the continued production of new slaves. As these changes took hold – and as high-density slavery became dominant in Atlantic Africa – slavery became increasingly closed. The incorporation of slaves took longer. Masters and slaves were more often in conflict. Slaves were not regarded as lesser kin, but as objects to be bought, sold, and used. This was resisted by slaves, who fought for inclusion.

Despite these changes in Atlantic Africa, the transformation of slavery into a central productive institution only occurred after the abolition of the slave trade in the early to mid-nineteenth century. Women and children were in many places still incorporated. For men, mobility into positions of authority or responsibility remained possible. Slaves sought out and gained political and economic privileges. Slave labor was intensified, but slaves worked much as they always had, mostly in loosely supervised small groups attached to farms on which they lived as well. Many slaves remained only marginally connected to productive activities and worked instead within households, were killed as sacrifices, married as wives, or used as government officials. Finally, there was a marked regional difference in slave use between West and West Central Africa. Fewer slaves were retained for productive use in West Central Africa; instead, the societies and states of this region simply chose to export as many slaves as possible: "In general the export trade drained population from productive sectors, except in a few places where became an important

[35] See, for example, Manning, *Slavery and African Life.*

component of production."[36] However, even in this region the use of slaves in production occurred in a number of places, including Luanda and Benguela.

What happened in the many parts of Africa that were not impacted – or only marginally impacted – by Atlantic commerce and the transatlantic slave trade? In these cases slavery was unnecessary because other forms of labor or political mobilization proved effective. But slavery also dominated places that were very far removed from the transatlantic slave trade. Access to various combinations of commerce, horses, firearms, credit, and markets continued to offer some Africans opportunities to acquire outsiders. In the Islamic West African Savanna, for example, slavery remained centrally important to the economics and politics of numerous states between 1600 and 1800. No large imperial state emerged to fill the void after the fall of Songhay in 1591. Instead, states jostled for dominance. Some states – especially those in the Western Sudan – sold slaves into both the Saharan and transatlantic slave trades, and used slaves in production and in politics. But most states in the Savanna zone– including the Hausa city-states, Dar Fur, and Borno – had no ties to the transatlantic slave trade. These states raided for slaves, sold slaves across the desert in exchange for commodities, and used slaves in productive tasks ranging from weaving to mining to farming. Indeed, the number of slaves exported across the Sahara desert approached the total number of slaves exported across the Atlantic (although the trans-Saharan trade took place over a longer time). For the region as a whole, the percentage of those held in slavery easily reached 25 percent, with the highest concentrations in centers of political and economic development. The period between 1600 and 1800 accentuated patterns of the previous period. Slavery continued to be a central institution. Along the Swahili coast of Eastern Africa, the Indian Ocean trade continued to encourage the growth of commerce and credit between 1600 and 1800. Slaves also remained important as producers, objects of exchange, and as domestic servants and retainers for the elite, although the scale and scope of slavery really expanded only in the nineteenth century, along with the formalization of Omani domination and commercial control of the coast. In South Africa, European settlers imported tens of thousands of slaves into the Cape Colony, where they were used in urban and rural tasks. The expansion of the Dutch East India Company led

---

[36] Lovejoy, *Transformations in Slavery*, 127.

to European settlement at Cape Town, which produced an increasing demand for labor. Although many South African farmers were poor, some generated a substantial income, had access to credit, and purchased slaves supplied by the Dutch East India Company. By the 1700s, slave labor was absolutely essential to the production of cereal crops and grapes (for wine), and its importance endured well into the nineteenth century. The transatlantic slave trade did not directly impact South Africa, but the consolidation of slavery in the region was indeed tied to, in the words of Paul E. Lovejoy, "the expansion of the European economy ... and the growth of trade with Asia."[37] The centrality of slavery would only increase for large parts of Africa in the nineteenth century.

The Transformative Nineteenth Century

Africans experienced dramatic change during the nineteenth century. In 1800, the transatlantic slave trade was still in high gear, and Europeans remained largely confined to the coast. By the end of the century, the transatlantic slave trade had been abolished, and Europeans were in the process of occupying large parts of the continent. Islamic revolutions swept through the West African Savanna. In East Africa, the Omani Arabs built a commercial empire on the Swahili coast. This all led to a major economic reorientation, focused on commodity production and international trade. Slavery changed as well. The number of slaves held in captivity continued to expand, especially in the areas of greatest economic and political growth. More slaves were used in economically important roles. Slavery continued to play an important role in the consolidation of new states. Some of these states developed strong and stable political institutions by using slaves, while others used slaves to build states that were primarily geared to pillage and war. Overall, the major historical changes of the period led to the creation or further consolidation of high-density slavery, which became the dominant form of slavery in large parts of Africa. By the end of the nineteenth century, slavery had indeed · become a central institution.

Great Britain abolished the transatlantic slave trade in 1807. In subsequent decades, other nations followed suit. Although abolition was

[37] Lovejoy, *Transformations in Slavery*, 133.

not initially effective – approximately 3,446,000 slaves were exported via the Atlantic in the nineteenth century – it became increasingly difficult for Africans to export slaves. Instead, the trade of so-called legitimate commodities (palm oil and groundnuts, for example) expanded as European demand increasingly turned to those products. The end of the slave trade had variable impact on Africa. The rulers of a few states in Atlantic Africa – like Oyo – experienced a crisis of adaptation after abolition. Some rulers were unable to adapt to the end of the slave trade. Other rulers and merchants, however, dealt with the potential economic impact of abolition by retaining an increasing number of slaves in Africa. The commercial and military networks that supplied slaves for the transatlantic slave trade were reoriented to meet African demand. Africans used slaves to produce legitimate commodities that were in high demand. They also produced goods consumed by ruling elites (as slaves had done long before the nineteenth century). Thus, the abolition of the transatlantic slave trade led to the expansion of high-density slavery in Africa. Slaves worked on agricultural estates throughout Atlantic Africa. They produced commodities that were centrally important to the success and survival of rulers and states. These agricultural estates varied in size. Slaves still worked in small groups, and had their own plots of land to farm and significant opportunity for mobility. But increasingly, the creation of slave-dominated agricultural estates – as well as the widespread use of slaves in craft production and mining – led to the increased exploitation of slaves and to fewer opportunities for any kind of social mobility. Slaves certainly resisted these changes, but often had little ability to force masters to provide them with privileges.

The consolidation of a system of slave supply, exchange, and production also occurred in the Islamic Savanna of West Africa and the Swahili Coast of East Africa. In the Savanna, a series of revolutionary Islamic holy wars led to the creation of large, stable Islamic states, the most successful being the Sokoto Caliphate. Although the rulers of these states were firmly opposed to the enslavement of other "good" Muslims, they had no compunctions about enslaving "bad" Muslims or non-Muslims. The holy wars of the West African Savanna produced *millions* of slaves, as did the raids and wars that continued afterward. By the end of the century, 25–30 percent (or more) of local populations labored in slavery; indeed, the state founded in 1818 by Seku Ahmadu – with its capital at Hamdullahi – relied extensively on

slave labor. Although many of the slaves continued to work in noneconomic roles – as concubines, officials, domestic servants – many more
were put to work on agricultural estates or in salt mines. Slaves still
had options that led to the amelioration of their working conditions or
eventual manumission – as slaves did virtually everywhere they were
used – but in the nineteenth century slaves worked longer and harder
in a productive capacity; in short, social mobility took longer and was
more contested than ever before. Those slaves who did not work in the
fields provided essential political, military, and reproductive labor. As
soldiers, slaves went to war to protect the state and to provide a steady
supply of slaves. As government officials, slaves managed taxation and
other vital state functions. As concubines, slaves helped the ruling elite
reproduce itself via childbearing, child-rearing, and as basic labor in
the service of elite households. On the East African coast, Omani
Arabs – and Swahili merchants – invested heavily in the production
of cloves, as well as other agricultural products (coconuts, cereals),
which led to the expansion of slavery along the coast. Slaves and ivory
were brought from the interior and sold into the Indian Ocean trade
or retained for use as labor in agricultural estates that specialized in
commodity production. Close to a *million* slaves were held on the coast
by the end of the nineteenth century. Although the size of agricultural
estates varied – as did the importance of slavery in production – the
nature of slavery changed. Customary protections that were formerly
offered to slaves were revoked in order to increase their productive
capacity and to enhance the overall control of masters. Finally, the
expansion of slavery took place far beyond these two regions. For
example, Egypt invaded the upper Nile Valley – now mainly Sudan –
in an effort to seize slaves for use as soldiers in Egyptian armies. New
irrigation techniques that came along with Egyptian rule expanded
agricultural production, which eventually led to the extensive use of
slave labor. In South Africa, Afrikaner frontiersmen migrated away
from the Cape into the interior of South Africa beginning in the 1830s,
where they built independent states. Afrikaners continued to raid and
use slaves, although their dependence on slavery was cloaked by claiming that they were "apprentices."

The consolidation of high-density slavery and new political structures also led to disorder and conflict. In West Africa, new predatory
states emerged – like Rabih's state, for example – that conquered huge
parts of the Savanna while raiding, trading, and using slaves. This
state was not bureaucratically stable like the Sokoto Caliphate, but

essentially lived off plunder. In the interior of East Africa, the demand for slaves along the coast led to increasing violence and instability. Commercial credit and caravans moved many slaves along routes to the coast, but the distinction between slave trading and raiding was often blurry, as coastal adventurers and entrepreneurs regularly acquired slaves by using violence. In other cases, predatory states – like that of Msiri or the Cokwe – were made possible only by raiding, selling, and using slaves. Thus, the demand for slaves on the Swahili Coast helped lead to the expansion of slave trading and slave use into the interior.

Conclusion: Slavery in African History

In this chapter I focused not merely on the "whys" of African slavery but also on the ways that different forms of slavery (political, domestic, productive) became dominant and changed over time. By the end of the nineteenth century, slavery was a central institution throughout the continent. More Africans were held in high-density slavery, and slavery was fundamentally tied to markets and production. Even in places where low-density slavery predominated, slavery dynamically changed and sometimes became a central institution. These changes were part of a contingent – and even a contradictory – process. People did not always take the long view, even as political, economic, or social forces encouraged them to acquire and use slaves. Slavery was not simply a nineteenth-century phenomenon. Nor was it primarily a response to external pressure generated in Europe, the Indian Ocean, or the Mediterranean; rather, slavery was a very old institution grounded in the earliest political, social, and economic struggles Africans faced. Although the forms of slavery varied dramatically, in the end, slaving allowed insiders to acquire outsiders and use them in ways that enhanced the insiders' power. The way slave owners used – and took advantage of – that inequality varied: sometimes slaves were acquired to add members to a lineage, to be used as soldiers, married, or placed on farms to produce commodities for a market. The ways slaves were acquired and used in turn shaped the extent to which slavery became closed, open, or something in between. Early African slavery was a way for the ambitious or powerful to expand their numbers and resources; slavery was largely concerned with securing access to the reproductive potential of outsiders. Over time, credit, commerce, and technology transformed African political and economic structures. Large, stable, and often highly militarized states were created by insiders who depended on outsiders as slaves. Slaves were used in specifically productive roles, but also helped build or protect new states and their rulers as soldiers, officials, and concubines. In short, slaves came to play a central role in the continuation of states, the ruling classes, government institutions, local households, and entire economies. The use of outsiders in this way had consequences, of course, which often led to further change, as other Africans adopted the slavers' strategies. We will now turn to a closer examination of the historical dynamics – the practice – of slavery in particular contexts, beginning with the complexities of slavery in decentralized societies.

CHAPTER 3

Slavery without States

Introduction

A Balanta man, Mam Nambtacha, described how Balanta communities dealt with the captives they acquired in the past, and focused on the way that children might eventually be incorporated after a long period of time living within a household:

> People went to distant *tabancas* [villages] to conduct *ostemoré* [a raid]. They carried away cows and other goods.... Captives could also be taken. The families could pay something and in the end could gain the liberty of the captured people. If the families could not pay, the captives stayed in the houses of their captors. For example, in the *tabanca* of Cumbumba, there was once an old man called Mpas Na Uale who was said to be in the subgroup Mansoanca. He had been captured in *ostemoré*. Since his family did not have the courage to pay a ransom and retrieve him from the *tabanca* of Cumbumba, Mpas Na Uale stayed there until he died. At that point he was not Balanta Mansoanca but a Balanta Nhacra. The practice of *ostemoré* was one of the things that led to the mixing of the Balanta with other ethnic groups.[1]

★ ★ ★

Early Africans were pioneers. In the previous chapter we saw that between 12000 and 9000 BCE, Africans began moving into a variety

---

[1] Hawthorne, *Planting Rice, Harvesting Slaves*, 140.

of ecological niches and gradually invented new subsistence strategies. Africans developed pastoralism as early as 7000 BCE and domesticated a variety of indigenous African food crops as early as 6000 BCE. Later – perhaps by 600 BCE – some early Africans mastered ironworking to produce better tools and weapons. These innovations gradually spread throughout the African continent. By 1000 CE, farming and ironworking were the building blocks of many African economies and societies. This transformed Africa. Between 2500 BCE and 1600 CE, settlements became larger and less mobile. New kinds of social and political systems emerged, which were often centered on the development of complex and hierarchal state systems. Slavery was deeply embedded in many of these early states and was often essential to their development.

While new kinds of states emerged out of these agricultural and iron revolutions, many Africans remained outside or only marginally connected to them. State formation was but one "pathway to complexity."[2] Africans living outside states were not contained in a timeless world of simplicity and disorganization. Complexity developed in the absence of formal state systems. Nor did decentralized political complexity inevitably lead to the development of states. Africans often strenuously avoided incorporation in states. Many Africans lived in communities that were *not* organized via centralized, purely political institutions (i.e., kingship), but were instead based mostly on kinship, with cross-cutting associations centered on age or achievement helping adjudicate communitywide decisions and organize labor. Although some scholars call these societies "stateless," the terms "horizontal" or "decentralized" fit better because they highlight the fact that these societies had both politics and a complex organization. Furthermore, decentralized communities sometimes existed within states and managed to retain significant amounts of independence. States seldom possessed the means to order the worlds of all of their subjects.

This chapter addresses the history of slavery in decentralized and kinship-oriented societies. I am primarily concerned with simple state systems and minimal but nascent inequality. I explore societies that existed outside the authority of states, people who lived within state systems but who remained effectively outside state-based

---

[2] To borrow the phrase coined by Susan Keech McIntosh. See McIntosh (ed.), *Beyond Chiefdoms: Pathways to Complexity in Africa* (Cambridge: Cambridge University Press, 1999).

institutions, and early decentralized polities dominated by big men. We have already observed that age (oldest-youngest) and sexual (male-female) divisions determined the allocation of power in many decentralized societies.[3] These societies focused on their own continuation – or reproduction – within the domestic economy. People consumed what they produced. Their goal was to increase the numbers of persons attached to the corporate unit to maximize labor output as well as to provide social insurance in bad times. In these societies, size did matter. Slaves were important political resources in decentralized communities, especially in the entourages of chiefs and big men. Although slave labor was sometimes essential to the reproduction of decentralized societies, the more market-oriented and stratified the society, the more slave labor came to be envisioned as a central means to produce a surplus – for either consumption or sale. In short, low-density slavery was not *only* a social or political institution. In some decentralized societies slavery became essential, widespread, and economically oriented. Even in these cases, however, most slaves were used and conceptualized within the overarching structures of kinship, which often encouraged the incorporation of slaves, sometimes quite rapidly and sometimes over the course of generations. That is, slaves regularly became junior members of kinship groups. Although they were – in theory – perpetual juniors, this too depended on how well they integrated and performed.

Thus, low-density slavery in decentralized societies had dynamic dimensions. Slaves facilitated reproduction in a variety of ways, whether by simply producing food or by cementing the political dominance of lineage elders, for example. Most important, slavery was a central strategy used by elites to consolidate and expand their own political and economic power. In societies where age structured access (or the lack of access) to resources, slavery allowed, in the words of Miller, some people to "bypass" both the "biological limits of human reproduction" and the slow social advancement that was normally governed by age and seniority.[4] That is, slavery offered insiders new opportunities and advantages that could not be realized by simply controlling kin. To understand when and why slavery emerged in

---

[3] See Lovejoy, *Transformations in Slavery*, 12–13.
[4] Joseph C. Miller, "Africa" in Paul Finkelman and Joseph C. Miller (eds.), *The Macmillan Encyclopedia of World Slavery* (London: Simon & Schuster Macmillan, 1998), 30 and Miller, *The Problem of Slavery as History*, 48–49.

these kinds of societies, we must first turn to the development of complex corporate groups based on kinship, and to the ways in which the political and social contradictions that emerged *within* those groups helped generate slavery.

Inventing Households, Lineages, and Kinship

As Africans colonized the continent, they invented methods to gain access to the productive and reproductive capacities of people. Many Africans did not own the land they worked or ruled. They instead acquired "use rights," which were the rights to use land by claiming membership in a household, descent group, or larger community.[5] The ownership of land did not generate wealth or capital in and of itself. Labor was required to produce goods that could be owned, consumed, or exchanged. Africans aimed not to control land, which was often easily available, but instead to control what the land produced. In other words, with a surplus of land, people became more valuable. There were numerous ways to mobilize people – by kinship or age, for example – but control over people *through slavery* offered perhaps the most efficient means of both claiming what was produced and increasing that production. Slaves made it possible for their owners to realize the potential wealth and status that could be generated from their use rights over land.

If land was available, it needed hands to work it. If states remained absent, corporate systems were necessary to organize that work and to help ensure survival and prosperity. The invention of kinship was a complex and long-term process that began very early in African history. For thousands of years, early Africans migrated and colonized new ecological frontiers. Before the Iron Age (c. 600 BCE–c. 1000 CE), much of this expansion was a product of the Bantu migrations, which were long-term and gradual movements of members of the Bantu language family across the African continent south of the equator. There were also many smaller migrations – such as those of the Cushites, Lwo, and Kwa, for example. The early Africans who colonized new frontiers had problems they needed to solve. They had

---

[5] See John Thornton, *Africa and Africans in the Making of the Atlantic World*, 1400–1680 (Cambridge: Cambridge University Press, 1992), 76. There were, of course, other methods. Thornton also emphasizes taxation.

to develop the means to exploit local environments. They also needed
to distinguish themselves from those who already occupied the land
into which they were moving. As a solution, they created corporate
groups based on kinship. Lineages integrated native and newcomer
through real or fictive family or kinship ties, served as an organizational structure that facilitated the expansion of labor, and governed
the acquisition and maintenance of use rights over land. By attaching and integrating people into their societies, newcomers increased
their own knowledge of, and control over, critical resources.[6] For early
Africans facing new environments and preexisting populations,

> [t]he safest course ... lay in expanding the kin group internally, by
> acquiring adherents who could qualify as kinsmen rather than by
> bringing in mere followers, who, in time, might become competitors.
> Compared to the allegiance of strangers, rights over kinsmen were more
> reliable. At the same time, externally, one also sought alliances with
> other local groups, and these were best achieved through ties of kinship
> and marriage. In both instances, kinship provided a ready-made pattern
> for binding relations in a frontier area that otherwise represented an
> institutional vacuum for newcomers.[7]

In other words, Africans aimed to accumulate what we have already
called a wealth in people. Over time, population densities increased,
access to land became more difficult, and the invention of ironworking produced new tools and better weapons. As methods of accumulation broadened and new means of violence emerged, possibilities
for conflict over power and resources increased. Broadly egalitarian
and openly incorporative systems were less necessary in this new
environment. This promoted early political centralization in the form
of big men. These competitive men aimed to control more people
and resources than anyone else did. To do so, big men needed to
prevent fission – or separation – of the lineage into smaller groups
led by competitors. They also sought to impose a much less egalitarian order within the corporate group while increasing the number of dependents they controlled. That is, they wanted power over

---

[6] See Kairn A. Klieman, *The Pygmies Were Our Compass: Bantu and Batwa in the History
of West Central Africa, Early Times to c. 1900 C.E.* (Portsmouth, NH: Heinemann,
2003), 72–73.

[7] Igor Kopytoff, "The Internal African Frontier: The Making of African Political
Culture" in I. Kopytoff (ed.), *The African Frontier: The Reproduction of Traditional
African Societies* (Bloomington: Indiana University Press, 1987), 44 as cited by
Klieman, *The Pygmies Were Our Compass*, 73.

others rather than broader equality. Lineage power brokers and big men increasingly made political decisions, controlled the allocation of resources – especially land – and played a central role in adjudicating disputes. Bilateral kinship – which encouraged open and fluid affiliation with both the mother's (matrilineal) and father's (patrilineal) lineages – receded, and unilineal forms of descent – which restricted affiliation to the mother's *or* the father's lineages and provided clearer lines of inheritance and succession for increasingly complex communities – came to dominate lineage kinship structures. A broad range of kinship relations fell under the terms "matrilineal" and "patrilineal." As Vansina notes, it is crucial to consider not just descent, but also patterns of "succession, inheritance, name-giving, [and] exogamy" that did not always reflect the "rules" of either form of unilineal descent. Those terms simply refer to the dominant principle among many in a region.[8] Unilineal descent permitted new kinds of accumulation via inheritance and marriage strategies and further encouraged the concentration of power in the hands of senior members – the big men – of the lineages and kinship groups: "[T]he advantage of a unilineally defined corporate group was to limit the number of claimants and to arrange them in a certain order of succession."[9] Big men increasingly claimed special status, often as the original founder of the lineage, and then used that status to enhance their authority and claims over goods (e.g., cows), people (e.g., women and children), and power. Success brought its own rewards. People wanted to join the prosperous and powerful through alliance or incorporation. Lineage juniors gained protection from lineage membership, but they also took on economic, political, and social obligations to the broader corporate group. Over time, lineage juniors might become seniors as they aged and accumulated status, wealth, and clients, and as they married and produced children, who in turn became new junior members of the lineage. Thus, villages grew as centers of population and power and were dominated by particular lineages or households within lineages and tied to others by bonds of kinship and marriage. Bridewealth became common as a means to facilitate the exchange of people. The fathers of new husbands were expected to give part of their wealth (often in the form of metals, foodstuffs, and animals) to the fathers or

[8] See Jan Vansina, *How Societies Are Born: Governance in West Central Africa before* 1600 (Charlottesville: University of Virginia Press, 2005), 91–92.
[9] Vansina, *How Societies Are Born,* 93.

uncles of new brides. To understand the role of slavery in this historical process more fully, we need to understand better how slavery provided a common solution to the contradictions that emerged between
the ideals and actual practices of kinship.

Slavery and the Lineage Ideal

Although the invention of unilineal descent was a critical element
in both initiating and expanding slavery in decentralized societies,
previous scholarship on these societies – and on low-density slavery
in general – has tended to focus primarily on the *noneconomic* use of
slaves. The social and political use of slaves in low-density slavery was
of course a central reason for their existence, but slaves also played
critical roles in production and reproduction, which were interrelated
anyway (i.e., people produced food and thereby ensured reproduction). Second, the scholarship has not taken account of historical
change. Lineages, decentralized polities, and low-density slavery are
often treated as changeless, fixed, and static. Miller, for example,
noted that because all "[African societies] embedded individuals in
social hierarchies, wherein each person had a unique status defined
by a multiplicity of obligations as well as protections that they had
built up through their lives," they did not develop ideas about "personal autonomy," nor did mutually exclusive categories of "slave"
and "free" exist across all time and space.[10] Instead, I argue that not
only did slavery and freedom become salient categories, but also that
slavery was the answer to the fundamental historical contradictions
Africans living in decentralized communities faced. The question we
ought to ask, then, is: when and why was slavery used to attach people to corporate groups?

Few decentralized societies existed without any attachment to markets or production of a surplus. Sometimes people living in decentralized societies accumulated, sold, or traded the surplus they produced
to internal or external markets. Thus, the economics of decentralized
societies were often far more complex than historians have recognized. Slavery emerged both as a means to address contradictions

---

[10] Miller, "Introduction" in Campbell, Miers, and Miller (eds.), *Women and Slavery,*
   vol. I, 26.

between the values of accumulation and kinship and as a function of the development of a complex, surplus-producing economy. Kinship practice provided incentives, protections, and privileges to junior members of lineages and clans. Kinship ideology emphasized the ideals of reciprocity and limited accumulation. But, as frontiers closed off, populations increased, and new kinds of military and commercial technologies developed, conflicts over accumulation increased, as did tensions between the "haves" and "have-nots," men and women, and the old and young. These conflicts centered on tensions between the integrative, reciprocal ideals of lineage and kinship organizations (we are all in this together) and the realities of increasing inequality, the desire to accumulate, and the consolidation of big men (powerful men make the choices and accumulate the most). Ideas about reciprocity and belonging did not go away. Junior members used them to limit the power of lineage seniors and big men, who could not ignore kinship-based rules and expectations that dictated how insiders were to be treated. But slavery permitted the attachment of people to corporate groups who could make none of the claims of free members grounded in kinship: "The key aspect of slaving was moving individuals ... into new surroundings where they found themselves alone, disabled culturally, and hence in position of overwhelming vulnerability."[11]

From where did slaves come? The development of big men increased the number of prisoners available. Once prisoners were turned into slaves – rather than simply being killed – powerful men had access to the largest numbers of them. Male slaves became a crucial part of the big man's entourage. While kin could be challengers and clients could change allegiances, slaves could do neither, and thus were the big man's most reliable dependents. These slaves also enjoyed the perks that the big man's power brought. Female slaves produced children, who sometimes inherited slave status, which expanded the size of the big man's household. A slave woman who produced children and who

---

[11] Joseph C. Miller, "Domiciled and Dominated: Slaving as a History of Women" in Campbell, Miers, and Miller (eds.), *Women and Slavery, vol. II*, 287–288. While reduction to status as property was not the sole defining characteristic of slavery everywhere in Africa, see also Finley: "The slave is an outsider: that alone permits not only his uprooting but also his reduction from a person to a thing that can be owned." Moses Finley, "Slavery" in *International Encyclopedia of the Social Sciences* (New York, 1968), 307–313 as cited by Martin Klein, *Slavery and Colonial Rule in French West Africa* (Cambridge: Cambridge University Press, 1998), 15.

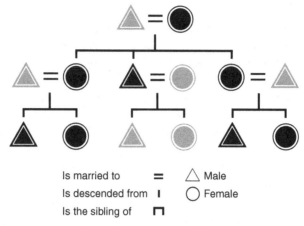

Is married to	=	△ Male
Is descended from	I	○ Female
Is the sibling of	⊓	

FIGURE 7. Matrilineal descent.

satisfied her master sexually could earn her master's favor and profit from the performance of her sons, as Klein notes:

> [S]laves may have liberated the chief or his wives from agricultural labour, or at least, reduced the need, and they probably provided food and drink for the chief's hospitality. The acquisition of slaves in early societies was one way either big men or descent groups increased their numbers and thus, their power.[12]

Specifically, the advantages slaves offered depended on whether matrilineal or patrilineal descent dominated. At its most basic, matrilineality simply meant that descent was traced through the maternal – or the mother's – line. A matrilineage was a multigenerational corporate group of members related to each other based on their ability to trace descent through females to the same female ancestor (Figure 7).

Both men and women inherited membership in the matrilineal line, but only women could pass that membership on to their descendants, as Figure 7 demonstrates. In matrilineages, fathers did not gain rights over their own children because they were unrelated to their wives' lineages and therefore not members of the matrilineage, who had the overall claim instead. The mother's brother (or maternal uncle from the perspective of "ego" in Figure 8) gained many of the specific "fatherly" claims and rights over his sister's children,

---

[12] Martin Klein, "Slavery and the Early State in Africa" in *Social Evolution & History* Vol. **8**, No. I (2009), 171–172.

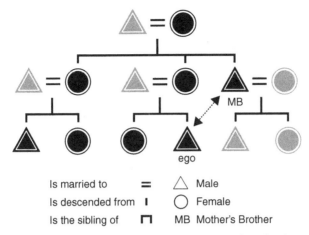

Is married to   =   △ Male
Is descended from   I   ○ Female
Is the sibling of   ⊓   MB Mother's Brother

FIGURE 8. Matrilineal descent and the mother's brother.

given that the matrilineage was composed of sisters and their brothers (from the same mother), as well as the children of the sisters and
of the daughters and so on (Figure 8). Thus, children did not inherit
their father's property. Fathers did not marry off their daughters and
gain bridewealth. Fathers did not control their children or grandchildren's labor power. A father's authority over his children was often less
important than that of the children's maternal uncle and matrilineage.
A typical matrilineage would contain, then, an older generation composed of brothers and sisters and the offspring of those sisters (who
were in effect claimed by the matrilineage via their mother's brothers)
via the maternal line.

The problem for matrilineages was that their population was limited by the number of a man's sisters who belonged to the matrilineage
(whereas in a patrilineal setting, a man could marry numerous wives
and produce children for his lineage). Only children of women affiliated with the matrilineage produced children who belonged. A man
literally *could not* produce children who "would be affiliated with his
own kin group" – they instead belonged to his wife's kin.[13] This produced tension. Fathers wanted to control their own children, while
uncles were concerned that they would lose control over those same
children, given that their sisters (the mothers of the children) lived with
their husbands outside of the uncles' direct, physical control. Here we

13 See Miers and Kopytoff (eds.), *Slavery in Africa*, 29.

see extensive, overlapping systems of authority, belonging, and kinship that enmeshed people within a swirling sea of possibilities that
also checked and balanced the assumption of too much authority. It is
easy to see why slaves were valuable in this kind of situation. Female
slaves married to powerful men produced children who belonged *only*
to the matrilineage of the father, in contrast to the "normal" pattern of
descent and belonging. Those children had no other claims placed on
them. Thus, it was possible through slavery to increase the number of
dependents significantly by marrying slave women, producing children
with them, and attaching them to the matrilineage whose labor power
was controlled purely by that father and the matrilineage of which he
was a part. Most important, these slave wives and children had no
other kinship networks on which to rely. They were wholly dependent
on the slave owner and father, which thereby enhanced the power of
the slave owner in lineage politics when he could greatly expand
the people under his control in this manner. The entire lineage also
benefited in terms of the expansion of the raw labor power of female
slaves. Finally, the children of female slaves sometimes inherited their
mother's slave status, as did subsequent generations, which meant that
the matrilineage itself could reduce the potential of internal competition and threats from these slaves over time. Male slaves acquired
were of course valued as clients, laborers, and retainers, but in addition, should they marry free women, children of those marriages did
not inherit slave status (which was carried via women). However, the
children of these sorts of unions had "no loyalties outside their lineage" because their fathers were slaves, which made them especially
valuable as lineage members.[14] Obviously, over time, the gradual incorporation of slaves was more likely than in highly commercialized and
high-density contexts, but the point remains that slaves were acquired
(and possessed value) because they could be *excluded* from all of the
normal rights (i.e., inheritance, fatherhood) possessed by kin and free
lineage members.

In the case of patrilineages, the value of slaves was more straight-
forward. Patrilineal descent refers to the practice of tracing descent
through the male line. A patrilineage was a multigenerational corporate group of people related through the male line to a common male
ancestor. A patrilineage was generally composed of a man, his wives, their
children, and so on (Figure 9). Fathers had claims over their children,

---

[14] Miers and Kopytoff, *Slavery in Africa*, 29.

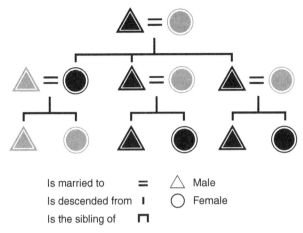

Is married to   =   △ Male

Is descended from | ○ Female

Is the sibling of   ⊓

FIGURE 9. Patrilineal descent.

who became part of the broader patrilineage. Married daughters left the lineage and produced children with their husbands, who then in turn became part of their husband's (and not their father's) lineage. Reproduction of the lineage, then, depended on men acquiring wives, producing children, and using female children to acquire bridewealth when they married. Why were slaves valued in this context? Although men did not vie for control over their children in the same manner as those in matrilineages, slaves also provided useful advantages as wives or concubines nonetheless. When lineage men married or took a slave as a concubine and produced children, those children, as well as the slave, were exclusively claimed by the owner – the father – and by the patrilineage. While the free wife and her children were protected by her kinship links outside the husband's control – via her own kinship and lineage ties and the payment of bridewealth – slaves were not. The male in this scenario not only increased his wealth in people – who helped ensure continued productivity and the reproduction of the lineage – but he gained more rights and powers over those persons, specifically because, as in matrilineal settings, they were excluded from normal kinship ties. The benefits for women in *some* of these contexts was that marriage to free males could provide important avenues for social integration into the master's/husbands/owner's society. In some societies, for example, the children of slave women who had children by free men actually inherited free status (although in their first generation they too might suffer because their kinship networks were shallower as a result of their mother's status). Females might also be married off to male slaves, whose children belonged to the owner. Finally, men in this context were acquired commonly, but they were usually used as labor, as soldiers, or to facilitate reproduction via a slave marriage.

The danger in presenting kinship as I have earlier is that African lineage and kin relationships are frozen in time. My purpose rather was to demonstrate that kinship relations and slavery were not focused unproblematically on the goal of social "integration." In the real world, kinship relations changed, were modified, or were blends of a variety of patterns, and people often had fluid and contingent understandings about kinship. As Rhiannon Stephens notes, "[S]ocieties have ... changed their models of descent and communities have developed specific forms of those models to serve their needs (or the needs of influential groups within them)."[15] The ideal descent systems found in the pages of textbooks changed in the real world – often in response to tensions and conflicts within societies or to new ecological or economic conditions. Kinship relations should be treated historically. Patrilineal and matrilineal patterns of descent influenced, but did not always determine, how slaves were used. Although kinship was a central factor that shaped slavery in decentralized societies, it is also important to note that slavery was also impacted by broader political, social, and economic changes as well. Nonetheless, slaves were acquired in low-density settings because they could be *excluded* from the kinship dynamic. This in turn allowed the powerful to expand their rights and claims over people in new ways.

Incorporation and Manumission in Decentralized Societies

Kinship-based slavery and slaving strategies had consequences. Continuing contradictions between slavery and the ideologies of kinship and descent often necessitated that outsiders *eventually* be integrated in a variety of ways – through their children, marriage, or via worldly success. The integration of slaves was a necessity at some point in nearly every place slaves were used. Africa was not unique in that

---

[15] See "Rhiannon Stephens, "Lineage and Society in Precolonial Uganda" in *Journal of African History* **50**, 2 (2009), 205. See also Neil Kodesh, "Networks of Knowledge: Clanship and Collective Well-being in Buganda" in *Journal of African History* **49**, 2 (2008), 197–216.

regard. But in decentralized and low-density settings, three factors facilitated what was sometimes rapid integration. First, these societies often had no structural position for slaves outside kinship. To use an example beyond Africa, the Iroquois could be brutal, torturing their prisoners, or they could totally integrate them because there was otherwise no structural slot for them. Many decentralized societies in Africa were in similar positions. Second, the intensity of face-to-face relationships coupled with the need to secure and access slave reproduction facilitated integration. At some point the continued existence of acculturated, long-term slaves within kinship-oriented groups produced social tensions over slave and free statuses. Some slaves could, for example, make claims as wives rather than workers, which facilitated integration, often along terms that favored the slave. Women could use sex and sexuality to enhance their social integration and connection to their masters, for example. Third, and unlike high-density slavery, centralized political institutions and standing armies did not exist. Lineages and houses were the largest political structures. The means of violence was, as a result, significantly smaller than in state-based systems. Large numbers of unattached slaves could represent a real risk in low-density settings. That risk was managed by providing mechanisms and means for the gradual assimilation of slaves over the course of generations.

But it is also critical not to overstate the integrative nature of low-density slavery. The issue was not simply about "integration" or "belonging" in the abstract. Rather, we need to understand the terms on which integration occurred; in other words, how and in what ways one could belong. This was not always a smooth or automatic process. Jonathon Glassman, for example, emphasizes that conflict was often at the center of integration:

> [S]laves were outsiders who were acquired by force, denied the rights and honor of full membership in local communities and kin groups.... The slaves resisted this alienating state of affairs most often by demanding what was denied them: more autonomous participation in local social reproduction, that is, fuller membership in local institutions of community and kinship. These demands gave rise to conflicts which ultimately determined the nature of the slave system. Sometimes these were partially resolved by the eventual absorption of the slave population into the non-slave community.[16]

[16] Jonathon Glassman, "The Bondsman's New Clothes: The Contradictory Consciousness of Slave Resistance on the Swahili Coast" in *Journal of African History* vol. 32, no. 2 (1991), 283–284.

Even female slaves, who were often the most quickly and easily integrated, were not offered the same privileges and protections as free
women enjoyed. Not all female slaves had the same opportunities to
gradually assimilate. Among the Mangbetu peoples of northeastern
Zaire, female slaves were not real wives because bridewealth was not
paid as part of the marriage and they brought no lineage to be joined
to her husbands. This meant that the slave wife was not worthy of
respect or honored in the same way as free wives were, as a Mangbetu
elder noted: "A free wife merited dignity and was dowered. A slave
wife had no dignity. She could not respond when her husband spoke.
You became her father, mother, brother, sister to her. She could not
leave. One preferred a free wife because she could go back to her family and bring back [gifts]."[17] Likewise, Robert Harms notes that in the
case of the Middle Zaire river region:

> The manipulation of marriages formed a clear contrast to the rights
> held by free women in marital arrangements. As a general rule, free girls
> had the right to refuse suitors. If a suitor paid earnest money while the
> girl was still young and she refused him when she reached the age of
> marriage, the father paid back the earnest money ... the matrilineage
> of a woman ... retained rights in her children ... a free woman who was
> unhappy with her husband could leave him and return to her parents.
> Slave women on the other hand, had no say in the choice of a husband
> and no control over their offspring.[18]

Overall, then, slavery and incorporation in decentralized contexts was
understood via idioms and practices of kinship. Decentralized societies
often had high rates of integration, but the integrative process was both
complex and contradictory. Because kinship in this context provided
the ideological basis for social organization, dominance and submission – as well as the degree to which one did or did not belong – were
expressed in those terms. Thus masters might be "fathers" and slaves
"children" – but those terms did not mean that slaves could claim the
same rights as free children, nor were those terms expressions of real
and substantive kinship ties. Rather, in decentralized settings, slaves
were attached to units using the operative language of power, which

---

[17] Curtis A. Keim, "Women Slavery among the Mangbetu" in Claire Robertson and
Martin Klein (eds.), *Women and Slavery in Africa* (Portsmouth, NH: Heinemann,
1997), 148.
[18] Robert Harms, "Sustaining the System: Trading Towns along the Middle Zaire" in
Robertson and Klein (eds), *Women and Slavery in Africa*, 105.

was in this case grounded in the benefits and inequalities of kinship. Incorporation – which I have noted numerous times was certainly more common in low-density settings – was not the automatic product of the way kinship worked or the assimilative character of these societies, but was a function of the nature of slavery as well as a product of the actions and goals of slaves – and masters – themselves.

Kinship and Slavery among the Anlo-Ewe, Kabre, and Mangbetu

To help illustrate these complexities, we now turn to the Anlo of West Africa. The Anlo initially practiced patrilineal descent. However, when Akwamu conquered the Anlo in the eighteenth century, they brought with them a matrilineal inheritance system. This involved nephews inheriting the acquired property of their maternal uncles. The otherwise patrilineal Anlo adopted this inheritance pattern. At the same time, many Anlo lineages and households were engaged in extensive competition over the acquisition of people. Why? Sandra Greene has demonstrated that some prosperous Anlo acquired numerous female slaves, whose availability reduced the need for husbands to demand that their wives spend the majority of their time in the husband's households. Slave wives could do the work and provide children instead. This led many Anlo wives to spend more time with their own kin, often in their brother's households. In turn, the brother of such a sister gained access not just to her labor power but also to that of her children, to add to that of his slaves and slave children, who were especially vulnerable – and who were known to work harder as a result – given they had no kin to protect and include them. Wealthy families benefited from this informal arrangement most because they had the capital to accumulate slaves, which made the whole process possible. Poorer households looked for ways to follow the pattern by seeking to control the marriages of their daughters more fully via matrilateral cross-cousin marriage. When a man betrothed his daughter to his sister's son (who were matrilateral cousins), the father of the bride could then claim his nephew's labor because the father of bride was obliged to pass on his acquired property to his new son-in-law and nephew. The father of the bride also had the right to claim the labor of the children produced by the union of his daughter and nephew, because their grandchildren inherited his acquired property as well.

All of this labor could then be added to that of slave wives and children – if available – to produce and expand the household. Regardless,
poorer households and lineages remained competitive via the manipu-
lation of kinship. Slavery introduced a new dynamic into kinship relations. As slaves, they remained outside normal kinship relationships.
They were valuable for their work and reproductive potential in ways
that changed the dynamics of the kinship relationships that they were
beyond.

Likewise, the Kabre, who occupied parts of northern Togo in West
Africa, sold their own children into the transatlantic slave trade. This
illustrates the complex interactions between kinship, accumulation,
and slavery. Charles Piot has argued that the Kabre practiced a pres-
tational economy – that is, an economy that was focused on the "cir-
culation of things-as-gifts."[19] The value of the things was based on
the differing needs of the buyer and/or seller, which meant that the
value of a goat, for example, might change depending on how much
the buyer needed it or how much the seller needed to sell, as well as
how much labor it required to produce that particular object. Things
were not exchanged for currency, but for other things. However, the
real objective was to convert those things into people by giving of gifts
or loans – in the form of, for example, land, animals, or beer – to others in order to establish personal ties. The goal was to build relationships with other people by giving, exchanging, borrowing, and loaning
goods in the hopes of eventually creating a longer-term bond – known
as *ikpanture*. When this happens, "Kabre say that the two individuals and their houses, have 'become one' and that the tie cannot be
broken."[20]

The ownership of things was tied to their labor inputs; in other
words, if one expended labor to sow fields, the crop was theirs for that
reason (not because they owned the land but because they expended
the necessary muscle power to sow and harvest the crop). It was
possible to have multiple claims of ownership to the same item. For
example, the food, farms, or money of a person could be claimed by
another if it was not in use – all land had multiple potential owners
and many might have access to that land to farm if it was not otherwise being used by another. This was also – and here we (finally) move

---

[19] Charles Piot, "Of Slaves and the Gift: Kabre Sale of Kin During the Era of the Slave
Trade" in *Journal of African History* 37, 1 (1996), 36.
[20] Piot, "Of Slaves and the Gift, 37.

back to kinship – true of persons. Although the Kabre were patrilineal, a "mother's brother is said to 'own' his sister's children until they complete their initiations."[21] Only after initiation is the father able to claim the labor power of his children. Thus, people who accumulated things (and persons) risked that others would claim those things unless they were in use. The best strategy, then, was not to accumulate extensive amounts of land or animals, for example, but to lend out those goods, and to thereby preserve them from the claims of others while also using them to build relationship and ties – and access – to people. The goal was not to simply accumulate property, but rather to circulate that property as widely as possible in the hopes of building to *ikpanture* and also to immobilize other people's claims to that property.

In the era of the transatlantic slave trade, the Kabre – specifically the mother's brother – were known to have sold their children to slavers. Why? Given the nature of the Kabre economy and the dual claims to children of father's and mother's brothers, children were sold by mother's brothers in order to take advantage of the stronger claim to those children *before* their father could make such a claim. Furthermore, those children were sold for cowries – a form of currency – that could then be claimed by the mother's brother and lent out or circulated to establish personal ties. This dynamic would have been impossible should a mother's brother not make the claim to those children when he could. Otherwise, he would have failed to immobilize the father's claim and would not have been able to acquire things – in the form of cowries – that he could in turn convert into people via lending, as Piot notes: "[A] mother's brother didn't simply keep the cowries for himself; he gave some to the child's mothers (his sister), some to its father, some to his own mother's brother, and so on.... Thus he redistributed the cowries back along the chain of people who had produced the child."[22] Certainly, the Kabre example tells us little about low-density slaveholding *within* their particular society, but it does demonstrate how kinship could be manipulated to encourage accumulation and the ways in which access to slaves might powerfully impact the strategies of Africans, especially the powerful.

One final example: slavery among the Mangbetu peoples of northeastern Zaire disrupted the normal politics of kinship and helped a big man consolidate power. Nabiembali used male slaves to secure

---

[21] Piot, "Of Slaves and the Gift, 41.
[22] Piot, "Of Slaves and the Gift, 46.

power in a new and revolutionary manner. Rather than relying on kin, Nabiembali used a group of male slaves to produce goods and fight in wars. Using these slaves, he gained political control over all the lineages in the region, which had previously been governed by elder men based on kinship. He also "used his male slaves against some of his own sons.... He refused to recognize the sons' claim to power.... He could ignore their demands – which were legitimate under the lineage system of rule – because he had the support of his slave Dakpala and other non-Mangbetu factions."[23] Thus, Nabiembali acquired substantial political power by ignoring kinship and relying on slaves instead.

Work and Labor in Low-Density Slavery

We have no way of knowing precisely how many slaves were used in decentralized societies. We can infer that slave use was common, but given the paucity of source material, we will never have anything resembling a precise percentage or number. Moreover, local social and political structures often rendered slaves unnecessary or restricted their use. Hawthorne notes, for example, that the existence of age grades among the Balanta led to a desire to acquire women and especially children rather than adult males. Why? Male slaves were difficult to integrate into age grades: "Since members of male age grades were bound together through the course of their lives, passing as a group from one social rank to the next ... captured grown men (or even adolescents) could not be incorporated into *tabanca* [village] life."[24] Because outsiders could not be members of the age grades, they literally had no place in the community. Children, on the other hand, could be brought into age grades early on or, in the case of women, could be integrated through marriage. Although slaves were by definition outsiders, the *possibility* of integrating them was essential for slavery to function as an institution. The Balanta therefore either killed the men they raided or sold them to Atlantic traders, while they retained children (and women, whom they also sold) in larger numbers for use as labor and as wives.

Decentralized societies varied widely in terms of their complexity, occupational specializations, and organization. While they tended to

---

[23] Keim, "Women Slavery among the Mangbetu," 146–147.
[24] Hawthorne, *Planting Rice and Harvesting Slaves*, 141.

be organized around kinship structures, some were almost completely acephalous and unattached to commerce or markets, while others were significantly stratified and engaged in specialized craft production and the exchange of goods via commercial networks. In general, most people worked as farmers and organized themselves in domestic units. The more complex added groups of people who were specialists in a variety of occupations (e.g., hunting, fishing, blacksmithing, ritual/religious). Others developed trade and market systems, as well as extensive cross-cutting associations (councils, age grades, title-holding societies) to make and enforce communitywide decisions.

This all impacted how slaves worked. In the least stratified and market-oriented societies, slaves worked at numerous tasks, mostly related to the production of foodstuffs for the domestic unit or as domestic labor (hauling water, building fires, clearing bush, etc.). That work, while useful, was no different than the work performed by free men. Slaves could have been easily replaced by free men; their role in productive labor was often of minor importance compared with their roles as domestic servants or political retainers. More often the actual work of slaves was important in decentralized societies, even if it was balanced by social and political uses. Because the limiting factor of production was the number of hands one controlled versus the amount of land one held, slavery increased the overall productive output. This freed people from some labor-intensive tasks, facilitated occupational specialization and increased food production, which ensured continued household and lineage reproduction. More hands at work meant that more food was produced to be consumed, stored for insurance in bad times, or exchanged for goods that were not produced locally. Although slaves produced these goods, they had no claims over them in exchange for their labor, unlike free men and even women. Thus, slavery facilitated the reproduction of the corporate group *and* the accumulation of wealth in the hands of politically powerful men as their heads.

The Diola societies of southern Senegal, Gambia, and Guinea-Bissau, for example, were decentralized wet rice farmers. The slaves acquired by the Diola were used for a variety of purposes, including as a supplement to household agricultural labor. However, the labor they provided for the cultivation of rice was less important than their role in expanding the numbers and therefore the prestige of the household to which they were attached. This prestige gave free members of the household better access to, and enhanced influence in, assemblies and religious rituals associated with a number of spirit shrines. Male slaves worked their own rice paddies and might eventually be permitted to marry, but masters retained the right to take their livestock and a portion of their rice. Female slaves were usually married to free men, and their children acquired the status of their fathers whether slave or free. The slaves worked their own rice paddies using their own household labor and consumed much of what they produced. Clearly, this kind of slavery was not tied to rationalized commodity production for internal or external markets, but was linked instead to domestic and household reproduction as well as to the desire of the free to aggregate dependents for religious, social, and political activities.[25]

In contrast, the Sena of Mozambique used slaves more directly for productive purposes. Barbara and Allen Isaacman noted that the agricultural output of the Sena was quite low: "[T]he size of the surplus that a lineage segment could accumulate varied in direct proportion to the number of its economically productive members."[26] Adding dependents therefore led to greater wealth. Particular lineages enhanced their positions by exchanging their perishable agricultural surplus for a nonperishable status item or to add further to the lineage via bridewealth or slavery. Once slaves were acquired, they referred to their master and his family using kinship terminology, such as *baba* for father. If captured as children, they guarded livestock, collected firewood, and worked in the fields alongside free children. Eventually, an acquired slave would be married – usually to a member of his owner's family – which provided economic and political benefits for the master as well as an avenue of incorporation for the slave. The acquisition of slaves expanded the productive capacity of lineages, its access to people, and its access to other status items, which enhanced the overall power and status of the lineage. Access to political power was directly related to the size of the lineage: "A large following enabled the lineage to mobilize a disproportionate number of people in times of internal conflict.... The absence of a standing army meant that larger lineage segments also played a more prominent role in the defense of the village," which enhanced the prestige and power of that particular

---

[25] See Robert Baum, "Slaves Without Rulers: Domestic Slavery Among the Diola of Senegambia" in Spaulding and Beswick (eds.), *African Systems of Slavery*, 45–66.

[26] Barbara Isaacman and Allen Isaacman, "Slavery and Social Stratification among the Sena of Mozambique" in Miers and Kopytoff (eds.), *Slavery in Africa*, 107.

lineage.[27] By no means was slavery *the* central means of production, nor was slaving *the* central means of acquiring dependents; nonetheless, slavery was useful for interrelated economic, political, and social reasons, tied to both production and reproduction.

The importance of slavery to *both* production and reproduction further explains why females were usually the most highly desired slaves. Female slaves were acquired to produce children, for sex, and for work. We know that slaves in low-density contexts were not used on plantations, and no doubt played a less central economic role than in high-density slavery, but the existing sexual division of labor required women to perform most of the agricultural tasks in the fields: "The dominant ... pattern was for women slaves to do the same things free women did, which meant most of the agricultural and virtually all of the domestic work."[28] In short, female slaves worked and possessed added reproductive and sexual advantages that male slaves generally did not, especially in this kind of context, as Harms notes of the Middle Zaire river region:

> [T]he people who profited most directly from the labor of slave girls were not the male masters, but their senior wives. While it would take a senior wife years to bear and raise enough children to form a working group from which she could extract a surplus, she could quickly create a large working group if her husband bought slave girls. The key difference between free and slave girls lay in the relative ease with which the latter could be recruited. Slave recruitment allowed senior wives at Bonga, for example, to leave the agricultural work to the slave girls while they concentrated on local commerce and social functions.[29]

The Igbo, Slavery, and Economic Change in a Decentralized Society

The Igbo now occupy a large region of southeastern Nigeria. At some point in the past (a precise date is impossible to find), the Igbo came to share a broad set of political and cultural beliefs including, among many others, similar religious beliefs, ideas about governance, power

---

[27] Isaacman and Isaacman, "Slavery and Social Stratification among the Sena of Mozambique," 117.

[28] Robertson and Klein (eds.), *Women and Slavery in Africa*, 11.

[29] Robert Harms, "Sustaining the System: Trading Towns along the Middle Zaire" in Robertson and Klein (eds.), *Women and Slavery in Africa*, 101.

and authority, kinship structures, and methods of farming. Igbo communities were not homogeneous. They were profoundly heterogeneous. But at some point in time people came to consider themselves Igbo and came to demarcate particular – and always changing – practices and beliefs as "Igbo." All in all, the Igbo emerged out of both the agricultural and iron revolutions. They developed an intricate and extensive market and trading system as well as a largely dispersed, decentralized system of authority and governance that seldom included kings or centralized political power.

Because most Igbo lived in decentralized communities, the largest political unit was the village, although as Ugo Nwokeji notes, some Igbo developed forms of centralized authority.[30] Igbo villages were composed of a number of patrilineages, which shared common descent and occupied a common territory. Although there were significant variations, most Igbo communities were organized around kinship, village assemblies, and sometimes informal councils. Decisions were generally made in village assemblies, which were made up of free men who debated political and economic questions. The process of decision making was shaped by the contributions of older and/or high-achieving men, who were often the heads of the village patrilineages. They sometimes sat on councils but in many cases simply contributed to debate and discussion. Because they possessed greater authority and prestige, they often guided and influenced decision making: "[P]recolonial Igbo society had a political system in which no individual or institution was paramount, in the sense of serving as the sole or exclusive source of all political authority. Power and authority were decentralized, so that political roles were diffuse."[31] Religious authorities also played important roles in adjudicating moral and legal issues, as did age grade associations (composed of a variety of men based on their specific ages) and other associational groups (title-granting societies, professional guilds).

Inequality and conflicts over accumulation existed, of course. Age, ability, wealth, and descent were critical variables for the acquisition of status and power. In many Igbo communities, one key to prestige and power came with formal entry into titled associations. Successful

---

[30] See G. Ugo Nwokeji, *The Slave Trade and Culture in the Bight of Biafra: An African Society in the Atlantic World* (Cambridge: Cambridge University Press, 2010), 14–15.

[31] Ebere Nwaubani, "Chieftancy Among the Igbo: A Guest on Center Stage" in *The International Journal of African Historical Studies* 27, 2 (1994), 348.

men throughout Igboland used some of their wealth to purchase titles – which were ranked from lowest to highest in prestige – and which were to be purchased and taken in a prescribed order after an often grueling set of rituals were performed. By taking a title, a man was permitted to wear its symbol (often an ivory anklet or a colored hat) that outwardly signified power and success. This historical dynamic differed in its specifics from lineage to lineage and village to village, but, as Victor Uchendu notes, the common general practice was for prestige/status to be "achieved by those who could convert their wealth into less tangible symbols by buying 'positions' in exclusive clubs and secret societies."[32] In Igboland, seniority brought status, but so did achievement, leadership, and descent (the heads of powerful patrilineages were often in the best initial position to accumulate people, wealth, and titles).

Early in Igbo history, slaves were used as extra hands or for domestic and prestige purposes. Gradually, two forms of servitude emerged throughout Igboland. The *ohu* were regular slaves owned by persons, while the *osu* were so-called cult slaves, who were permanently attached to religious authorities. Until the nineteenth century, *ohu* slavery was common enough throughout Igboland, but was not an essential part of the economic and social structure. Slaves were acquired for a mixed bag of reasons, including economic (for agricultural and domestic labor), political (to help in raids and plunder), or social (as status symbols, ritual sacrifice). Most slaves were captured in war and kidnapping, although an increasing number were bought and sold in slave markets held throughout the region or sent into slavery as a result of crimes committed. Younger slaves were especially desired. They were more easily controlled than adults were. Unlike most of Africa, until the middle of the nineteenth century, male slaves were valued over female. This was likely a result of the vital role men played in yam production and the value placed on that labor.[33]

Slavery was highly variable in Igboland, but in general *ohu* slaves worked a number of specific days for their masters and a number of days for themselves. Sometimes slaves worked an assigned plot of personal land on the days they worked for themselves. Slaves worked alongside members of the households or lineages to which they were attached on the days they worked for their masters, where they often worked harder

---

[32] Victor Uchendu, "The Igbo" in Miers and Kopytoff (eds.), *Slavery in Africa*, 124.
[33] In general, see Nwokeji, *The Slave Trade and Culture in the Bight of Biafra*.

and were subject to more and different kinds of discipline. Limits on workdays were not always respected. In nineteenth-century Aboh, slaves were supposed to work for their master every fourth day in a four-day market week (and therefore worked three days for themselves), but they also had to work as members of their master's war canoes and therefore worked for entire weeks at a time. Most slaves lived in the same compounds as their masters, but in some rare cases they lived in separate slave villages. Routes to manumission existed, although that process was often long and took place over a number of years, sometimes generations. Slaves were often left with continuing social, economic, and political disabilities, including being responsible for continued labor for their master, an inability to marry the freeborn, weak legal protections, and an inability to acquire titles other than slave titles. Freed slaves might found junior lineages of servile origins. The association with slave status remained a social stigma, sometimes for generations. Most often, manumission came via incorporation, which often occurred after a slave proved himself a member of the community through extraordinary service (killing an enemy or an animal), by acquiring land, or via self-redemption (paying the master a fee). Uchendu has described the manumission cycle for slaves, although it probably never functioned as smoothly or was conflict free for the slaves:

> A child slave might be attached to the household of one of his master's wives, where he strengthened its labor force and therefore gained his subsistence. Approaching adulthood, he was allowed to earn an independent income by hiring himself out one day in the four-day week. He could invest his income in livestock and take their increase. This acquisition of wealth, which is recognized by the Igbo as an important index of social status, seemed to complete the process. In the case of women, marriage quickened the process of manumission provided that it was a union between [a] slave woman and her master or another freeman. On the other hand, marriages between slaves tended to perpetuate a slave lineage, with all the attached stigma.

The nature of the incorporation process varied across Igboland. In Owerri, for example, the process was arduous and long. The price for self-redemption was the full purchase price of the slave in question plus 100 percent interest and even with that fee: "the mere payment of a fee did not bring complete acceptance in the ranks of the freeborn."[34] Women had wider opportunity for marriage to freeborn Igbo, but were negatively impacted by the inability to own land, which

---

[34] Nwokeji, *The Slave Trade and Culture in the Bight of Biafra*, 326.

was a central avenue to manumission and a demonstration of full citizenship. This undermined some avenues to manumission for women while favoring men.

Although low-density slavery predominated in Igboland, high-density slavery developed in some places. A decentralized society like the Igbo could develop high-density slavery if the economic and political conditions were right. Early slaving began as Igbo communities grew in coherence and size. Igboland was (and is) one of the most densely populated regions of Africa. Unlike many other parts of Africa, land was not easily available and was in high demand. This made slaves even more valuable. In some cases slaves were acquired specifically for the skills they might contribute to the household and patrilineage. As the open frontier diminished, Igbo slavers were motivated by the desire to secure exploitable extra hands who could be used for a wide variety of purposes, and who were not subject to normal kinship and lineage rules. Slaves worked harder than free persons did. Slave production thereby aided domestic and lineage reproduction within the subsistence oriented economy of the early Igbo. *Ohu* slaves both supplemented household labor and increased the power and status of the heads of households and the broader patrilineages to which they belonged. Between the seventeenth and nineteenth centuries, Igbo production and trade increased regionally and internationally. Much of the region developed substantial trade linkages with the coast and traded commodities – including human beings – in large numbers. This also meant that the region was flooded with new kinds of commercial goods as part of that trade. Igbo communities were increasingly involved in the production of goods for the coastal and Igbo markets, which included the production of palm oil, cotton, and yams even as the trade in slaves diminished over the course of the nineteenth century. An Igbo elder from Asaba noted:

> Asaba bought and sold slaves. They bought them primarily for burial ceremonies and for services such as manual labor on their farms and for the production of palm oil and other needs. Each quarter of Asaba had its "slave camp" ... from among whom about six or eight men could be taken against their will for a burial ceremony of an Obi or titled man. They were used also as a means of exchange..... Most slaves bought were either from the East or some section of the northern region adjacent to the East.[35]

---

[35] Elizabeth Isichei, "Historical Change in an Ibo Polity: Asaba to 1885" in *Journal of African History* **10**, 3 (1969), 424.

Historians of slavery have tended to argue that slavery in Igboland was *transformed* as a result of two major and external factors: the transatlantic slave trade and the rise of the trade in nonhuman commodities, the so-called legitimate trade, which developed after the transatlantic slave trade was abolished. In general, these historians believe that this era encouraged the spread of slavery, given the huge demand for slaves and commercialization of the trade to the coast.[36] The transatlantic slave trade and rise of legitimate commerce also changed the ways slaves were perceived and used. In general, it is argued, Africans moved toward the use of chattel slaves in the production of commodities. In some cases, this led to the creation of true slave societies, in which slaves were used in production in ways that were absolutely central to the entire political economy.

It would be silly to deny that the low-density slavery of Igboland was not impacted by the massive changes at work in the eighteenth and nineteenth centuries. More slaves worked to produce palm oil than ever before, and there were more slaves than in previous centuries. In places – especially in areas dominated by Igbo slavers known as the Aro – social stratification increased, along with militarization, the intensity of slave exploitation, and slave rebelliousness. Masters and slaves were more than ever in conflict over work, incorporation, and the overall moral economy, especially in areas where slaves were used intensively in production. However, slavery was not new to the Igbo. Slaves were still used as household and lineage labor. The production of palm oil was but one strategy used to sustain and protect Igbo villages, as well as to generate wealth for the powerful in Igbo society. Slaves never became the sole producers of palm oil. The production of palm oil was performed by small-scale farmers using household labor according to preexisting Igbo land tenure systems. Certainly, the heads of lineages had access to larger amounts of communal land attached to their positions and therefore in these centuries used larger numbers of slaves in production than ever before, but even here the ideological shift was not necessarily that dramatic. Igbo lineage heads already used slavery and understood how it could provide extra labor beyond kinship. The Igbo had long used slaves because they offered a means to escape and work around the kinship-defined norms of obligation and reciprocity. In this case, moving slaves into the production of palm oil did not require a massive shift in how the Igbo viewed and

---

[36] See especially Lovejoy, *Transformations in Slavery*.

understood slavery, although in places the *scale* of that labor increased as did slave resistance to these demands. Thus, by the end of the nineteenth century, in some parts of Igboland high-density slavery became more common, but, in general, for most Igbo, low-density slavery – grounded in notions of kinship, focused on local households and the domestic, and that used slaves in a wide variety of roles – was predominant. For slaves, it *is* clear that some objected to the increased demands on their labor associated with palm oil, but there was little they could actually do about it other than run away, rebel, or look for other avenues toward freedom/incorporation. Slavery in Igboland – while changed – remained tied to the nuances and understandings of freedom and slavery that existed long before the nineteenth century

Conclusion

Although decentralized societies have often been ignored or simplified by historians, in this chapter I have argued that by examining them we might better answer some of the central questions about slavery in Africa. The extended family-kin-descent structures of decentralized societies protected their members, facilitated the extraction of labor, and ensured reproduction. Slavery emerged in these societies partly as a result of the increasing and profound contradiction between the ideals of kinship and its actual practice over time. As big men came to dominate some kinship units, and as new kinds of technologies emerged that enhanced preexisting inequalities, slavery became a useful strategy to acquire new kinds of dependents who had few if any of the protections granted to kin. In some cases, this was a primarily political strategy. Slaves were used as retainers or as status and prestige objects that enhanced the numbers and power of particular lineages or other kinship-based corporate groups. In other cases, however, slavery was an economic strategy, aiming at the acquisition of dependents who worked to produce goods that might enrich their owners – as well as the broader kin or lineage group – in a variety of ways.

In most decentralized contexts, low-density slavery predominated. The opportunities for slaves to struggle for incorporation – and the willingness of masters to grant those kinds of changes – were more common and likely than in high-density slavery. Marginality and belonging were conceptualized and enforced through a kinship idiom rather than through the actual buying and selling of persons (although that could and did happen).[37] In some cases, highly stratified and economically productive decentralized societies developed systems that moved them closer to high-density slavery. The ability to both gain *access to* the labor power of vulnerable people and to *extract* most of what was produced by that vulnerable labor became critical to the reproduction of some decentralized societies. In conclusion, slavery – and the invention and elaboration of kinship and descent structures – was fundamentally tied to political economies that valued people. In the next chapter, we turn to the ways that slavery underlay and facilitated the creation and expansion of African states.

[37] See Willis and Miers, 481, who note that while kinship and seniority remained the key "organizing principles" for most of these societies, the "implications" and practice of those principles were often "reinterpreted" – and in some cases remade, especially in the nineteenth century in places where slavery became very common.

CHAPTER 4

Slavery and African States

Introduction

In August 1710, Andries Barendse requested his freedom. He based his request on the fact that he had been born in the Cape Town slave lodge and had worked as a mason for the Dutch East India Company (as its slave) for more than twenty years. The Council of Policy agreed and freed him. Andries was then given a job to work for the Company as a mason at a rate of pay of 10 guilders per month, only 1 guilder more than the starting pay for a teenage soldier or sailor in the service of the Company. Over the course of 170 years of Company rule in South Africa, only 108 of its slaves were given their freedom in this manner.[1]

★ ★ ★

At the end of the nineteenth century, during a civil war in Kano (located in what is now northern Nigeria)Emirate of the Sokoto Caliphate, *Dan Rimi* Nuhu, a powerful royal slave official, soldier, and titleholder, crowned the rebel pretender, Yusufu, as emir. Nuhu had long supported Yusufu's cause and claim. Nuhu was a well-known and powerful slave in the palace, but he had joined the war camp of Yusufu early on in the struggle. When Nuhu arrived on horseback, Yusufu said, "Our trip is successful, our trip is successful since Nuhu

---

[1] Robert C. Shell, *Children of Bondage: A Social History of the Slave Society at the Cape of Good Hope*, 1652–1838 (Hanover, NH: Wesleyan University Press, 1994), 186.

has joined us, he has joined our camp!" Thereafter, Nuhu transformed Yusufu's military camp into the proper seat of a rival emir. He gave Yusufu the royal regalia and insisted that he follow Kano court protocol. With Nuhu's support the rebels later took the Kano throne. Afterward, the royal slaves and their families who supported the new emir gained a substantial amount of power.[2]

★ ★ ★

The ruler of Ibadan between 1870 and 1885, Momoh Latoosa, promoted numerous slaves to important military and political positions. Iadgana and Kannike, slave captains of Hausa and Kanuri descent, respectively, each commanded armies of approximately 1,000 infantry and 1,000 cavalry. These elite slaves acquired horses, farms, and drummers and even had their own harems of women. Young slaves were placed with these powerful senior slaves to be trained for war. One observer from the time noted that these slaves were "more richly dressed and make more show than their lord. Whatever the misfortune of the house these are never of course sold; they remain the guardian of the house and of their master's sons."[3]

★ ★ ★

Although many African societies were decentralized, with political structures organized around kinship, Africans also built a wide range of state systems. African states from 1000 CE onward were common and successful. Kinship and statehood were not mutually exclusive. Many African states emerged out of preexisting lineage and kinship structures. States often developed as a means to enhance the political and economic opportunities presented in lineage systems, as big men sought to consolidate and expand their power beyond the limitations of kinship. In other cases, kinship simply served as an available model for the state structures Africans created. If slaves were valuable as the "ultimate kin" in lineages, they were even more valuable as political resources and labor for the emerging political elites of many African states.

This chapter focuses on the role of slavery in the development and consolidation of African states. In some instances, *political* slavery – or

---

[2] Stilwell, *Paradoxes of Power*, 221–222.
[3] Samuel Johnson, *The History of the Yorubas* (Cambridge: Cambridge University Press, 2010), 326.

the use of slaves for political purposes – was widespread and structurally essential. Slaves played a central role in the reproduction of African states; slavery became essential to the continuation of state institutions and the political elite. How? Slavery enhanced elite material and ideological power by increasing a ruler's ability to secure political power, prestige, and wealth from nonelite subjects. State institutions depended on these resources. For example, slaves increased a ruler's (and therefore the state's) control over taxation, food and craft production, and the military. Slaves enhanced the coercive power of the state and its rulers in their capacity as bodyguards and soldiers. They served as reliable bodies of dependents who facilitated political centralization by securing succession to the throne and by providing bureaucratic continuity in systems that were otherwise outgrowths of households and lineages. As well, slaves embodied and secured the rulers' access to wealth in people. For slaves who gained access to state institutions, dependency became an avenue to power. These privileged slaves fashioned their own ideologies and forged bonds with the free elite that brought them closer to belonging (or that allowed them to better negotiate the terms of their bondage). For rulers, slavery provided a body of dependents over whom they exercised unique kinds of power and whose reproduction they could better control. The danger for rulers was that these same slaves might gain enough power to undermine their control over the state and its institutions.

Theories of State and State Formation

The question of what constitutes a state has vexed political scientists and historians. Our goal here is not simply to define statehood, but rather to examine the role of slaves in African states. Nonetheless, we do need to establish a general understanding of the meaning of state. A state can simply be described as "a society in which there is a centralized and specialized institution of government."[4] Going further, some theorists have developed more complex descriptions. R. Cohen, for example, argues that an early state is "a centralized and hierarchically organized political system in which the central authority

---

[4] J. Haas, *The Evolution of the Prehistoric State* (New York: New York University Press, 1982), 3 as cited by Graham Connah, *African Civilizations: An Archeological Perspective* (Cambridge: Cambridge University Press, 1987), 6.

has control over the greatest amount of coercive force in the society. Sub-units are tied into their hierarchy through their relations to officials appointed by and responsible to a ruler or a monarchical head of state."[5] Thus, inequality was usually a fundamental component of state formation. So were the creation of political and legal institutions and the control of the means of violence. Some scholars have argued that states emerged as a result of economic/social conflict among people, via military conquest, through trade/economic change, over the competition to control specific material resources, and/or out of the desire of many within society to gain access to the protection or benefits of statehood. States emerged for any and all of these reasons. Rather than developing an overarching *theory* of state formation, it is more important to understand how and why states developed at particular times. This is especially critical because the formation of states was not a unidirectional or evolutionary process. Political centralization might have emerged as the product of economic, social, and political change, which may or may not have resulted in the creation of centralized states elsewhere. As John Lonsdale argues, state formation was a slow, sometimes erratic process that was profoundly imperfect and contingent on individual decision making.[6]

The Practice of Statehood in Africa

African states shared unique qualities, which further complicates our analysis. African states were deeply influenced by kinship and were often initially outgrowths of those structures. In addition, some states were founded by migrants who lacked local political allies or resources. They sought to project and legitimate their power, while looking to either incorporate or marginalize preexisting populations. The political elites of early African states – whether or not they were founded by migrants – normally sought to control people rather than impose direct territorial control over the regions they claimed. However, in some cases, especially in West Africa, territorial control was also a feature of state power. Because African states tended to expand beyond

---

[5] R. Cohen, "State Origins: A Reappraisal" in H. Claessen and P. Skalnik (eds.), *The Early State* (The Hague: Mouton, 1978), 36 also cited by Klein, "Slavery and the Early State," 170.

[6] John Lonsdale, "States and Social Processes in Africa: A Historiographical Survey" in *African Studies Review* 24, 2–3 (1981), 172–173.

kinship through the attachment of occupational, religious, and military specialists, Miller has felicitously labeled them "composite polities."[7] These states were composed of kin and clients, on whom the political elite depended for their political power and economic well-being (rather than simply depending on the direct control of land).

In many early African states, rulers were *not* singular and supreme leaders, who dominated the means of coercion and had direct territorial authority, but were simply a first among equals. Sometimes their power was offset by occupational or political associations, by groups of lineage or clan heads, or by members of a governing council. The Mende in Sierra Leone, for example, formed polities of up to 20,000 people, but the power of rulers was constrained by the authority of the *Poro* secret society, which regulated the harvesting of palm fruit and fishing, fixed prices for certain commodities, and adjudicated disputes. The overall role of the ruler in early African states was to mediate among the different constituencies that made up the state as well as to guarantee that the state had important ritual or supernatural protections, which they – as ruler – provided and safeguarded. As Susan Keech McIntosh concludes, early African states had their basis in "ritual, personal, and charismatic authority rather than in effective coercion and control."[8]

Although these kinds of political strategies were both innovative and successful, many early African states were, as a result, composed of competing power blocs that resisted further centralization. This in turn produced a common and repetitive pattern: rulers attempted to centralize power, acquire legitimacy, and thereby overcome the composite and decentralized structure of African states by using slaves. To understand this as a process, we must examine the nature of horizontal and vertical power. McIntosh argues that African states exhibited "relatively weak vertical political control and extremely complex horizontal integration," which were designed to "decentralize or distribute" power. McIntosh sees this as the primary feature of many – if not most – African states.[9] In other words, McIntosh believes that

---

[7] Miller, *Women and Slavery, vol. I*, 20–21.
[8] McIntosh, "Pathways to Complexity: An African Perspective" in McIntosh (ed.), *Beyond Chiefdoms*, 15.
[9] McIntosh, "Pathways to Complexity," 16. For a thoughtful case study in the context of powerful kingship, see Holly Hanson, "Mapping Conflict: Heterarchy and Accountability in the Ancient Capital of Buganda" in *Journal of African History* **50**, 2 (2009), 179–202.

.

African states privileged horizontal integration. The constituent elements of the state were bound together in cooperative and often noncoercive horizontal relationships. I think that removing the elements
of conflict, inequality, exploitation, and stratification from any analysis of African state formation is profoundly mistaken. Because power
was dispersed horizontally in early states, ambitious rulers and their
households sought further state centralization via coercion to enhance
their own power over other state constituencies – as well as over common people and material resources. Because this new kind of vertical power often lacked legitimacy and broader support, revolutionary
elites turned to slaves. In short, rulers used slaves to enforce their will
over people and things because they could not mobilize the support
of free people. Over time, these kinds of rulers aimed to centralize
their power further by creating new institutions (or by destroying old
ones) that limited singular power, by establishing or gaining control
over the coercive apparatus of the state, by securing more control over
important resources, and by developing new rituals that advertised
the power of the ruler. Slavery was absolutely vital to these centralizing processes, to the discussion of which we will now turn.

Slavery, Centralization, and Legitimacy

Heterogeneous, horizontal government sometimes worked so well
that rulers remained only a first among equals. State power operated
through horizontal connections rather than vertical hierarchies. More
often, however, the drive to centralize power meant that rulers sought
to impose new kinds of power and authority over others. This led to
the use of slaves in politics. Rulers used slaves to create institutions
that moved beyond kinship as well as to establish *singular* authority.
The process was not just related to material circumstances (demography, ecology, technology) but to nonmaterial circumstances as well.
As Paul Roscoe notes, "[The potential for political centralization
exists] wherever humans have wants that can best or only be satisfied
through the agency of others, since these conditions promote struggles for domination to satisfy these wants."[10] Thus, and as Roscoe also

[10] Paul Roscoe, "Practice and Political Centralization" in *Current Anthropology* 34, 2
(1993), 114–115 also cited by David L. Schoenbrun, "The (In)visible Roots of
Bunyoro-Kitara and Buganda in the Lakes Region" in McIntosh (ed.), *Beyond
Chiefdoms*, 145.

notes, political centralization basically describes the centralization of "relational power" or, in other words, "the concentration of power over others in the hands of a few," which can vary in terms of its effectiveness (how much power), extent (the numbers and kinds of people subject to that power), and level of institutionalization (to what extent that power becomes embedded in institutions).[11] Slavery enhanced all three kinds of centralization. Slavery encouraged the consolidation of power in fewer hands, increased the extent of that power, and led to new kinds of institutions and state structures.

States and their rulers used slaves in different ways depending on whether a state was in its early stages or whether it had consolidated into a mature system. Mature states used slaves in a broad range of institutional and political capacities. States that lacked the most legitimacy – often expansive states founded through violence by new men who were not associated with preexisting power structures – used slaves to terrorize, conquer, and enslave *because* they were institutionally weak. For rulers, legitimacy was usually a critical question early on. Slaves were used most coercively at this point. Slaves were a reliable body of dependents for new rulers who lacked legitimacy and political support. At some point, the rulers of mature states no longer needed to establish their legitimacy to the same degree, yet slavery often expanded. Why? Once slavery was established, it was easy to find other uses for slaves. And they were useful. Mature states used slaves to centralize authority, to police their populations, and/or to expand militarily. Slaves tended to remain loyal to their ruler and were very good at their work. Over time, if the state survived, slaves built and staffed mature state institutions and symbolically represented the ruler's hard-won political legitimacy. Slaves were used, then, in overlapping roles as soldiers, enforcers, and bureaucrats.

The problem for many African elites was that they relied on networks of brothers, uncles, sisters, mothers, and children for political support. Although this might at first appear to favor the ruler, in practice, people related to the ruling house via kinship competed directly with the ruler for power. Periods after the death of a ruler were particularly fraught, as the various constituent elements of the state sought to determine succession. Meanwhile, other non-kin elites struggled to limit the ruler's power over them, often by restricting the ruler's decision-making and military power. Rulers therefore needed to aggregate

---

[11] Roscoe, "Practice and Political Centralization," 114.

dependents who literally *could not* compete with them as kin and who lacked the ability to claim the same kinds of legitimacy as could other groups associated with the state. The use of slaves was, then, a product of the rulers' – and the early states' – need for *dependent* and socially *isolated* clients in the context of intense political competition. Rulers sought to centralize state power in the hands of a single person or a single household, which transformed horizontal relationships into something that looked much more vertical. As was the case in decentralized societies, the value of slaves in this process lay in their status as kinless outsiders who lacked an independent basis of political power because they gained power only through the ruler to whom they were bonded. Slaves were, in short, more vulnerable and less of a threat to the ruler, as Meillassoux notes:

> [The] deprivations which excluded slaves from civil society were also at the origin of their progress in the circles of power ... the slave owed what he was to his master ... only his master could grant him the attributes of a person, albeit fictitious and precarious. The slave owed his master everything, including his loyalty ... since the slave was naturally excluded from inheritance and from succession within the master's lineage, he had no possible claim to possessions or titles. He was thus not involved in rivalries between collaterals or other pretenders to power occasioned by kinship.[12]

State power was further centralized through slavery via the use of slave wives and concubines. Rulers sought to control reproduction. They used female slavery to control the politics of succession and reproduction. Although many rulers married free women, they also produced numerous children with their slave concubines. On one level, this was simply a means to expand the size of the royal household and to provide labor for the palace or capital (such as food production, food preparation, and domestic service). There was a lot of work to be done in the palaces of the powerful. The work of female slaves sustained many African political elites and states. In Dar Fur, for example, 500 slave women were used just to bring water to the palace of Sultan 'Ali Dinar. But also important was the fact that the children of female slaves had fewer kinship allies and resources than did the children of free women. While the children of concubines – who were usually free if the father was free – certainly competed for the throne and manipulated the links with their mothers and the harem to enhance their

[12] See Meillassoux, *The Anthropology of Slavery*, 138–139.

power, their ability to draw on wide and extended kinship networks did not exist. This was a significant advantage for the ruler, who was also the father of these children: "Through sons by slave women, male household heads concentrated and controlled assets they had accumulated into at least the succeeding generation, without having to guard against jealous or grasping in-laws."[13] In the Kingdom of Kongo, for example, many female slaves were kept by elite men as slave wives and concubines. By the time of King Álvaro II (reigned, 1587–1614), female slaves played important roles in the expansion of central power and the determination of royal succession. To reduce the power of free clans, Kongo kings began designating royal sons of slave wives to succeed the throne, which eliminated the sons of free wives from consideration. Previous kings had failed to secure the succession of their favorites. Succession had become very complicated, in part because each potential heir was embedded in webs of clan and kin affiliations. This created tension. Some clans grew in power over others. The sons of slave wives had no such ties or problems. They bore no connections, and had no responsibilities, to the powerful kin groups that competed with the king. Although this practice did not continue for the entire history of the kingdom, it was nonetheless important between 1587 and 1622.

This is why so many rulers used eunuchs in positions of power. Eunuchs – slaves who had their penises and/or testicles removed as boys – were the ultimate slaves. They had no physical ability to produce children, which rendered them completely kinless in perpetuity. Their unique status, as neither male nor female, bound them even more closely to their master. They had no – or very few – other social options. Without their master, who provided for them a place in the political, administrative, or military system, they belonged nowhere. They benefited from this relationship as well. The senior eunuch in Wadai, for example, supervised numerous villages and the Arab population, which made him extremely rich. The use of eunuchs and virile slaves to institutionalize revolutionary regimes often produced conflicts, as political elites and nonelites sought to contest state authority via violence, flight, or negotiation. Rarely, influential slaves seized political power for themselves. But overall, between the years 1000 and 1900 CE rulers throughout the continent used slaves to effect dramatic structural transformations in African states.

---

[13] Miller, *Women and Slavery, vol. I*, xviii.

For example, by the fifteenth century, the kings of Kano headed a government in which their power was dependent on the loyalty of close relatives, some of whom had claims to the throne. The power of the Kano *sarki* ("king" in Hausa) was also counterbalanced by non-royal free officials, who had a central role in the choice of a king's successors. This produced tension between the kings and the nobility of Kano. A series of powerful free officeholders repeatedly aligned themselves against the throne. The kings of Kano attempted to check the power of these freeborn officials by installing slaves into powerful positions. By centralizing power, the kings of Kano attempted to transcend the kinship divisions that weakened their position. Through slaving – and the elimination of kinship ties that came with slavery – the kings acquired a group of officeholders on whom they could rely and control. Most importantly, in comparison to the freeborn aristocracy, the kings could more easily alter the provenance of slave offices or change and replace individual slave officeholders.

Some of the best evidence for this comes during the reign of *Sarkin Kano* Muhammad Rumfa (reigned 1463–1499). Rumfa transformed the Kano government by expanding and centralizing his own power via the appointment of numerous slaves to high political positions. This was the culmination of centuries of slave use. Kano had long been involved in capturing and trading slaves, but the intensity and scope of state-sponsored slave raiding increased over time. *The Kano Chronicle* records that, during the period between 1438 and 1450, a free official, who held the title of *galadima*, was so successful prosecuting wars that slaves "became very numerous." He founded 21 towns where he left 500 male and 500 female slaves. On the *galadima's* return to Kano, he gave the king "three thousand slaves."[14] Before Rumfa, these practices produced political instability. Free officials enriched themselves through slaving and deposed a number of kings. To regain control of the government, Rumfa initiated new policies. Most importantly, he built a new palace from which he ruled and settled hundreds of slaves who reported only to him. He placed those slaves in charge of key departments, including the armory, storehouses, treasury, police, prisons, and communications. Other slaves served as bodyguards and soldiers and were also based in the new palace. Rumfa's use of slaves

---

[14] *The Kano Chronicle* in H. R. Palmer (ed.), *Sudanese Memoirs, Being Mainly Translations of a Number of Arabic Manuscripts Relating to the Western and Central Sudan* (Lagos: Government Printer. Reprinted 1967 by London: Frank Cass), 76.

in this political way greatly enhanced his power and became a hallmark of Kano government. In addition, Rumfa appointed eunuchs to high state offices or placed them in charge of domestic and household activities. For example, one eunuch was placed in charge of the royal bedchamber, and another supervised the king's harem. These reforms did not end elite competition in Kano. Kings were deposed after Rumfa's reign. But slavery ensured that kingly power was recognized and centralized. Subsequent kings had far more resources at their disposal than they did before Rumfa's reforms.

Attempts to centralize power through slavery occurred far beyond Kano. In Axum (located close to what is now Ethiopia), palace slaves counterbalanced the power of free officials – often drawn from the king's own family – between 200 and 600 CE. Centralization through slavery also occurred in places and times ranging from fifteenth-century Kanem, where kings created an extensive network of slave officials – including eunuchs – to offset the power of the free elite and thereby enhance their own administrative and political power, to sixteenth-century Morocco, seventeenth-century Kajoor, eighteenth-century Oyo and Dar Fur, and nineteenth-century Dahomey, Sokoto Caliphate, and Borno. There are three major ways in which slaves facilitated state formation, expansion, and political centralization: their use coercively as soldiers, bureaucratically as officials and experts, and ritually as markers of kingly status and as enforcers of royal protocol.

Slavery, State Violence, and Coercion

Rulers used slaves because they could better control them – and believed them more loyal – than free persons. Slave soldiers made up important parts of state armies that were used to conquer other states or to defend against external threats. Rulers benefited immensely from the acquisition of loyal troops who could be used to make good their imperial ambitions. In addition, many African states lacked the technological and bureaucratic capacity to fully project their power over the people and territory they claimed. Although they were strong at the core, state power weakened in the periphery, where rulers could not mobilize labor or collect tribute or taxes. African rulers used slave soldiers to project their authority and power into those regions. Rulers needed to employ violence and exact reprisals over populations far from the core and over whom they had little direct control. Slaves were used to ensure (sometimes through force) that taxes were paid and tribute collected. States that aimed to effect territorial control, or to control particular resources (salt or gold, for example), used slave soldiers to police and protect those regions. These same slaves might be directly involved in slaving. Slaving was a major economic and political activity for some African states. Slave soldiers waged wars that produced future generations of slaves, who might either be used internally or shipped into the regional and international slave trades, which further generated wealth for the ruling elite. When sold into one of the external slave trades, slaves were exchanged for important commodities that "reinforced state military power," including horses, steel blades, chain armor, and guns.[15] In short, slave soldiers made the reproduction of slavery institutionally possible.

Slaves were used as soldiers (versus simply as hooligans and enforcers) because they could be trained more systematically than non-slave soldiers. In Africa, free soldiers might be called up periodically from the population of free farmers or craftsmen. In other cases, nonroyal aristocrats served as the core of the military or at least as the commanders of regular soldiers. Whatever the specifics of local military organization, in contrast to slave soldiers, free soldiers were normally part-time soldiers, whose time in service was limited. Slave soldiers were trained and employed primarily as soldiers; they had no farms to which to return at the end of campaigns. As a result, slaves often composed the core of the professional fighting force, tied closely to the singular ruler. This is not to argue that free soldiers were absent. Nor were free soldiers ineffective or poorly trained. The fighting core of the army was often composed of excellent and free soldiers. But the use of slaves offered important advantages over free soldiers. They helped political elites overcome the organizational weaknesses of some African states. Freed from local ties, loyal to ruler, professional, and often deadly, bodies of slave dependents offered rulers coercive opportunities far greater than possibly disloyal free retainers, who had multiple interests to balance. Whereas rulers were sometimes limited in their ability to mobilize free populations or had less control over free troops (who served under free officials and who could empower

[15] Ralph Austen, "Imperial Reach versus Institutional Grasp: Superstates of the West and Central African Sudan in Comparative Perspective" in *The Journal of Early Modern History* **13** (2009), 525.

competitors), they were certainly not faced with those same problems when using slaves.

Slave soldiers were used most widely in West Africa. Although the West African region was diverse, with the interior influenced by Islam and trans-Saharan networks and the non-Islamic coast tied to European commerce, slaves were used in similar ways: as bodyguards, militarized retainers, and soldiers. The kings and aristocrats of the numerous states along the seventeenth-century Gold Coast, for example, began to employ slaves as soldiers to bolster the size of their armies but also to reduce the power and independence of the *asafo* – the professional association of soldiers who often acted independently of the rulers. The value of slaves as soldiers was recognized by European visitors to the region, one of whom noted that "only slaves could be commanded in war."[16] Meanwhile, in the same region, the kings of Akwamu possessed an extensive army of slave soldiers, as one visitor noted: "[H]e has for warfare the best and most experienced slaves to be found in the entire country."[17] In seventeenth- and eighteenth-century Asante, slaves were used as soldiers and helped support and supply the army. Although the organization of the Asante army is subject to some debate, for most of Asante's history, troops were called to war (and war captains appointed) as needed under the overall authority of the king or *asantehene*. These troops were drawn from both the slave and free populations. Most of the soldiers, if free, already possessed guns – which were not provided by the state – because firearms were a mark of status and manhood. Those slaves who were called to war were provided with guns, which they were otherwise forbidden from owning. This marked them as perpetual minors – distinct and different from freeborn soldiers: "Thus ... the possession of a gun was an indicator of adult male status; slaves went to war, carried weapons and accoutrements in the bag that belonged to their master, and might even fight – but they were disbarred from the adult male right of owning or bearing their own gun,"[18] which in

---

[16] John Thornton, "Armed Slaves and Political Authority in Africa in the Era of the Slave Trade, 1450–1800" in Christopher Leslie Brown and Philip D. Morgan (eds.), *Arming Slaves" From Classical Times to the Modern Age* (New Haven, CT: Yale University Press, 2006), 85, citing Willem Bosman, *A New and Accurate Description of the Coast of Guinea* (London, 1705; reprint London, 1967), 180.

[17] Thornton, "Armed Slaves and Political Authority," 85.

[18] T. C. McCaskie, *State and Society in Pre-Colonial Asante* (Cambridge: Cambridge University Press, 1995), 98.

turn signified their social isolation, dependence, and exclusion from the broader corporate group. Dependency provided avenues to power for slaves in Asante, but – as was the case throughout Africa – the realities of slave status could not be easily eliminated. Slaves were occasionally used to form a royal bodyguard for the *asantehene,* which occurred in a variety of periods, but seems to have been most common later in Asante history. In 1764, during the reign of *Asantehene* Osei Kwadwo, "[m]ultitudes of prisoners were taken. The adults were sacrificed or sold as slaves ... and all the male children were educated at the King's expense to become soldiers of a new bodyguard which he formed."[19] In the 1880s, a group of northern slaves made up a special corps of riflemen attached to the *Asantehene* Mensa Bonsu in the capital, Kumase. Bonsu's use of slave soldiers stemmed from his political weakness and his inability to gain the trust and loyalty of Asante's population.

The use of slave soldiers increased as states became more closely involved in the transatlantic slave trade and European commerce. By the nineteenth century, female slaves in Dahomey – called "amazons" by European visitors – guarded the king, became a crack fighting force, and were involved in a number of foreign wars (Figure 10). In Oyo, many regular soldiers were slaves, who literally built the empire, while various kings eventually created a bodyguard corps composed of slaves to offset the power of the free elite and administer the provinces. Even more important – at least for a state that depended so heavily on cavalry – slaves from the Islamic interior (who had knowledge and experience with horses) were captured and put to use as expert horsemen and animal caretakers, a vital resource as Oyo the kingdom became Oyo the empire. After Oyo fell in 1835, "new" Oyo used slaves on an even larger scale, mainly in the palace as political and military instruments of the king. The other Yoruba states that emerged in the period relied on slave soldiers to fight their extensive wars. Lovejoy notes that Kurumi, a warlord in the region, conquered the town of Ijaye in 1829. By 1859, he had amassed 300 slave wives and an army of 1,000 slaves. Likewise, by the 1850s, Ibadan imported several thousand slaves per year. The rulers of Ibadan trained and used the best male slaves as soldiers. The Ibadan warlord Ogunmola had 1,800 slave soldiers in the 1870s.[20] In the case of Yorubaland in the nineteenth century, slave

[19] Emmanuel Terray, "Contribution à une étude de l'armée asante" in *Cahiers d'Études Africaines* 16, 61/62 (1976), 313.
[20] Lovejoy, *Transformations in Slavery,* 179–180.

FIGURE 10. Female soldier in Dahomey. In Frederick E. Forbes, *Dahomey and the Dahomans: being the journals of two missions to the king of Dahomey, and residence at his capital, in the years 1849 and 1850* (London, 1851; reprinted in 1966), vol. 2, facing page 23. Courtesy of the UVM Bailey-Howe Library.

soldiers helped facilitate a nearly constant series of wars between the various city-states (i.e., Abeokuta, Ibadan, Ijebu, Ondo). They also maintained the continual cycle of slaving necessary to provide new soldiers, as well as slave wives for the soldiers and slave farmers (who produced the food that fed the armies). Slave farmers in turn secured a ruler's control over vital foodstuffs and commodities on which the elite depended.

Slave soldiers were also used extensively in the interior of West Africa. In Songhay, slave soldiers made up the majority of the standing army. Under Askia Dawud (reigned 1549–1583), the ruler's army numbered up to 30,000, which was composed mostly of slave cavalry.[21]

[21] John Thornton, *Warfare in Atlantic Africa*, 1500–1800 (London: Routledge, 2000), 35.

In addition to warring against external enemies, this slave force helped offset the strength of regional armies raised and controlled by officials in the provinces and to capture more slaves for internal use and trade. Some slaves supervised the slave farms that fed the political elite. One of Askia Dawud's sons was recorded as saying: "It is enough for him to lead one expedition to any settlement of the infidels, and before the night passes he will have collected war spoils numbering 10 thousand slaves or more."[22] Even more ironically, the Moroccan army that crossed the Sahara Desert to conquer Songhay in the 1590s was composed of well-trained slaves armed with guns.

Likewise, in Borno and the Sokoto Caliphate, rulers established crack forces of slaves, armed with guns, as bodyguards and political enforcers. Both states used slaves extensively as cavalry. In the case of Borno, according to Ahmed ibn Fartua, who wrote in 1582/83, the Mai (or King) of Borno, Idris Aloma, acquired "Turkish musketeers and numerous household slaves who had become skilled in firing muskets.... Hence the Sultan was able to kill ... with muskets, and there was no need for other weapons, so that God gave him a great victory by reason of his superiority of arms."[23] In 1870, it was estimated that the ruler of Borno was protected by a standing army of 3,000 slaves, armed with guns, spears, and bows. In the Sokoto Caliphate, numerous emirs established slave regiments armed with guns, especially in the 1890s, as some sought increased independence from the central authority at Sokoto. In the Emirate of Kano, one current occupant of the emir's palace noted that in the past the people equipped with guns in Kano were the "slaves" of the emir who were "trained like soldiers" in the use of guns and "military tactics" by two slave officials who held the titles of *sallama* and *shettima*.[24] In nineteenth-century Dar Fur, slaves were settled in specialist communities supervised by officials appointed by the sultan. Some of these slaves were formed into specialized military units. Others manufactured horse armor used by the Dar Fur cavalry. The use of military slaves was a common pattern replicated in numerous other states across the Sudanic Belt of

---

[22] Michal Tymowski, "Treasury Systems, Types of Territorial Control, Reciprocity and Exploitation Limits in an African Pre-Colonial State: The Case of Songhay in the Late 15th–16th Century" in *Hemispheres: Studies on Cultures and Societies* **19** (2004), 174–175, citing the *Ta'rīkh al-Fattāsh*.

[23] Imam Ahmed Ibn Fartua, *The History of the First Twelve Years of the Reign of Mai Idris Alooma of Bornu* (London: Fran Cass, 1970), 11–12.

[24] Interview with Lamido, July 7, 2000, in Kano, Nigeria.

Africa, including Sennar, Wadai, Bagirmi, Segu, and Kaarta, to name just a few.

Slave soldiers were used outside West Africa as well, ranging from the Nile Valley and Ethiopia through to parts of the North African Maghreb and parts of Eastern and Central Africa. In the sixteenth-century Kingdom of Ndongo, for example, military specialists were recruited from the ranks of slaves, who lived in special villages that supported them. By the end of the sixteenth century in the Kingdom of Kongo, there were likely 4,000–5,000 slave soldiers led by each of four Kongo nobles, which together composed the bodyguard of King Álvaro II (reigned 1587–1614). As royal authority declined and internal conflict increased in the Kongo during the seventeenth century, kings and members of the aristocracy used slave soldiers more extensively. In 1665, after King António's defeat at the Battle of Mbwila by the Portuguese and their African allies (a force that included 4,000 slave soldiers!), the Portuguese captured thousands of Kongo slave soldiers. Afterward, rivals of the Kongo kings used slave soldiers as they competed for the throne. In 1685, one such pretender had "six thousand slaves at his command."[25] The seventeenth-century Moroccan Sultan Isma'il ibn al-Sharif (reigned 1672–1727) built an army of slave soldiers numbering roughly 50,000 men, which he used to effect political centralization and wage war. In the nineteenth-century central African state of Kanyok, slaves – known as the *biin mazemb* (people of the rear) – were formed in separate regiments under the charge of a slave official or free royal officers. In battle, they were placed in the most dangerous and vulnerable positions. Slave soldiers were also used extensively in Ethiopia as provincial rulers came to compete for central power in the late eighteenth and nineteenth centuries. Lastly, Egypt conquered Sudan in the nineteenth century using slave soldiers.

Although slave soldiers were commonly used, regional and chronological variations were important. Unlike West Africa, in Eastern and Central Africa slave soldiers came to be used most often in the nineteenth century. Why? The nineteenth century was a period of tremendous and violent change. Older political systems were being destroyed and replaced with new kinds of militarized states. In parts of eastern Africa, especially, slaves were armed during this period of disorder

[25] Linda M. Heywood, "Slavery and Its Transformation in the Kingdom of Kongo: 1491–1800" in *Journal of African History* 50, 1 (2009), 1–22.

and warfare. New men sought to build new states that were rooted in slaving and military power and not in old forms of legitimacy (kinship or religious sanction to rule, for example). Thus, slaves were used here, as they were in West Africa, because rulers sought to mobilize supporters, but eastern Africa represents an extreme: states were less developed, and rulers built states without substantially drawing on – or sometimes even seeking – broader legitimacy from history or the people they ruled. With this kind of state building, it is easy to see the value of slavery.

In the nineteenth century, Arab and Swahili state builders and traders penetrated the interior of eastern Africa from the coast to find the Nyamwezi people (from what is now Tanzania) and the Yao (from the regions of modern Mozambique and Malawi) building polities and taking advantage of the burgeoning trade in people. Two people perhaps best exemplify these trends: Mirambo and Tippu Tib. Mirambo – whose name meant "corpses" – was a new breed of ruler who came to power in an era of disruption. He liked to claim that he sought peace and the recreation of an older Nyamwezi social order (and thereby drew on past traditions and ideals), but he carved out a new state in the interior of Tanzania between the 1860s and 1870s that bore little relationship with the past. Mirambo built a state through violence. Although he was from a Nyamwezi elite family, Mirambo relied mostly on young men, many of whom were slaves. Together with free followers they were known as *rugu ruga*, or rootless, unattached, unmarried young men with reputations for violence, slaving, and robbery. These men had generally been captured or bought in exchange for ivory as children. Trained and armed with guns (and other weapons), they served as the core of Mirambo's army, and were rewarded with the loot – including other slaves who could be sold for profit – generated by the conflict, as well as with higher, supervisory ranks in the military, especially as commanders of slave soldiers on the frontiers of Mirambo's empire. It was noted at the time that as a leader Mirambo had a special preference for young soldiers:

> [Mirambo] preferred boys or young men to accompany him to war; he never took middle-aged or old men, as they were sure to be troubled with wives or children, and did not fight half so well as the young fellows who listened to his words. Said he, "They have sharper eyes, and their young limbs enable them to move with the ease of serpents or the rapidity of zebras, and a few words will give them the hearts of lions. In all my wars with the Arabs, it was an army of youths that gave me

victory, boys without beards. Fifteen of my young men died one day because I said I must have a certain red cloth that was thrown down as a challenge. No, no, give me youths for war in open field, and men for the stockaded village."[26]

Mirambo sought to gain control over important trade routes running to Lake Victoria and Lake Tanganyika – as well as those to the coast – which brought him into regular conflict with coastal Swahili and Arab merchants as well as local kings and chiefs. Mirambo and his slave and free soldiers regularly fought enemy armies and conducted extensive guerrilla campaigns. At the same time they made a quick profit by stealing and enslaving, as Richard Reid notes: "Mirambo was increasingly interested in a form of 'total war', which involved the targeting of towns and villages. Often, his warfare did not involve the clashing of armies in open country, but rather taking the battle to political and economic centers."[27] Mirambo certainly hoped to build a settled, territorial state, but did so by using war and slavery to gain commercial and political predominance. Mirambo did not rely on the loyalty or goodwill of his subjects, but acted independently of them by relying on slaves and unattached men who owed their lives and success to Mirambo and to the grim and devastating cycle of violence they initiated and perpetuated. Ironically, the men on whom Mirambo relied and Mirambo's own behavior made it all but impossible to actually create a peaceful or stable state system: "[Mirambo's core followers] were soldiers, who delight in war & bloodshed and who are led by a chief whose every thought is directed towards conquest, plunder & the acquisition of territory."[28]

Tippu Tib was one of Mirambo's foes, and he used slaves for parallel reasons: they were an efficient way to mobilize and control labor in the context of the creation of a new state. He literally had no other way to create a state in an area where he had no roots or support. Tippu Tib came from the Swahili coast to the interior (now the eastern Congo) with a large group of dependents in the 1860s. He eventually established a town – Kasongo – in the interior that was also a commercial trading post. However, this region was largely decentralized, and as a result he was unable to mobilize local labor or gain much in the way

[26] Richard Reid, *War in Pre-Colonial Eastern Africa* (Athens: Ohio University Press, 2007), 158.

[27] Reid, *War in Pre-Colonial Eastern Africa*, 65.

[28] Reid, *War in Pre-Colonial Eastern Africa*, 99.

of local support. He therefore used slaves. These slaves raided local villages and towns in the region (often using guns), hunted for ivory, served as concubines, were used as porters, enslaved local populations, and were sold in exchange for ivory. Some also were put to work farming on the plantations that surrounded Kasongo. Those who were slave soldiers were probably never sold, but they were indeed of slave status. By the 1880s, Tippu Tib had established a loosely connected trading state that was protected by an army numbering well into the thousands.

By the nineteenth century, similar kinds of states were created in parts of West Africa, although this was less common than in eastern Africa. Guns, terror, and slaving became central routes to political power. For example, both Samori in upper Guinea and Rabih bin Fadlallah in the Lake Chad region built new states via conquest by using violence and slave soldiers. Of Rabih and his imitators, Cordell provides the following description, which sums up the nature of these states and the role of slaving and slavery in them perfectly:

> Starting with small, well-armed forces that accompanied them from the Sudan, they became warlords with their own armies created through the Turko-Egyptian practice of slave recruitment.... Because they were operating in non-Muslim zones among small-scale societies, their arms and organizations gave them a tremendous military advantage. They raided for slaves, integrating boys and young men into their detachments, taking girls and young women into their followings, and giving the others to northern traders in exchange for additional arms, powder, and the standard goods of long-distance trade.[29]

Slavery, Governance, and the Creation of State Institutions

Some scholars have argued that African states were weak and transitory. Ralph Austen calls this the "anti-state paradigm of indigenous African politics."[30] My view is that African states were not always territorially, institutionally, and demographically weak. Some state rulers

---

[29] Dennis Cordell, *Dar al-Kuti and the Last Years of the Trans-Saharan Slave Trade* (Madison: University of Wisconsin Press, 1982), as cited by Klein, "Slavery and the Early State," 185.

[30] Austen, "Imperial Reach Versus Institutional Grasp," 510. See also Jeffrey Herbst, *States and Power in Africa: Comparative Lessons in Authority and Control* (Princeton, NJ: Princeton University Press, 2000).

expanded their institutional capacities through the use of slaves in ways that *created* new and effective institutions, which produced political legitimacy. Slavery was not simply a product of the structural weaknesses of African states or the quest for political legitimacy. Nor did slaving always lead to destructive violence and disorder. Instead, slaves often became the institutional and bureaucratic backbone for the administration of state territories, tax systems, and other central government functions. As was the case with slave soldiers, slaves staffed these positions because the ruler – their master – benefited from their loyalty and from their unique dependence. Slaves were also used to supervise labor, especially the production of food and crops, which provided the material basis for the privileged position of the ruler and the free elite. Thus, the use of slaves in *politics* was tied into the broader *economic* use of agricultural slaves. As political elites became dependent on slave labor to produce food and other essential commodities, they turned increasingly to elite slaves to manage this production and to keep the growing number of agricultural slaves in line.

Slaves did not dominate the administration of every African state. Nor did African politics always lead to slavery. Free persons regularly played central roles as government officials. They sometimes worked alongside slaves. In other cases, slaves were not used in government positions at all. Nonetheless, the use of slaves was common in places where states were institutionally complex and secure. States that merely looked to raid had little need for complex government institutions. Thus, the warrior states of the nineteenth century used slaves differently than those that were more stable and bureaucratic. When states sought to project territorial authority or impose themselves on populations in noncoercive ways (through taxation for example), African elites used slaves to build and operate the machinery of government. Why? Household-style governments were usually at the center of African states. These kinds of governments were characterized by highly personalized politics. Powerful men and their retinues conducted government, and in a real sense *were* the government. If the household literally *was* the government, a central question remains: how was government to work in practice? How were officials to be trained? How could rulers devolve power and control over state functions without risking their positions? The answer was slavery. By using slaves, rulers created a professional body of officials within patrimonial and non-bureaucratic structures. Slaves were more easily and systematically trained and promoted (often according to merit) because – as slaves – they stood outside kinship. They were subject to unique methods of training, for long periods of time, and ruthlessly demoted (or executed) should they fail or become a threat. In nineteenth-century Borno, for example, Barca Gana was made *kacella*, which was a powerful slave office in the government. He acted as general and as the governor of six huge districts. He had more than fifty female and one hundred male slaves in his household, owned horses and wore gorgeous clothes. The ruler of Borno at this time, Shehu al-Kanemi, mistakenly sent Barca a horse that he had meant to send as a present to another chief. When al-Kanemi asked Barca for the horse back, Barca grew so incensed at the request that he sent back all the horses that al-Kanemi had ever given to him saying he would henceforth walk rather than ride. Al-Kanemi then sent for Barca. In front of the court, al-Kanemi stripped Barca, placed the leather girdle around his loins, which signified slave status, and reproached him for his ingratitude. He then ordered that he be sold. According to a European observer at the court, Barca, humbled and disgraced, then "fell on his knees … and acknowledged the justness of his punishment."[31] The following day al-Kanemi commuted the sentence.

Compared to free officials, masters could better control slave reproduction. Masters sometimes sought to prevent slave reproduction completely, and regularly used eunuchs. In other cases, slaves were prevented from passing on the rewards of their positions to their followers or families (this could happen among free officials as well, but normally limitations were imposed on the amount a king could extract). Finally, by placing slaves in positions that controlled production or taxation, masters ensured that they would gain access to the wealth so produced; indeed, rulers often used government slaves to acquire material forms of wealth (such as wives, cows, gold, cowries) as part of their official duties, which they then redeployed to create unequal political and economic relationships with other elite or non-elite persons. Slavery thereby helped expand a ruler's power over people by increasing a ruler's ability to make people into dependents.

Overall, the social and political disabilities of slaves meant that they could be more efficiently and safely placed in charge of state activities.

[31] E. W. Bovill, *Missions to the Niger* vol. III (Cambridge: Cambridge University Press, 1966, 378 cited by Anders J. Bjørkelo, *State and Society in Three Central Sudanic Kingdoms: Kanem Bornu, Bagirmi and Wadai* (PhD dissertation, University of Bergen, 1976), 201.

Slavery helped rulers overcome the institutional weaknesses of household-style governments. In sixteenth-century Kingdom of Kongo, for example, slaves were used as skilled couriers. By the seventeenth century, the kings of Kongo appointed slaves to the council as a means to expand royal authority. The council played an important role in administration and political decision making, including making declarations of war. Indeed, beginning in the 1580s, the Kongo kings inherited the slaves of deceased or demoted titleholders, which resulted in a massive expansion in the number of slaves attached to the royal household. Many slaves personally looked after the king, commanded the king's bodyguard, or supervised the agricultural estates that fed the Kongo capital city of São Salvador. Slaves were used extensively in South Africa under Dutch rule both in productive and nonproductive capacities. Although South Africa was dramatically different from the Kongo – and was tied more closely to Europe – slaves were used for political purposes. In addition to working on the plantations that surrounded Cape Town, slaves worked in the town itself. They performed skilled and unskilled work. Some slaves worked on company farms, while others maintained the town's roads, acted as interpreters, masons, smiths, wheel-wrights, wagon drivers, cooks, grave diggers, miners, police, and as executioner's assistants. These slaves kept Cape Town in order and maintained the power of the Company. In the capital of the Lunda kingdom of central Africa, by the 1700s a group of officials known as the *mazemb* played an important role in the ruler's (known as the *mwant yav*) household and government. They lived to the rear side of the king's enclosure. Although scholars tend to be vague about their status, they were likely of slave status. The most important titleholders among the *mazemb* slaves included the market supervisor, the "stakeholder" during the period after the death of a king, crown maker, beer-pourer, and jackal-jester. The most powerful titleholder was the *kanamoub* who commanded the king's rear guard (which was also composed of persons of slave status).[32] Some among the *mazemb* even nominated candidates to become the next king.

The use of slaves as government officials and skilled labor was even more common in West Africa. In fifteenth-century Songhay, for example, slaves were used as government officials, but also as skilled weavers, blacksmiths, and supervisors of slave estates that produced the

---

[32] See J. Jeffrey Cooper, *The Seduction of Ruwej: Reconstructing the Ruund History (the Nuclear Lunda, Zaire, Angola, Zambia* (PhD dissertation, Yale University, 1978), 107.

food that sustained the political elite. In the Kingdom of Benin, *Oba* (king) Ewuare (reigned c. 1440–1472) created a complex hierarchy of officials to administer the state and empire. The so-called town chiefs and palace chiefs were nonhereditary appointments held at the pleasure of the *oba*. Although these chiefs were generally from free and influential families, both the *oba* and the free elite possessed numerous slaves in their retinues. Some of those slaves were appointed to administrative and government positions. For example, Idiaghe – one of Ewuare's slaves – became *iyase*, which was one of the highest titled positions in the state. As *iyase* he also commanded the Benin army. One oral tradition states that Ewuare appointed his slave "to avoid unnecessary rising and opposition, and also to enjoy peace and security throughout his reign."[33] Some traditions claim he was freed first, which is doubtful. He became a political problem for the *oba* despite his slave status. One tradition notes that the *oba* "encountered more worries, more rising and more opposition from his own slave than he would have from any ordinary man in the land."[34]

The *obas* of fifteenth- and sixteenth-century Benin also depended on guild associations, composed of artisans who developed specific skills related to a wide variety of tasks, including ironworking or blacksmithing, leather working, carving, hunting, drumming, and dancing. These guilds were associated with the palace. When new skills were needed, the *oba* often created new guilds composed of his slaves. If a preexisting guild grew short of artisans, *obas* attached some of their slaves to the guild and solved the problem. Some scholars argue that slaves had to be emancipated before they joined the guilds, which is based largely on evidence from the twentieth century. These scholars may be correct, but it is also possible that emancipation did not occur or occurred after some years of guild service. There were certainly numerous slaves in the kingdom. Imperial Benin regularly went to war and captured many slaves as a result. At the same time, in 1516, *Oba* Esigie prohibited the sale of male slaves into the external slave trade, which meant those male slaves had to be used internally within the kingdom.

In later periods, such as in eighteenth-century Dar Fur, slaves specialized in agricultural production or in the care of horses, while

---

[33] J.U. Egharevba, *Concise Lives of the Famous Iyases of Benin* (Lagos: Temi-Asunwori Press, 1947), 9, as cited by Osarhieme Benson Osadolor, *The Military System of Benin Kingdom, c.* 1440–1897 (PhD dissertation, University of Hamburg, 2001), 97.

[34] Egharevba, 9, as cited by Osadolor, 97.

one slave – a eunuch called the *ab shaykh dali* – acted as the governor of the eastern provinces and controller of the palace. In nineteenth-century Borno, a European traveller noted that "the sheikh has a large enclosure of huts, within a wall, where he generally has from five hundred to eight hundred slaves of both sexes, under the charge of four eunuchs, who are employed preparing cotton and spinning the linen."[35] In the Kingdom of Dahomey, female slaves served as ministers of state, kingly counselors, governors of provinces, and state traders. By the nineteenth century, these slaves stood at the center of a huge royal household and administrative system centered on the palace at Abomey where they acquired wealth, power, and high rank as a result of their slave status. In nineteenth-century Ibadan, a slave known as Sobaloju – or the eye of the king – served as the intermediary between the king (in this case Latoosa) and the public.

Political slavery was also a central institution in the Sokoto Caliphate. The Sokoto Caliphate became one of the largest and most complex states of the precolonial period. The caliph in theory ruled from Sokoto, but much of the actual power was in the hands of the emirs and their officials who governed various emirates. Slaves were used in every emirate-level government. They were systematically recruited, trained, and used to administer the collection of taxes, supervise agricultural production, train soldiers (sometimes in the use of guns), act as military leaders, and collect information as spies. They developed a host of additional skills, including animal husbandry, the care of horses, military logistics, military intelligence, construction and building, and the supervision of a variety of palace institutions, including the armory, treasury, and the blacksmithing operations.

Slavery, Prestige, and Ritual: Projecting Political Power

Slaves were associated with new ideas about the rituals of power and the sacred position of many rulers. They played important roles in representing, confirming, and enhancing the right of rulers to actually rule. As the singular power of rulers grew, new symbols and rituals denoted and reinforced their unique status. Some rulers wore special clothing or took possession of sacred objects, while others surrounded themselves with slaves to publically display their power, and

[35] Bovill, 482, as cited by Bjørkelo, 162.

still others sacrificed human beings – often slaves – to demonstrate the extent of royal power or to affirm their special connection to the supernatural. Successful rulers became singular figures who sat at the top of a pyramid of relationships. Slaves enforced royal protocol and stood at the center of public spectacles of royal power. The presence of slaves visually demonstrated the ruler's special role and authority. Rulers used slaves in this capacity because they were uniquely dependent and liminal beings; slaves could not claim the same kind of honor as free persons could. Only slaves could attend to the ruler's domestic and daily needs because only they were capable of crossing sacred physical and ritual boundaries.

Luba kings in Central Africa used slaves to play the royal drum (which some say was made from the skin of a sacrificed slave). The slave drummer was said to have had his nose and ears cut off. The drum was played only upon the enthronement or death of a king or at the death of one of his children. Female slaves were often sacrificed by being buried alive along with deceased Luba kings. In Oyo, some slaves were used as musicians and performers at the king's court. In sixteenth-century Songhay, the king was flanked by 700 eunuchs during his audiences at court on Fridays. Slave women also sang and entertained at the Songhay court. Leo Africanus visited Songhay during the reign of Askia Muhammad I, around 1508, and made note of the pomp, size, and grandeur of the court:

> [T]he king possess[es] a special palace reserved for an enormous number of wives, concubines, slaves and eunuchs whose job it is to look after these women. There is a substantial guard of horsemen and foot soldiers armed with bows. Between the public and private gates of his palace is a large courtyard surrounded by a wall. On each side of this courtyard is a gallery used for audiences. Although the king deals with all his affairs himself, he is assisted by numerous functionaries – secretaries, counselors, captains, treasurers and stewards.[36]

In Benin, Asante, and Dahomey, slaves and war captives were selected for human sacrifice. In all three cases, sacrifices had political and religious meanings. Sacrifices occurred at royal funerals or during special religious or political ceremonies. Although there were multiple reasons for the practice, often slave sacrifice demonstrated royal power,

---

[36] John Hunwick, "Songhay, Borno and the Hausa States, 1450–1600" in J. F. A. Ajayi and Michael Crowder (eds.), *History of West Africa* (New York: Longman, 1985), 348.

symbolized a ruler's ability to communicate with the supernatural, and advertised a ruler's vast wealth in the people. In the eighteenth century at the Annual Customs of Dahomey – also known as the "Watering of the Graves" – war captives and slaves were sacrificed to commemorate deceased kings in numbers ranging from 40 to 300. In the 1780s, King Kpengla of Dahomey explained his motives for so doing: "You have seen me kill many men at the Customs ... this gives grandeur to my Customs, far beyond the display of fine things which I buy. This makes my enemies fear me, and gives me such a name in the bush."[37] It is interesting to note that the two kings best known for the scale of human sacrifice in Dahomey, Agaja and Gezo, were both usurpers and lacked legitimacy. The use of slaves in this way once again helped rulers overcome their own lack of legitimacy. Likewise in Benin, human sacrifices were offered at a variety of festivals honoring deceased kings and the reigning king's deceased father.

Case Study: Oyo

In Oyo, slaves were used to centralize power and counter the power of free aristocrats, as bodyguards to enhance the authority of kings, and as soldiers to expand the state. Oyo emerged as a kingdom in the Yoruba heartland of what is now southeastern Nigeria. Although the state was initially focused on a single town called old Oyo (or Oyo Ile), which was surrounded by more powerful neighbors, by 1600 Oyo emerged as an expansive imperial state in its own right. During the seventeenth century, the state became involved in the transatlantic slave trade and undertook a series of military campaigns, initiated by *Alafin* (king or "owner of the palace" in Yoruba) Ajagbo. By the time of *Alafin* Abiodun (reigned 1774–1789), the kingdom consisted of six core provinces, with further territories beyond the core that extended far to the south, southwest, and east, all of which paid tribute to Oyo in one form or another.[38] While this expansion created the Oyo Empire, it also produced tensions within the Oyo state. Those

---

[37] Quoted by Robin Law, "Human Sacrifice in Pre-Colonial West Africa" in *African Affairs* **84**, 334 (1985), 74.

[38] See Robin Law, *The Oyo Empire c. 1600–1836: A West African Imperialism in the Era of the Atlantic Slave Trade* (Oxford: Oxford University Press, 1977) and I.A. Akinjogbin, *Dahomey and Its Neighbours, 1708–1818* (Cambridge: Cambridge University Press, 1967).

tensions revolved around struggles between the *alafin* and the royal council over the centralization of kingly power.

In brief, Oyo government operated on a number of levels. First, powerful men – usually the heads of Oyo-based lineages located in specific parts of the city – controlled resources and accumulated large numbers of people as followers. The men at the head of large patrilineages claimed possession of particular political positions or offices within the Oyo government: "The Oyo chiefs were thus representatives of the component lineages of the city, and served, to some degree, as spokesmen of lineage interests in the determination of national policy."[39] Second, Oyo government consisted of the *alafin* and his household, which occupied the palace in Oyo. The *alafin* was the overall head of state and performed judicial and ritual functions. But, for much of the seventeenth century, the *alafin's* power was constrained by the royal council, or *Oyo Mesi*, which was composed of persons from nonroyal but elite lineages (in other words, these were aristocrats but they could not normally aspire to become kings). The council of the *Oyo Mesi* was headed by the *basorun*, who also commanded the state army. The king was required to consult the *Oyo Mesi*, although in theory the *alafin* had the final word. In addition, the *Oyo Mesi* played a critical role in selecting new kings. By the early 1700s they – through the *basorun* – made the final decision about which of the candidates selected by the royal lineage would actually become *alafin*. If they were disappointed with a given *alafin*, the *Oyo Mesi* could formally repudiate the king and compel him to commit suicide. Given that the *basorun* commanded the army, and together with the *Oyo Mesi* had an important role in the determination of succession, they wielded considerable influence with the king. They sometimes undermined kingly power. The *alafin's* position could also be put at risk from members of his own household, some of whom – as kin and as members of the royal lineage – had a claim to the throne or controlled government offices that made them potential threats to the *alafin*.

This constitutional structure was stretched to the breaking point during Oyo's period of greatest military expansion. The tensions inherent in the system produced conflicts over power and authority. A series of *Oyo Mesi* and *alafins* aimed to increase their power at the expense of the other. This was a complex process. A bewildering number of *alafins* reigned in the seventeenth and eighteenth centuries, ranging

---

[39] Law, *The Oyo Empire*, 64.

from very successful kings, like Ojigi who conquered Dahomey but who was nonetheless forced to abdicate and commit suicide, to those who were less successful, like Osinyago, who was poisoned as a result of a conflict between members of the royal lineage itself. In short, the seventeenth and eighteenth centuries witnessed the astounding success of Oyo's imperial ambitions and were beset by intense political conflict. Six of the nine persons holding the position of *alafin* were forced to commit suicide between approximately 1690 and 1754. Why was the state so plagued by internal conflicts at the height of its power?

Oyo was increasingly involved in slaving. Oyo shipped many captives into the transatlantic slave trade and many more were retained within Oyo. The seventeenth-century *alafins* used slaves to further political centralization and to boost their authority over the *Oyo Mesi* and members of the royal household. The *alafins* placed thousands of slaves in the palace administration to protect the interests of the king. Most important, these slaves governed the newly acquired outlying provinces. The aim of the *alafin* in this period was to increase kingly power by replacing horizontal political ties between the king and the aristocracy with vertical ties dominated by the king and his slaves.

The seventeenth-century *alafins* controlled three kinds of slaves: eunuchs, titled officials, and the so-called *ilari*. Many eunuchs guarded the king's wives and performed important domestic duties. Others had vital political roles that helped kings centralize power. For example, the so-called eunuch of the middle (*ona iwefa*) played an important role in the administration of justice. The Eunuch of the right (*otun iwefa*) supervised the cult of the god Sango. The eunuch of the left (*osi iwefa*) administered the collection of the *alafin's* revenues. In addition, these eunuchs headed the palace administration and acted as go-betweens with free Oyo chiefs. Another group of slaves, known as the *ilari*, meaning "scar-head" in recognition of their shaved and scarified heads, served as the king's bodyguards, messengers outside the palace, and collectors of taxes. Finally, regular titled slaves served in administrative and ritual capacities, from court historians to executioners. Robin Law considers the most important of these slaves to have been the "master of the horse" or *olokun esin* who supervised the kings horses and stables.[40] Indeed, *alafins* sent slaves (called *ajele*) out to each important provincial town, where they watched over the

---

[40] Law, *The Oyo Empire*, 68–69.

towns and ensured loyalty. They were known as "those who serve as the kings eyes."[41] Tribute from Dahomey and Egbaland was supervised by palace slaves drawn from the *ilari*. *Alafin* Ajagbo created a provincial military commander who reported only to him who was initially from the *ilari*. He thereby gained control over the provincial armies (vs. the *Oyo Mesi's* control of the metropolitan army). As Law notes, "[T]he process of imperial expansion created the resources that made centralization possible.... Successful wars yielded slaves, who could be incorporated into the palace bureaucracy ... the revenues from tribute and the expanding slave trade yielded wealth in luxury goods which the *Alafin* could distribute in order to secure the loyalty of his personal staff."[42]

Seventeenth-century *alafins* used imperial expansion and slavery to create a complex administrative system, control succession, and bypass the role of the *Oyo Mesi*. But the *Oyo Mesi* were also enriched by imperial expansion. They maintained control over the army at the capital and struggled to reduce the growing power of the *alafins*. This led to conflict, which culminated when *Basorun* Gaha seized power in 1754. Gaha dismissed the slaves and ruled mostly through close clients and kin. Despite the constant removals of *alafins*, for most of the seventeenth century palace slavery persisted, which, until Gaha, gave each new *alafin* access to power via slaves to challenge the authority of the *Oyo Mesi*. Gaha's rule only lasted until 1774, when *Alafin* Abiodun seized power, executed many of Gaha's supporters, rebuilt the slave-based administration, and enlarged his bodyguard of slave soldiers. Abiodun ruled until 1789, when Oyo was at the height of its power. However, even Abiodun's successes failed to completely resolve the state's constitutional struggles. Although slavery effected state centralization, it failed to fully transform the state, which eventually led to civil war and the destruction of Oyo by 1835–1836.

Case Study: Slave Soldiers and the *Prazeiros*

In the seventeenth century, the Portuguese crown established a number of estates in the Zambesi Valley of southeastern Africa. The estates – known as *prazos* – were given to Portuguese settlers. The

---

[41] Law, *The Oyo Empire*, 110.
[42] Law, *The Oyo Empire*, 241.

prazeiros eventually became independent forces in local politics, intermarried with local women, formed alliances with African states, and served as middlemen in the centuries-old trade from the interior to the coast. Many also adopted the symbols and customs of local political elites. They were initially small in number, lacked local legitimacy, and had no monetary or military support from the Portuguese crown. They aimed not to create commercial farms, but to trade in ivory and slaves as well as extract wealth from local, African producers. Given that they had little legitimacy, were exploitative, and could not attract labor, the *prazeiros* turned to slaving as a means to acquire soldiers and retainers. They used these slaves to enforce order, protect their estates from enemies, and extract wealth in the form of labor and taxes from local farmers. These armed slaves came to be known as the Chikunda by the eighteenth century, when they numbered about 50,000 men who were divided up between different *prazeiros*.

Chikunda slave soldiers were initially acquired from regions as far away from the Zambesi Valley as possible to enhance their cultural isolation. They lived in slave villages set apart from local populations, supervised by a slave chief. *Prazeiros* assigned loyal slaves to supervise the villages of free farmers. The Chikunda ensured their master's orders were followed. They recruited and forced local farmers to work on a variety of projects. Many also waged war on African or *prazeiro* neighbors. Most important, the slaves supervised the collection of an annual tax owed to the *prazeiro* and supervised or forced the sale of a number of crops (sorghum, maize) at below market prices to the *prazeiro* at harvest time. Chikunda slave soldiers basically became enforcers: when a village failed to provide its share of tax or crops, villagers were punished by whipping or even murder. Likewise, when farmers rebelled against a *prazeiro*, they found themselves on the receiving end of intense Chikunda violence. The Chikunda also engaged in numerous nonmilitary activities, including work as porters, traders, hunters, and canoe men.

In the context of an inability to mobilize labor, lack of political legitimacy and institutional weakness, an emerging Afro-Portuguese political elite turned to slaving to consolidate their power and to produce wealth: "The multiple functions that the Chikunda performed highlight how closely military slavery, economic production, and political consolidation were linked.... Military slavery was an engine of economic production and a means of producing and solidifying *prazeiro's* privileged class position."[43] But it was much more than that. The Chikunda themselves had aims and desires. Although the Chikunda were certainly slaves, and were subject to harsh discipline and punishment if they rebelled, they used their access to power and wealth to build a meaningful identity. They sought not to leave slavery, for it offered to them significant opportunities within a broader system of exploitation, but rather looked to define the terms of their subjugation. Absolute and autonomous freedom was not the goal for these slaves. Chikunda slave soldiers created an identity based on valor, courage, strength, and military prowess that were expressed via meaningful rituals. They set themselves apart from free farmers, built a unified slave culture, and overcame the fact that they initially spoke different languages and came from very different regions. They also established kinship connections by creating families based on patrilineal descent, developed their own language – Chi-Chikunda – and marked their status via special body markings and facial tattoos. Thus, the Chikunda were well-armed and fearsome soldiers who shared a common identity based on military success and valor. They were still slaves, however. They could not dispose of property and were often punished by the *prazeiros* for being disobedient. On the other hand, *prazeiro* masters were often terrified of their own slaves and knew they could push them only so far, which provided opportunities for these slaves to negotiate and modify the terms of their bondage. By the nineteenth century that relationship had broken down. The *prazeiros'* own economic fortunes declined, which led them to sell some of their Chikunda, which in turn led to Chikunda resistance and rebellion. By the 1830s, external invasions finished off the remaining *prazos*. But many of the Chikunda remained. As freemen, they founded a number of states of their own.

Conclusion: Slavery and the Reproduction of African States

The daily world of a slave in charge of the imperial treasury, the army, a harem, or even the collection of taxes was very different from that of a slave who toiled away on a farm or who cleaned out the stables. Yet the vulnerability and social isolation that led to the widespread use of slaves in domestic and agricultural tasks also led to their use in states,

---

[43] Allen Isaacman and Derek Peterson, "Making the Chikunda: Military Slavery and Ethnicity in Southern Africa, 1750–1900" in *Arming Slaves*, 104.

as agents of centralization, soldiers, concubines, and bureaucrats. For the ruler, slaves were the perfect antidote to relying on unpredictable kin or clients. The *social* and *political* cost of using slaves in some positions was less than using free persons. Free people expected rewards and challenged their patrons or allies. They made claims based on *belonging* that undermined elite power. Slaves simply could not make these claims, nor could they make the challenges. Slavery became a means to cement loyalty through institutionalized violence, coercion, and persuasion. For the "patron" they were the perfect "clients." Yet, this only tells part of the story. For slaves in positions of power, their dependency offered them numerous avenues to shape the conditions of their own bondage. Male elite slaves married and had children, others grew rich, and still others became so powerful their own masters shook in fear of their wrath. Some elite slaves took up arms and killed or overthrew their masters, but most sought to remain within the system that enslaved them. Because absolute freedom would have reduced their power, most elite slaves sought to integrate themselves more closely to the free elite. For men, political and military opportunities became a route to belonging. For women, integration and belonging occurred most often via marriage, concubinage, and childrearing, which also provided opportunities to reshape the master-slave dynamic. Political slavery provided for a fair degree of status mobility for some slaves. Where it was used extensively, open rather than closed slavery predominated. What is most interesting is the desexualized male – a eunuch – stands as the ideal example of male elite slavery, whereas the sexualized female – a concubine – stands as the ideal example of female slavery, which powerfully illustrates the gendered dynamics of slavery in this political context.

Throughout Africa political slavery became central to the reproduction of states and state institutions. Slavery underlay the privileged class position enjoyed by rulers and aristocrats. Food production, defense, and taxation were literally in the hands of elite slaves. In other words, slavery was essential to the "struggle for control of economic resources, control of knowledge, ceremonies and symbols, and control of armed forces."[44] Rulers used elite slaves to facilitate the

---

[44] J. Cameron Monroe, "Continuity, Revolution or Evolution on the Slave Coast of West Africa? Royal Architecture and Political Order in Precolonial Dahomey" in *Journal of African History* **48**, 3 (2007), 355, citing Norman Yofee, *Myths of the Archaic State: Evolution of the Earliest Cities, States, and Civilizations* (Cambridge: Cambridge University Press, 2005), 38.

extraction of resources from their subjects. Female slaves provided a great deal of the domestic and reproductive labor on which political elites depended. Elite slaves supervised nonelite slaves as well as free farmers and thereby facilitated "production" by making the state more efficient.

What about the road not taken? In large parts of Central and West-Central Africa, states reproduced themselves not by using slaves as officials – or even as soldiers – but by relying on the enslavement and export of slaves into the Atlantic system, which was a different method of institutional reproduction altogether. Some states did not use slaves at all. Shaka's Zulu state became a military powerhouse in the nineteenth century. Located in the eastern part of southern Africa, Shaka and his predecessor Dingiswayo presided over military expansion and acquired control over huge number of cattle. How can we explain the use of slaves by some states and not by others? The states that avoided the use of slaves as political or military agents were effectively controlled by a powerful institutionally legitimate monarch – like Shaka – who had few elite competitors for power, which were highly incorporative and expansionistic, and were able to mobilize and effectively control large freeborn populations, obviating the need for slaves. In the Zulu state, unmarried adult men lived and trained together in age-based infantry regiments, which fought together on the battlefield. The organization and use of these regiments helped weaken territorially based kinship relationships and protections. In exchange, people looked to build horizontal relationships with one another as soldiers and hoped to establish vertical relationships with the monarch. Bravery and success in war encouraged integration and cohesion. Success on the battlefield brought worldly success. Men and women looked to integrate themselves into the state rather than resist it: "Shaka and his successors formed a broad Zulu empire through military conquest and intensive incorporation of conquered people into the new polity. While Zulu institutions such as *amabutho* age-sets linked to scattered royal homesteads brought youth together from around the kingdom and socialized them into a new cosmopolitan Zulu identity."[45] In Asante, government and administration remained largely free of slaves, which was a result of the creation in the eighteenth century of a patrimonial bureaucracy based partially on merit.

[45] Paul K. Bjerk, "'They Poured Themselves into the Milk': Zulu Political Philosophy Under Shaka" in *Journal of African History* 47 (2006), 3.

In other cases, age grade systems or initiation societies throughout Africa provided an alternative means of political mobilization, and limited the power of the ruler to such an extent that slaving never became a viable political strategy.

States used slaves for different reasons at different times. Some simply used slaves as thugs to loot and rob, while others built complex administrative institutions using slaves, and still others were used to centralize power in the hands of rulers. Although political slavery helped build the practical and ideological hegemony of numerous states, it also produced contradictions. The belonging, honor, and power offered to royal slaves meant that they could destabilize the very states that used them. The delicate and dialectical balance between master and slave sometimes tipped in favor of the slaves. If anything, the role of slavery in African states illustrates just how important the actions and ideas of slaves were to the rise and fall of African states. We will now turn to the everyday slaves who worked in fields, farms, and industries to assess the economic impact of slavery in Africa and the extent to which African states and societies depended on slaves in production.

CHAPTER 5

Slavery and African Economies

Introduction

In 1685, Michel Jajolet de La Courbe visited a slave agricultural estate of a powerful official of Waalo, a Wolof state in what is now Senegal. These large farms produced food crops that fed the Wolof political elite and were exchanged for livestock and animal products. La Courbe noted that after his arrival on the estate, he found the man he sought "in the middle of his field with his sword at his side and his spear in his hand, which encouraged his people in their work." He noted that the slaves "numbered more than sixty, and were naked. Each one held a small rounded iron hoe with a cutting blade at the end, which was attached to a handle and which they used to cut down the weeds and work the soil at the same time, working only the top surface of the soil. All of this was accomplished to the sound and rhythm of the energetic music of six griots, who played drums and sang. It was a pleasure to watch them move as if they were possessed, quickening or slowing the pace of their work as the beat of the drums rose and fell."[1]

★ ★ ★

In South Africa, by the middle of the eighteenth century, many slaves worked the wheat and wine farms that surrounded Cape Town. At the height of the harvest, slaves performed numerous tasks. According to

[1] James Searing, "Slaves and Peasants: Power and Dependency in the Wolof States, 1700–1850" in *The International Journal of African Historical Studies* **21**, 3 (1988), 477.

O. F. Mentzel, who observed these farms in the 1730s, "Every grape cutter at the vintage has a small basket, made of thin split Spanish reed standing next to him which when full, is carried to the pressing house ... a 'balie' or barrel ... when is pierced at the bottom and along the sides with holes made with a half-inch drill, stands on a trestle in a second larger barrel, without holes except for a bung hole, through which the must that is trodden out, passes into a pail or barrel placed beneath it. A slave stands in the perforated barrel, holds on to a short piece of rope stretched above him and treads the grapes with which it is filled with bare feet."[2]

★ ★ ★

In nineteenth-century Dar Fur, a tradition stated:

> The Slaves must do the work in the house; if they are unwilling to work they must be beaten with a whip or must be beaten with the stick. Then they begin to cry [and] be willing to work. Their language is difficult; people don't understand them. If we find a girl among them, who pleases us, then she doesn't need to do any housework. I make her my wife, so that we can sleep together in bed and 'eat the skin,' so that we will have children. Then she becomes pregnant and has a child. If it is a boy, then everything is fine.[3]

★ ★ ★

All slaves in Africa worked. The nature, intensity, and importance of that work varied substantially. Although slaves were used for economic purposes, their value ranged along a continuum from societies in which slavery was marginal to those in which slavery was a central economic institution. Over time, parts of the African continent experienced significant economic growth that was tied to the production of commodities for local use and that fed into regional and international exchange networks. In these regions, high-density, productive slavery developed as early as the eleventh century, because an increasing number of Africans used slave labor in vital sectors of the economy. As has already been observed, Finley explained this transition by distinguishing between a *society with slaves* and a *slave society*.[4] Although

---

[2] Cited by Robert Ross in *Cape of Torments: Slavery and Resistance in South Africa* (London: Routledge and Kegan Paul, 1983), 27.

[3] Quoted by Lovejoy, *Transformations in Slavery*, 223.

[4] Finley argued that slavery was "transformed as an institution when slaves play an essential role in the economy ... in slave societies hired labor was rare and slave labor

Finley wrote about slavery in global terms, scholars of African history have documented what they believe to be a similar transition. Lovejoy argued that a slave "mode of production" – a social, political, and economic system based on slavery – developed in Africa. For Lovejoy, this occurred when slaves were used in production and "the social and economic structure of a particular society included an integrated system of enslavement, slave trade, and the domestic use of slaves."[5] Lovejoy's argument is persuasive. However, it focuses primarily on external forces – especially the transatlantic slave trade – as the central impetus for transitions in African slavery, rather than concentrating on the internal forces that led to the use of slaves in production.

Why, then, did so many states and merchants move toward the large-scale, labor-intensive use of slaves in production? This chapter answers that question by focusing on the political, social, demographic, technological, and environmental challenges faced by Africans as they built economies. This emphatically does not ignore the impact of external forces on slavery. The transatlantic, Indian Ocean, and trans-Saharan slave trades were dramatically linked to the growth and transformation of slavery in parts of Africa. These trades increased the availability of slaves, expanded slave use, and influenced African social and political structures by enhancing social differentiation and stimulating political violence. The impact of external forces, however, was complex and highly variable. Both internal and external forces produced the economic use of slaves – even in places with large external slave trades. Africans used slavery to overcome local limitations on production, growth, and surplus extraction. This does not mean that slavery was timeless and unchanging, but rather that African producers aimed to increase their access to labor – and the productivity of that labor – through coercion, which most often took the form of slavery.

Economic specialization and growth in Africa became highly dependent on slavery. Slavery became economically essential in two major ways. The earliest economic use of slaves was tied to the growth of states and their governing political elites. Slave production sustained the elite. Slavery became vital to the "elite economy" of the court,

the rule whenever enterprise was too big for family to conduct unaided. That rule extended from agriculture to manufacture and mining." See Moses Finley, "Slavery" in *The International Encyclopedia of the Social Sciences* 14 (1968), 310.

[5] Lovejoy, *Transformations in Slavery*, 10–12.

palace, and military. Slavery did not necessarily have a large impact on the overall economy, which remained in the hands of free producers and merchants. Indeed, warfare and plunder were often (although not always) the most essential economic sector. A cycle of war and slaving developed that increased the internal African demand for slaves. Slaves were acquired through violence and were then used in production. They maintained and expanded a state's military capacity and system of governance by providing food, clothing, and other commodities to the elite. Over time, the use of slaves trickled down to nonelite households. Slaves became available, which often encouraged small-scale production for the market. In later periods (often in the nineteenth century, although not always), entire African economies became closely tied to slave labor. Slaves were widely used by elite and nonelite producers. Slaves produced commodities that were traded for profit or exchanged for other valuable goods. In time, producers at both the household and state levels grew dependent on these exchanges. Most important, Africans came to depend on slave rather than free labor for the production of essential goods.

This transition was partially grounded in preexisting African moral economies. Scholars have often viewed the use of slaves in production and the use of slaves within lineages as fundamentally oppositional, instead of seeking to understand how those slaveries were related. It often made sense to use slave labor because slavery was already an established reality, which offered a ready way to acquire workers within preexisting systems of labor mobilization. Slaves *had* to do the assigned work, and owners appropriated nearly all of what slaves produced. This was not always a conscious calculation, of course, but as Cooper noted: "The economic exploitation of slaves allowed an elite to enrich itself without challenging directly the village- or kinship-based economy.... Power in African societies, it is commonly said, comes from people. It is also directed at people."[6] The economic reliance on slaves further increased their marginality and the intensity of their exploitation. Complex communities that depended on slave labor developed well-defined structural positions for slaves. This was not a one-off shift that ended any other change. The transition to high-density slavery could stick or be a relatively short experiment that faded as conditions changed. High-density slavery produced its own contradictions: because integration was less common and more difficult, masters and

---

[6] Frederick Cooper, "The Problem of Slavery in African Studies" in *Journal of African History* **20**, 1 (1979), 116.

slaves might end up in direct conflict more often, as masters sought more from their slaves and slaves sought to hold onto work routines and social ties that ameliorated slavery.

Land, Labor, and Agriculture in Africa

Slaves were used most often in agricultural production. Why? Africans faced unique challenges. Land was usually available, but shortages of labor and fixed capital constrained economic growth. Although historians do not have access to sources that provide precise population figures, scholars have developed estimates counting backward from early colonial population figures. J.D. Durand estimated that in 1750, the population of the continent south of the Sahara ranged from 54 million to 135 million, whereas Patrick Manning estimated a population of between 48 million and 63 million, although he excluded much of southern Africa from the calculation. The population density per square kilometer ranged from 2.3 to 5.8 according to Durand and 2.3 to 3.0 according to Manning. Estimates suggest that overall population densities increased from 1.9 persons per square kilometer in 1500 to 4.4 in 1900.[7] These are only estimates but they offer some comparative perspective. In Europe, population densities ranged from twenty-three to twenty-seven persons per square kilometer (excluding Russia). Compared to European figures, African population densities were low and unevenly distributed. However, the numbers do not take into account regional and ecological variations or political decisions that might have restricted land use in some places. Thornton estimated that the Lower Guinea Coast of West Africa had a population density of thirty to forty people per square kilometer. Parts of the Ethiopian highlands, the Great Lakes region (now Uganda, Burundi, and Rwanda), and the highlands of southern Africa (in what became Great Zimbabwe) also had high population concentrations. African land abundance sometimes took a backseat to the fact that local populations sought to exploit very limited but especially fertile land. These farmers used terracing, irrigation, and fertilizing to intensively farm small amounts of available land. This process of agricultural inten-

---

[7] See Christopher Clapham, "The Political Economy of African Population Change" in *Population and Development Review* **32** (2006), 98.

sification "should be seen as a process that is only worthwhile under certain conditions, and historically these have not been widespread."[8]

What about birthrates? Despite the shortage of labor, African birthrates were not tremendously high. Africans often limited births – as did rural families in preindustrial Europe – in response to adverse conditions. Although labor in the form of people – human hands to clear the fields, till the soil, and carry the water – was highly valued, actual birthrates did not always keep up with that demand. In addition, labor mobility – via the migration of human beings – might have restricted labor availability in regions that lost migrants. Thus, as Dennis Cordell noted, "African societies, like all societies, have sought to assure their survival as societies, but this "vital force" did not translate into uniform patterns of demographic behavior. Nor ... did African families and societies seek necessarily to maximize births. They sought to assure social reproduction, but this goal could be attained in a number of ways."[9]

We can safely posit that overall population densities were relatively low, and land relatively available, but there were significant variations over time and place. Labor scarcity and land abundance *could* hinder productivity and reduce overall economic output. These factors help explain the reliance on coerced labor in the form of slavery, but what about places where populations were larger and land was less available? In these cases, the absolute density of populations mattered less than the social organization of production and reproduction. Local African households were often self-sufficient in food production and economically autonomous.[10] Although households might produce goods for exchange, they worked for themselves independently at a subsistence level. As self-sustaining economic units, local households could withdraw from market relationships. This local self-sufficiency made it very difficult for larger producers – usually states and merchants – to mobilize free, household-based labor. In other words, because the free populations of complex states were often relatively autonomous,

[8] Adams, W. H., "When islands expand: intensification and sustainability' in M. Widgren and J. E. G. Sutton, eds., *Islands of intensive agriculture in eastern Africa* (Nairobi, 2004), 136 and cited by Gareth Austin, "Resources, Techniques, and Strategies South of the Sahara: Revising the Factor Endowments Perspective on African Economic Development, 1500–2000" in *Economic History Review* **61**, 3 (2007), 592.
[9] Dennis D. Cordell, "African Historical Demography in the Years Since Edinburgh" in *History in Africa* **27** (2000), 75.
[10] Austin, "Resources, Techniques, and Strategies," 590.

weakly integrated into the state, and in some cases widely scattered, the acquisition of free labor was difficult and costly (in terms of the resources needed to coerce or attract that labor). Labor scarcity was accentuated everywhere by seasonal variation in demand. It was during the rainy season that much of the planting, weeding, and even harvesting occurred. The demand for labor was the greatest when it was needed the most. Even in places with relatively dense populations, obtaining labor was expensive and difficult, especially at times of peak demand. In 1796–1797, Mungo Park offered a useful description that illustrates differential seasonal labor demands:

> Few people work harder, when occasion requires, than the Mandingoes; but not having many opportunities of turning to advantage the superfluous produce of their labour, they are content with cultivating as much ground only as is necessary for their own support. The labours of the field give them pretty full employment during the rains; and in the dry season, the people who live in the vicinity of large rivers employ themselves chiefly in fishing.... Others of the natives employ themselves in hunting.... While the men are occupied in these pursuits, the women are very diligent in manufacturing cotton cloth.... A woman with common diligence will spin from six to nine garments of this cloth in one year, which, according to its fineness, will sell for a minkalli and a half or two minkallies each.[11]

Despite land abundance, Africans were not always, in the words of Gareth Austin, "resource rich." Africans faced environmental challenges that "restricted human economic activity" and varied over time.[12] On the most basic level, changes in the land dramatically altered what Africans produced. For example, in 1600, the different ecological zones that supported camel herding, cattle herding, or rain-fed agriculture were 200–300 kilometers farther north than they were in 1850, by which time the "Sahelian Cattle Zone had descended south into lands that had once been primarily agricultural; the farming frontier receding in advance of it."[13] Even in environmentally stable situations, the cost of effectively exploiting land availability was

---

[11] Cited by Austin, "Resources, Techniques, and Strategies," 598.

[12] James C. McCann, "Climate and Causation in African History" in *The International Journal of African Historical Studies* 32, 2/3 (1999), 262, citing Reid Bryson and Christine Paddock, "On the Climates of History," in Robert I. Rotberg and Theodore K. Rabb (eds.), *Climate and History: Studies in Interdisciplinary History* (Princeton, NJ: Princeton University Press, 1981), 3–4.

[13] McCann, "Climate and Causation," 269, citing James Webb, *The Desert Frontier: Ecological and Economic Change along the Western Sahel* (Madison: University of Wisconsin Press, 1995), 3–4.

high. Why? Soils were often of poor quality and easily eroded, rainfall was unreliable and concentrated in a specific rainy season, and in huge belts of tropical Africa, sleeping sickness (trypanosomiasis) made the use of animals impossible. As a result, extensive and labor-intensive hoe agriculture dominated much of Africa, which remained dependent on climatic fluctuations. To increase production, Africans first required extensive amounts of land in order to maintain long fallow periods that rejuvenated soil fertility. In some forest zones, farms laid fallow for twenty-five years before they could be successfully cultivated. In other cases, the fallow period ranged from one to ten years. With this system of land rotation and recurrent cultivation, the only way to dramatically increase output was to increase labor inputs – or the number of workers.[14]

The availability of labor was limited by many factors: political organization, population size, the nature of local landholding systems, production and farming techniques, environmental conditions, and the time of year that labor was required. Africans needed to maximize access to *available* human labor power. Many states and producers therefore sought to gain control over people to overcome the limiting factors that made the mobilization of free labor difficult. Africans used slavery to intensify production, which created surpluses of desired commodities that had both economic and political value. The surest route to expanded economic and political power lay in the intensive exploitation of slave labor. High-density slaveholding consolidated in centers of economic growth. Two separate Africa's emerged between 1000 and 1900: one in which slavery became a fundamental part of the political economy and another in which the political economy remained rooted in local, free, or client-based household production. There was often an overlap between non-slave and slave zones in Africa; free producers coexisted with slave producers, even in regions that used slaves extensively. We will now turn to the places where economic change and political innovation led to the consolidation of political economies that were dependent on high-density slavery before 1800: the Savanna and Sahelian zones of West Africa, parts of

---

[14] See Ralph Austen and Daniel Headrick, "The Role of Technology in the African Past" in *African Studies Review* 26, 3/4 (1982), 169, who note: "In pre-colonial Africa the predominant source of energy was human. Some areas used non-human energy for transportation: sailing dhows on the Indian Ocean, canoes on various rivers, pack animals in the Sudan. But agriculture and manufacturing were everywhere strictly human."

the West African coastal and forest zones, the Cape Colony in South
Africa, parts of Central Africa, including the Kingdom of Kongo and
the Luba and Lunda empires, and the Kingdom of Buganda in East
Africa.

High-Density Slavery in the Sahel and Savanna to 1800

The West African Sahel and Savanna were centers of high-density
slavery. Sudanic states of this region were some of the first to make
widespread economic use of slaves. Some scholars have argued that
Islam was most influential in the process, whereas others believe that
the trans-Saharan trade led to the increased use of slaves. It is certain
that Islam influenced how slaves were treated and that the trans-Saharan trade helped increase the number of slaves available. However, the
use of slaves in the Savanna and Sahel regions was otherwise driven
by internal developments. The dynamic economy that developed in
this region was based in part on local agricultural production and
large-scale inter-ecological trade between the forest, Savanna, Sahel,
and desert zones. States consolidated and expanded over the centuries
in an east–west pattern and gradually came to dominate north–south
trade routes. Two major groups played a role in these processes: merchants (who were heavily involved in the exchange of commodities
and maintained extensive commercial connections), and rulers (who
were basically hereditary monarchs) and aristocrats (who founded the
states, governed them, and fought on horseback – and who themselves may have emerged from warlike Saharan raiders). The rulers
of Sudanic states profited from their important position astride these
routes, especially via the taxation of goods exchanged by merchants,
mainly in the form of gold, salt, gum arabic, ostrich feathers, and
slaves. Rulers also extracted tribute from conquered territories. In
good times, rulers created stable political conditions, which in turn
helped boost trade and merchant profits. Over time, rulers built palaces to advertise their power and serve as royal courts where their
governments were based. They also raised large armies – especially
cavalry when horses were available – which they used both in regular
warfare and to raid for plunder.

These rulers needed to acquire labor that was not otherwise available in order to feed and provide for their armies and palace resi-
dents and retinues. Rulers, and sometimes merchants, had access to

large amounts of land on which they wanted to produce crops and commodities. Given the nature of agriculture in the region – and the dominance of smallholder production at the local level – the acquisition and mobilization of labor became a key problem. By establishing large slave agricultural estates, rulers effectively built a dependent local economy from which they could extract necessary resources. Merchants were vital to the slave trade itself, which helped make slaves available for sale, and in some places merchants became users of slaves as well. Austen perhaps described the situation best:

> [A]ll of these states gained more of their material support from captured or inherited slaves than free subjects. For purposes of supplying food and other agricultural goods to the rulers, many of these slaves were settled near the capital, thus reinforcing the sense of a state exercising power only at its center and collecting less regular 'tribute' from more distant, and potentially defecting, provinces.[15]

The ability of many Sudanic states to wage war and feed themselves became closely tied to the use of slaves; slaves essentially became the core producers for the warriors on horseback who dominated the states. Meillassoux argued that "[slavery was] intended for maintenance of the dominant class and the reproduction of its means of domination: war and the administration of war."[16] But, to reiterate, simply going to war and raiding was not enough. Certainly, selling captured slaves in trans-Saharan networks provided states with resources – in the form of horses especially – but the real issue was how to use captured slaves to overcome the limited supply of controllable labor, which was the basic problem these states faced. Thus, the roots of slavery were not to be found in Islamic, transatlantic, or trans-Saharan influences, but were in fact produced by the growth of local aristocracies and their ability to gain control over strategic resources.

Between 1000 to 1500 CE, high-density slavery became common throughout the western, central, and eastern Sudan. The regional economy was based on slave labor, which was tied to key productive sectors (especially agriculture, salt, and textiles), regional and international trade networks, as well as the overall capacity of Sudanic states to exercise power and reproduce themselves. Slaves were widely used, for example, in Ghana, Mali, Songhay, The Jolof Empire (Western Sudan), Kanem-Borno and the Hausa city-states (Central Sudan),

---

[15] Austen, "Imperial Reach Versus Institutional Grasp," 522.
[16] Meillassoux, *The Anthropology of Slavery*, 53.

Dar Fur, and the Funj Sultanate of Sennar (Eastern Sudan). Although these states had their own individual histories, they all were affected by similar historical processes between 500 and 1800 CE: the advent of warfare on horseback, the creation of political hierarchies based on kingship, the aristocratic control over land, the development of a desert-side economy that integrated these states into regional and international exchange networks – including the trans-Saharan trade – and, finally, all were faced with the need to expand agricultural and industrial production (such as salt mining).

Although there is a dearth of source material, the earliest states of the region – especially Ghana and Mali – used slaves extensively. Between 200 and 800 CE, Ghana's rulers built a populous capital city in the western Sahel (probably in what is now southeastern Mauritania and western Mali). The state was likely a product of the competition over scarce resources fueled by war on horseback, which led to the consolidation of a political elite. Ghana eventually developed a political system dominated by a king and an army, which was tied into trade networks throughout the Sahel and Savanna and that reached across the Sahara Desert. The state became an important southern terminus in trans-Saharan trade and was extensively involved in the gold and salt trades. Although Ghana relied mostly on the revenue raised from the taxation of trans-Saharan trade, it is likely, albeit not certain, that slaves were used in agricultural production. Slaving was certainly common, and a large number of slaves were taken in raids and sold into the trans-Saharan slave trade. According to Al-Bakri (c. 1014–1094), before 1054, the northern town and trading center of Awdaghust contained slaves "so numerous that one person among [its population] might possess a thousand."[17] Slaves were used in a variety of productive sectors, including ceramic production, metalworking, and textiles. Around the same time, states of the Senegal River Valley, including Takrur, raided for, traded, and used slaves. Mali, the state that dominated the region during the thirteenth and fourteenth centuries, also played a vital role in the slave, gold, and salt trades. Slaves worked in a variety of occupations and had important economic and political roles. On his pilgrimage to Mecca, Mansa Musa (ruler between c. 1312 and 1337) was preceded by 500 slaves carrying gold staves and

[17] N. Levtzion and J.F.P. Hopkins (eds.), *Corpus of Early Arabic Sources for West African History* (Cambridge: Cambridge University Press, 1980), 74.

accompanied by 14,000 female slaves. Although these numbers were probably exaggerated, they indicate that slaves were available and used in large numbers. It is also likely that slaves were used in agriculture, although here we are hampered by a lack of sources detailing how and where they worked.

We are on much surer ground when discussing the economic importance of slavery in Songhay. Starting in Gao, a small city along the Niger River in the thirteenth century, Songhay became a major imperial power by the sixteenth century. The state eventually controlled a vast amount of territory (1.4 million square miles), including the important cities of Jenne and Timbuktu, as well as a large portion of the Niger River. The state expanded through warfare. As a consequence, Songhay's rulers seized tens of thousands of captives over the course of its history. Like Mali, Songhay armies undertook expeditions solely to acquire slaves. In 1498, the number of slaves retained in Gao was so large that a special city quarter had to be built for them. Likewise, one of the sons of Askia Dawud claimed that raiding parties easily seized 10,000 slaves. Some of these captives were sold into the trans-Saharan slave trade, but many more were retained and used in a variety of ways, especially as agricultural laborers. Why? As the state grew in size, so too did its government and population. To feed the elite and their armies, the rulers of Songhay created a widespread system of agricultural slavery. Although the state was institutionally powerful and highly exploitative, there was a limit to its ability to extract goods and taxes from the free population. Compared to free farmers, slaves worked longer and harder, and much more of what they produced was claimed by the state. Thus, in the sixteenth century, the rulers of Songhay established agricultural estates, especially along the Niger River, where they used slaves as agricultural workers. These slave estates produced agricultural commodities and were sometimes bestowed as gifts to cement the loyalty of political allies. At least thirty agricultural estates existed from Dendi in the southeast to the Lake Debo region in the northwest. Some were quite large. The estate at Faran-Taka, for example, contained an estimated 1,700 to 2,700 slaves. Another estate in Dendi contained 200 slaves who were supervised by 4 slave officials. Slaves mainly grew rice and were supervised closely by slave officials. After harvesting, the rice was sent to Gao, the capital of Songhay, in boats that could carry around 20 tons per trip. Each year these estates produced a total of roughly 600 to 750 tons of rice, which helped feed the palace community in Gao (somewhere between 5,000 and 7,000 persons).[18] Other slave estates, some of which may have been owned by the nonroyal high officials of the Songhay court, produced a wide variety of cereal crops. Overall, according to the *Ta'rīkh al-Fattāsh*:

> The food that came from harvest of the farms was so abundant that no one knew how to evaluate it, nor even to be sure of its quantity. He owned plantations in all the lands that were under his dominion; that is, in Eeri, Dendi, Kulane, Kerei-Hausa, and Kerei-Gurma, as well as territories neighboring them on the way to Kukiya and Gao, as far as Kissu on the one hand, and the as far as the islands of Bamba and of Benga on the other. He also owned plantations in Aterem as far to the west as Kingui and Bunio as far to the east as the last port of Lake Debo. In some years, the yield that he drew from his farms surpassed four thousand sunnu [the name of a leather sack that held 200–250 liters] of grain.[19]

To what extent did regular people – free farmers – hold slaves? We simply do not have the data to know. But given the availability of slaves, and the consolidation of commercial and military systems that produced them in large numbers, it would be safe to assume that a proportion of small farmers would have bought a slave or two to help with the labor of farming and other domestic duties. Even the slaves sold into Saharan networks became workers. Some slaves worked in the salt mines of Taghaza and Taoudeni, others worked as agricultural laborers in the oases along trans-Saharan trade routes, while others smelted copper or pastured the flocks of their masters. Thus, the Berbers of the desert did not simply transport slaves across the desert, but used them as labor in central economic activities as well. The northern expansion of slaving and slaveholding was coupled with the southern expansion of the slaving frontier. The growing demand for slaves meant that the slave trade, slaveholding, and slave raiding became more common in the regions to the south of Songhay over time.

Further west, in the fifteenth century, the Jolof Empire dominated Senegambia. Its rulers used slaves extensively as laborers. A burgeoning trade in slaves brought horses and weapons into the region from the Sahara. This enhanced the slaving capacity of the empire, which in turn meant that more slaves were acquired to labor in the fields. When

---

[18] See Lovejoy, *Transformations in Slavery*, 32–33.
[19] Christopher Wise (ed.), *Ta'rīkh al-Fattāsh: The Timbuktu Chronicles, 1493–1599* by Al Hajj Mahmud Kati (Trenton, NJ: Africa World Press, 2011), 175–176.

the Portuguese first visited the region, they found that slavery was a well-established economic institution. Valentim Fernandes for example, made note of the numerous agricultural slaves who performed labor for their masters six days per week. Alvise Cadamosto, who traveled to the region in 1454, stated that the king of the Jolof Empire had no fixed income except that in each year the various "lords" of the region

> present him with horses, which are much esteemed owing to their scarcity, forage, beasts such as cows and goats, vegetables, millet and the like. The King supports himself by raids which result in many slaves from his own as well as neighboring countries. He employs these slaves in cultivating land allotted to him: but he also sells many to Azanaghi merchants in return for horses and other goods, and also to the Christians, since they have begun to trade with these blacks.[20]

In the sixteenth century, the Jolof Empire broke apart, leaving in its wake a number of Wolof states (Kajoor and Bawol, for example) that competed for supremacy. By the seventeenth century, these states were dominated by warrior aristocracies, which fought hard and played hard. They were known both for their success on the battlefield and for their hard drinking. The states closest to the coast – especially Kajoor and Bawol – acquired slaves from the interior and sent them into the transatlantic slave trade. They also used slaves extensively in agriculture and as weavers. Many of these slaves produced food for the local elites and Europeans. Slave-produced grain fed the slaves who waited on the coast to leave for the middle passage across the Atlantic. By the middle of the eighteenth century, the local production of grain and gum arabic along the Senegal River Valley demanded so much labor that it was partially responsible for the decline of the coastal slave trade. Africans chose to use slaves in production *rather* than trade them. To the north of the Senegal River, Berbers dominated the desert and Sahel of the Western Sudan. Even when European trade was robust, the Africans who lived closest to the desert and Sahel remained orientated toward the interior rather than the Atlantic. They continued to use slaves to acquire horses. Retained

---

[20] On Fernandes, see: Martin A. Klein, "Slavery in the Western Soudan" in Spaulding and Beswick (eds.), *African Systems of* Slavery, 18. On Cadamosto, see: A. Cadamosto, *The Voyages of Cadamosto* (London, 1937), 30 as cited by Martin A. Klein, "Servitude among the Wolof and Sereer of Senegambia" in Miers and Kopytoff (eds.), *Slavery in Africa*, 340.

slaves were used in northern oasis regions to cultivate dates, grains, and melons. Closer to the Savanna they cultivated grains for desert-side commercial communities, which merchants then traded throughout the Western Sudan. All in all, the expansion of commercial grain production throughout this region – whether orientated toward the coast or within the Savanna and Sahel – was made possible by the use of slave labor. According to James Searing:

> The slave estates of the Wolof nobility produced food crops rather than industrial or luxury crops, but they were still large-scale productive units. Although the first goal of these estates was to insure self-sufficiency in cereals for the large households of the aristocracy, there were important outlets for surplus production. The Wolof traded cereals for livestock and animal products with the Arab and Berber speakers of the Western Sahara. During the era of the Atlantic slave trade the Wolof traded their surplus cereals for European goods to supply slave ships with provisions, and to supply the coastal trade settlements, particularly Saint Louis.[21]

In the eighteenth century, the rise of Segu in 1712 further complicated regional politics. Segu depended on slave soldiers or *tonjon*, who viewed agricultural work as beneath them. The state was supported by thousands of other slaves, captured in a continual series of wars that also expanded Segu's borders. These slaves were mostly women who were sometimes wives as well. They labored in the fields in support of individual warriors. Others were put to work in state-owned farms. They were called *forabajonw* or "slaves of the big field." Skilled slaves became ironworkers who produced lead balls and repaired firearms. Yet others were redistributed to occupational groups (like the Somono fishermen) who provided important services for the state. Slaving in Segu was a "productive activity" in the words of Richard Roberts.[22] Some of Segu's slaves were acquired by Maraka Muslim merchants, who transported them into the transatlantic slave trade. In exchange, the *tonjon* of Segu received weapons and horses. Maraka merchants also retained slaves. The Maraka used these slaves as agricultural laborers on the many large agricultural estates that surrounded – and fed – Maraka towns. Slaves were used in textile production. Some of

---

[21] Searing, "Slaves and Peasants," 478.
[22] Richard Roberts, "Production and Reproduction of Warrior States: Segu Bambara and Segu Tokolor, c. 1712–1890" in *The International Journal of African Historical Studies* **13**, 3 (1980), 400.

this slave-grown produce, including cotton, was shipped and sold by the Maraka throughout the Western Sudan. Overall, the rulers and slave soldiers of Segu managed to create a state that was almost – but not completely – divorced from the labor and lives of free households. Segu did not need the labor of free people. Its economy and survival depended instead on war, pillage, slaving, and agricultural slavery, although many Bambara remained apart from this slave-based economy and worked on their own account as small farmers.

Moving to the east, in the Central Sudan, slaves were used widely in important economic roles. Slavery in Kanem-Borno, for example, corresponded to the broader patterns that characterized many Sudanic states. Kanem-Borno was founded around Lake Chad perhaps as early as 750 to 800 CE. Eventually a complex and hierarchical system emerged. The institution of kingship (king in Kanuri is *mai*) was controlled by the Saifawa dynasty from very early in Kanem-Borno's history through to the nineteenth century. The state eventually became a central part of the burgeoning trans-Saharan trade system, relied on horses as a central part of the military, and became increasingly influenced by Islam. At the center of this thriving economy was the regional and long-distance trade of commodities (slaves and salt, for example) as well as extensive agricultural, textile, and salt production. From an early period slavery and the slave trade were important features the economy. Slaves were sold locally and into the trans-Saharan slave trade. Those who were retained locally were used in many different tasks. At least by the reign of *Mai* Ali ibn Dunama (reigned c. 1465–1497), when a permanent capital was built at Birnin Gazargarmo, slaves were used in agricultural production. Dunama (and many other kings) distributed land in the form of estates to members of the titleholding aristocracy. Kings also retained land and slaves for their own use. Whereas free people might work and pay taxes on these lands, the titleholders acquired and settled slaves to work for them. Many of the settlements were located close to the capital and throughout the Komodugu Yo Valley. Over the centuries much changed in Kanem-Borno, but this system of land allocation and slave use persisted. Other slaves worked at preparing cotton and spinning textiles or managed cattle. Indeed, the capital was located within 100 kilometers of up to 200 salt-producing locations. Borno's salt industry was vast (producing perhaps 6,500 to 9,000 tons per year) and supplied salt across the entire Savanna. In many locations – usually in the desert where labor was hard to find – the work of salt production was done by slaves, who numbered well into the thousands until the industry declined, along with Borno's economy, during the drought of the mid-eighteenth century.[23]

It is likely that here too slave ownership was not restricted simply to the elite, but that all households would have – if possible – acquired a slave or two to help with domestic and agricultural work. A traveler to Borno made special note of the fact that nonelites owned slaves. Although the source comes from the nineteenth century, it no doubt reflected past practice:

> It can be understood that in small villages where every household is on its own, and where there is no beginning of a suitable division of labour to generate and maintain markets, the time of the inhabitants is fully occupied, and that even less well-to-do people cannot well dispense with the help of a few slaves. The domestic animals in particular are entrusted to the male slaves, who have to drive them to the pastures or cut fodder for them, while the female slaves help the mistress in all domestic duties.[24]

Lastly, the Hausa city-states, Dar Fur, and the Funj Sultanate of Sennar came to use slaves in a parallel process, namely the consolidation of a political elite, creation of political hierarchies, and development of a trans-Saharan trading system, which all served to increase the need for productive labor and made slaves more easily available via trade and war. In numerous Hausa city-states (especially Kano, Katsina, and Zazzau), slaves were used as laborers on agricultural estates administered either by the emir or by lesser officials who were given estates for their own use. Even before the nineteenth century, these estates produced agricultural commodities for local use, redistribution, and, eventually, sale. Slave production became essential to the city-states and their economies. Merchants in Hausaland acquired land and used slaves for similar purposes, although that process really took off later. Likewise, in Dar Fur, two Sultans – Tayrab (reigned c. 1752/3–1785/6) and 'Abd al Rahman (reigned c. 1787/8–1803) – settled slaves on agricultural estates near their capitals that produced food and other goods for both the army and the palace community.

---

[23] See, for example, Paul E. Lovejoy, *Salt of the Desert Sun: A History of Salt Production* (Cambridge: Cambridge University Press, 2003).

[24] Gustav Nachitgal, *The Sahara and the Sudan, Volume III: The Chad Basin and Bagirmi* (London: Christopher Hurst, 1987), 131–132, as cited by Humphrey J. Fisher, "Slavery and Seclusion in Northern Nigeria: A Further Note" in *The Journal of African History* **32**, 1 (1991), 125.

FIGURE 11. Slaves farming in East Africa in John Speke, *Journal of the Discovery of the Source of the Nile* (New York, 1869), 117. Courtesy of the UVM Bailey-Howe Library.

Some aristocrats accumulated as many as 600 slaves on their estates. In the Funj Sultanate of Sennar, Badi II (reigned 1644–1681) settled slaves around his capital. The slave population grew over the years to the point that in 1773 it numbered 14,000. Ostensibly used for military defense of the capital, these slaves contributed much more in their capacity as farmers who produced many vital necessities for the capital.

Slavery was a central economic activity in the Savanna and Sahel of West Africa. Large-scale agricultural slavery became common and essential to the states and merchants of the region (Figure 11). Slaves worked longer and harder than free people and produced more than free people who used comparable methods. Lovejoy and other scholars have used the word "plantation" to describe this system of slave production. I prefer "agricultural estates" in order to emphasize that there were distinctions between the two systems. Although large numbers of slaves were concentrated as units of production, there was no planter class, nor was there a single work regime for all "plantation slaves." Indeed, most slaves grew their own food, making the estates self-sufficient. These estates were often populated by newly captured slaves, who worked in supervised gangs. Over time, however, those slaves had children, and second-generation slaves usually renegotiated the terms of their own bondage. They worked in separate villages with less direct supervision. Although agricultural estates were a common feature of the landscape, no one knows how many slaves they absorbed. It seems likely that over the whole period (1000–1800 CE) we are dealing with a very large slave population (easily into the millions) that needed to be constantly renewed when slaves found their way out of slavery or died. This population was initially tied to the growth of large states, like Songhay and Kanem-Borno, but was not limited to those states. Thus, the dependence on slavery increased over time, so that by the nineteenth century the slave population was huge, ranging from 20 percent to 35 percent of the free population at minimum. In addition, smaller farmers used slaves, although we again have no firm idea of the numbers involved. Throughout this region, then, the labor of slaves was fundamental to the availability of food, the exchange of commodities, and even facilitated the development of Islamic learning and literacy, as it freed some Islamic scholars from the task of working to produce what they needed.

In the Orbit of the Atlantic World: Slavery and the Slave Trade in West Africa before 1800

If political consolidation, economic growth, African demography, and land use patterns produced an internal African demand for coerced labor in the Savanna and Sahel regions of West Africa, the emergence of high-density slavery in the forest and coastal zones of West Africa was driven by similar forces, but with a very important difference. States closest to the coast were enmeshed in European commercial networks. The pull of the Atlantic world meant that Africans produced goods and slaves that flowed out of Africa into the plantation economies of the New World. This has led many historians to argue that the transatlantic slave trade initiated a transformation in slavery. In other words, participation in the transatlantic slave trade increased the number of slaves in Africa and changed the way they were used. For many African societies, involvement in the trade increased slaveholding along parts of the West African coast. As the trade expanded, more slaves – especially women – were retained in Africa. Slavery became widespread. Slaves were also used more often in production and in less elite households. Slaves were valued not just for their local economic contributions but also for the returns they could bring once they were exported.

FIGURE 12. Slave coffle in Western Sudan in J. W. Buel, *Heroes of the Dark Continent* (New York, 1890), page 66, which was in turn taken from Joseph Simon Galliéni, *Mission d'exploration du Haut-Niger: Voyage au Soudan Francais* (Paris, 1885), p. 525. Courtesy of the UVM Bailey-Howe Library.

Between 1600 and 1800, numerous states established commercial networks that perfected slave production, marketing, and export tied directly to the transatlantic slave trade (Figure 12). Although a number of slaving states predated the transatlantic slave trade, many more were at least partially produced by the trade. The demand for slave labor also grew as a result of this *new* kind of political consolidation. African participation in the slave trade, then, created islands of prosperity and a degree of security for new slave-exporting states. But they were dependent on slavery and slaving for that security. In turn, the regions that were raided for slaves experienced increasing insecurity and violence. Slaving operations in the Savanna and Sahel zones certainly impacted the places from where Sudanic states drew their slaves, but the impact was more widely and deeply felt on the coast, given the large number of slaves exported, especially from 1700 onward.

Why did the rise in slave exports lead to both increased slave use and social differentiation within Africa? As economies became increasingly tied to trade, some Africans profited. The people who became rich from the slave trade and local elites (who were often one and the same) wanted to own and use slaves. High status came with slave ownership, as did many economic benefits. As more slaves were produced for the external trade, more slaves became available. These big men had the wealth and the opportunity to acquire slaves. The export of slaves along the West and West-Central coasts enabled African elites to acquire more slaves than ever before, whom they increasingly used in productive tasks or sold internally. They gradually built households that were full of slave wives, retainers, and workers, which in turn helped transform how members of these societies understood labor, marriage, and politics. Eventually millions of slaves were held in West and West-Central Africa. The African accumulation of slaves was further aided by the existence of complementary markets for slaves. European traders regularly purchased women and children, but tried as much as possible to buy males (for whom they paid the highest prices). Africans favored females. They sought to retain women and girls whenever possible. Thus, it often made economic sense for Africans to retain women and sell men. The impact of this overall transition was profound in some places, as Lovejoy notes:

> The influx of servile women, children, and older people reinforced social relationships based on dependency.... Increased stratification meant that the relative importance of ... dependent categories shifted. Strong men, government officials, wealthy merchants, and military leaders controlled large followings of slaves, junior kinsmen, pawns, women and clients. This group of powerful men formed the nucleus of a class society in which relatively few people dominated the instruments of warfare, commercial credit, and the means of production.[25]

I briefly discussed export numbers in Chapter 2, but it is useful to turn back to them again in order to provide fuller assessment of the scale of the trade. The volume of the slave trade was initially quite low, but it steadily increased from 1500 onward. Between 1450 and 1600, 409,000 Africans left Africa across the Atlantic, with the majority of 328,000 coming after 1500. That number rose to 1,348,000 between 1601 and 1700 and then to 6,090,000 between 1701 and

---

[25] Lovejoy, *Transformations in Slavery*, 113–114.

1800.[26] The massive increase in slave exports was possible because Africans extended the slaving frontiers deep into the continent. Slave production and commercial networks extended thousands of kilometers into the interior in some locations. Prices for slaves also rose substantially in this period. These numbers do not take into account the numbers of slaves killed in the wars and raids that produced slaves, nor the deaths that occurred from transport to sale on the coast. At least as many Africans were retained as were exported, perhaps as many as roughly 7 million. Many of the slaves produced in this period were either captured in wars or raids or kidnapped. After their initial captures, slaves were commonly sold numerous times along the slave route before they died, were retained in Africa, or made it to the coast to be shipped across the Atlantic. It is not too difficult to imagine suffering inflicted on the actual people behind these numbers. Although he was captured in the middle of the nineteenth century, Mahommah Gardo Baquaqua recorded his experiences of being kidnapped and sold perhaps twice before reaching the capital of Dahomey, where he finally lost hope and movingly described his state of mind:

> When we arrived here I began to give up all hopes of ever getting back to my home again, but had entertained hopes until this time of being able to make my escape, and by some means or other of once more seeing my native place, but at last, hope gave way; the last ray seemed fading away, and my heart felt sad and weary within me, as I thought of my mother, whom I loved most tenderly, and the thought of never more beholding her, added very much to my perplexities. I felt sad and lonely.[27]

The impact of the external slave trade, then, is clearly an important part of the history of slavery. But it is also essential to place the expansion of slavery into its local context – that is, the external slave trade and local factors interacted to produce high-density slavery. Internal forces had long shaped patterns of slave use. Free, smallholder agriculture remained dominant in many parts of the region. Slavery was an optimal way for rulers and merchants to boost output and gain better access to labor in the context of a system of shifting cultivation, continued smallholder independence, and the basic inability or unwillingness of states to attract, control, and squeeze free labor.

---

[26] Lovejoy, *Transformations in Slavery*, 47.
[27] Quoted by Robin Law, *Ouidah: The Social History of a West African Slaving 'Port'* (Athens, OH: Ohio University Press, 2004), 139.

Slaves were used in agricultural production for the reasons that they had always been: free labor was hard to control and political elites needed labor to provide food and goods to maintain their military and political capacity. Thus, the reasons that slaves were in high demand did not radically change as a result of the growth of the transatlantic slave trade before 1800. What was different – and this is a critical change – was that the slaving states and elites developed the military capacity and the commercial networks to produce a large number of slaves as a direct result of supplying externally generated demand. This enabled the eventual shift toward the wide-scale use of slaves in production, evident especially in the nineteenth century. To reiterate: more available slaves meant that Africans found more ways to use them to overcome factors that had long limited production and economic growth.

In the Gold Coast, slaving and slavery predated the transatlantic slave trade. Slavery was produced by a series of internal economic and political changes. Portuguese traders actually bought gold from Africans along what became the Gold Coast in exchange for slaves throughout the sixteenth century. Between 1485 and 1540, at least 12,000 slaves were imported into the Gold Coast and its environs.[28] That is, the *internal* demand for coerced labor was strong enough that Africans actually imported slaves from European traders. Moreover, slaves were imported into the region from the Savanna zone to the north from an early period, although we do not have the sources to provide a precise number.

How were these slaves used? Archeological evidence strongly suggests that a sedentary society based on agriculture well suited to the dense forest environment was in place before 1500 CE, perhaps as early as 800 CE. In this period, Akan speakers began the arduous process of clearing the rainforest and its high canopy to expand agricultural production, which was initially organized by large matrilineal kin groups. They also began the construction of earthworks (which may have been used as defensive fortifications, markers of the boundary between safe and dangerous space, or simply as barriers against elephants). Ivor Wilks posited that the era of population growth and agriculture production occurred in a "big bang" moment beginning in 1500. It is now clear that the transition to food production occurred

[28] Ray Kea, *Settlements, Trade and Polities in the Seventeenth Century Gold Coast* (Baltimore: Johns Hopkins University Press, 1982), 197.

over a longer time period.[29] Regardless, Wilks is correct that the clearance of the forest required a tremendous amount of labor. Between 300 and 700 tons of dense, heavy vegetation had to be cleared per acre of forest. This generated a demand for labor that greatly outstripped the capacity of free households. Slaves did this work. Slaves increased the amount of land available for agricultural production, although free households no doubt did most of the productive farming. The demand for slaves was also tied to gold mining, which likely originated as early as 900–1000 CE. Gold was in high demand in the Savanna, and was exchanged by Akan merchants for slaves. Gold mining drew the Akan into commercial relations with both the Savanna and the coast. Eventually, these economic and political changes ushered in a new era dominated by a number of independent Akan states. Africans living in this period witnessed dramatic change. Big men founded communities, gained access to gold, acquired slaves, cleared land, produced food, attracted more people, cleared even more land, and eventually built states. These men came to possess *obirempon* stools (a symbol of Akan chiefship) that were linked to control over a particular territory and its people. Up to roughly the end of the seventeenth century, these states, each with their own ruler or *afahene*, dominated the region.

From roughly 1500 to 1700, the emergence of the transatlantic trade along the Gold Coast helped further increase the population density of the interior and encouraged economic growth. The trade brought with it new crops (especially maize and manioc) and more slaves. Rulers used slaves in a variety of nonproductive ways (including as soldiers and concubines). But they also continued to use slaves in production, especially gold mining. As more slaves were acquired, gold mining expanded. In the 1600s, *afahene* bought slaves from the Dutch as well as from the northern Savanna traders. Akyem remained an important internal slave market well into the 1730s. In this period, somewhere between 80,000 and 160,000 slaves were imported for local use. They were concentrated in key gold mining areas, such as the Pra-Ofin basin or in areas where substantial forest clearance was necessary. As gold mining increased, so did urban-based craft production by free artisans. Neither miners nor artisans produced food, which in turn led to the need for more labor to produce food on greater amounts of

[29] Ivor Wilks, "The State of the Akan and the Akan States: A Discursion" in *Cahiers d'Etudes Africaines* **22**, 87/88 (1982), 237.

cleared land. This led to the increased use of slaves as productive and economically essential laborers in the 1600s.

How was the production of gold organized? Until about 1550, Ray Kea has demonstrated that a slave was able to reproduce his market price in 1.5 months of work, assuming that slave produced 48 dambas a day in gold. In one year, a single slave would have been able to produce enough gold for his or her master to buy four or five new slaves. Slaves not only produced gold; they also ensured that the slave population was reproduced. Many visitors to the Gold Coast made note of the use of slaves in gold mining. Valentim Fernandes wrote that at the end of the fifteenth century, seven gold mines owned by seven different kings were driven quite deeply into the ground, and "[t]he kings have slaves whom they put in the mines and to whom they give wives, and these the slaves take with them; and they bear and rear children in these mines."[30] The gold was in turn sold to Muslim merchants from the Savanna to the north in exchange for slaves, salt, and metalware. According to a Portuguese report written in 1572, gold mines were owned by a king who relied on slave miners, who lived in their own villages. Groups of slave and free cultivators, also located in their own settlements, supplied food to the miners. In the 1670s, close to what became Kumase, Samuel Brun made note of the numerous gold mines: "[V]ery often a large number of slaves disappear in the mine shafts because of a cavein."[31] In the 1690s, it was reported that gold was mined by slaves and that in "Petu, Sabu and Commendo, several hundreds of slaves are often seen to be seeking for gold."[32] However, by the 1600s, free persons were used in mine labor as well. They organized themselves much like free artisans and lived in specialized settlements near their place of work. Likewise, as the forests were cleared, fewer slaves were necessary to perform that labor.

This demographic and economic growth encouraged further state formation and ushered in a new era: the era of Greater Asante. In the interior, Asante became the dominant power. Osei Tutu, who was initially the leader of one among many Akan states, forged a union between his state, Kwaman (which was eventually renamed Kumase) and a number of surrounding Akan states. These states eventually crushed their main opponent – Denkyira – between 1699

---

[30] Cited by Kea, 201.
[31] Cited by Lovejoy, *Transformations in Slavery*, 121.
[32] Cited by Lovejoy, *Transformations in Slavery*, 121.

and 1701, when the union of the Akan states was formalized into the Asante Union. This union formed the basis of Asante's emergence as a centralized and militarized state system. Centered on the capital of Kumase and led by the *asantehene*, Asante expanded territorially throughout the eighteenth century via diplomacy and conquest. It eventually created an empire that was roughly the size of contemporary Ghana. The state had an effective army, complex administrative system, and was a center of gold and agricultural production, as well as a hub for a tremendous amount of trade. In the eighteenth century, Asante militarism was at its peak. The state and its elite benefited from warfare and imperial expansion, a process that some scholars have labeled predatory accumulation (the accumulation of wealth through predatory military activities). Asante did not wage war simply to secure slaves; rather, the state also had well-defined imperial and territorial ambitions it fulfilled through warfare. Thus, Asante's militarism was not only produced by the European demand for slaves coming from the coast, but was a function of both the state's political goals and the emergence of a culture that valorized military success and made it a precondition for elite advancement. Of course, Asante's military expansion led to the acquisition of tens of thousands of slaves after 1700. The number of slaves Asante exported into the transatlantic slave trade – and retained within Africa by big men – increased substantially as a result. Between 1701 and 1800, 881,200 slaves were exported from the Gold Coast region. Asante participated in the trade because it derived economic benefits from doing so; indeed, many valuable textiles and weapons were acquired as a result.

A new political economy emerged. People understood themselves as members of the broader Asante system. Gold dust became a unit of exchange. New kinds of taxes and levies were imposed. The administrative system grew in size and complexity. Perhaps most crucially, fewer slaves were needed to clear land (which had already been done in the core areas of Asante), and gold production declined and became a sector largely dominated by free labor. Thus, slave use within Asante changed as well. A number of major sectors of the Asante economy – hunting, crafts, agriculture, fishing, and trading, for example – all grew in this period. Conjugal family units cultivated the soil and produced enough food to keep the population of Asante reasonably well fed. But many of these farmers – who in the eighteenth century were better able to accumulate wealth – had the resources to acquire slaves and use them to help with farming and other household tasks.

Slaveholding increased over this period. These slaves were economically important but were used within households in small numbers per unit. Powerful Asante officials, big men, and merchants likewise accumulated many slaves and used them for economic and noneconomic purposes. In the region surrounding Kumase, slave laborers worked on plantation-style farms and fed the Asante political class in the capital. Slaves on these agricultural estates were allowed to keep a portion of what they produced to feed themselves, in a sharecropping system. Intensive slave production increased in the nineteenth century, when entire villages of slaves produced food to feed the capital. In one case, a visitor to Asante commented that one slave estate contained 8,000 "soldiers, slaves and vassals."[33] There is evidence that other urban centers of the region employed slaves in a similar manner; indeed, according to John Beecham, a British visitor to Asante, all the large towns of Asante were surrounded by "plantations" on which "slaves" labored. By 1817, this sector had developed to such as extent that Thomas Bowdich could note:

> The higher class could not support their numerous followers ... in the city and therefore employed them in plantations (in which small crooms [villages] were situated), generally within 2 or 3 miles of the capital, where their labours not only feed themselves but supply the wants of the chief, his family and the more immediate suite. The middling orders station their slaves for the same purpose and also to collect fruit and vegetables for sale, and when their children become more numerous, a part are generally sent to be supported by these slaves in the bush.[34]

Overall, Asante's history demonstrates that there was a complex correlation between the growth of the transatlantic slave trade, militarism, state formation, social differentiation, and the use of slaves *in* Africa. Asante had its own motives for slaving, which cannot be tied to just European demand. Likewise, the changing patterns of slave use in Asante cannot be linked to the growth of the transatlantic slave trade alone. Such growth must be understood in the context of the impact of Asante political consolidation, imperialism, and elite accumulation on the political economy, which no longer needed slaves for forest clearance and mining, but now used them more extensively in agricultural production and as part of its more militarized and imperial state

---

[33] T. C. McCaskie, *State and Society in Pre-Colonial Asante* (Cambridge: Cambridge University Press, 1995), 33.
[34] See Lovejoy, *Transformations in Slavery*, 172.

system. I want to be very clear here: I am not arguing the transatlantic slave trade did not benefit Asante, nor do I believe that the Asante did not take slaving into consideration when it waged war. Asante and its elite grew wealthy partially as a result of its participation in the trade. In other words, political elites became richer and more powerful because they had access to more slaves than ever before. The state also acquired vital military resources, such as guns and ammunition, as part of that trade. But, Asante's imperialism was produced by an Asante political class and culture that were influenced by many factors beyond simply its participation in the slave trade. Moreover, it was the internally generated transition to militarism and imperialism that helped produce the changing demands for slaves and labor within Asante itself.

What about elsewhere along the West African coast and its interior? To the east of Asante, along what became known as the Slave Coast and, even farther east, the Bight of Biafra, the transatlantic slave trade was directly involved in the political economy of African states and societies, including Oyo and Dahomey. Here too we see how the external trade both generated further internal demand for slaves and encouraged the formation of predatory slaving states. Up to 1800, most of the economic value of slavery came from the export of slaves rather than their internal use in productive capacities. For example, Dahomey was a predatory and militarized state that emerged on the Abomey plateau at the end of the seventeenth century. By the eighteenth century, Dahomey extended its hegemony far beyond the plateau, especially south toward the coast. King Agaja (reigned 1718–1740) conquered the kingdoms of Allada and Ouidah in 1724 and 1727, respectively. Although Dahomey had many reasons for going to war, the desire to manage their own role in the trade via direct access to European merchants was a central motive for this expansion. In this period, the state developed a centralized bureaucratic system that administered the kingdom and facilitated the enslavement of captives and their export. This was not a simple process. Rulers often struggled over the best means to control the trade and with the day-to-day difficulties of governing recently conquered territories. Despite these weaknesses, the state was formidable. Geared for war, it produced a large number of captives who were shipped from the Slave Coast across the Atlantic. In the eighteenth century alone, 1,223,200 slaves were exported from the Bight of Benin region, many of whom were produced by Dahomey. Dahomey, especially its rulers, profited from this

trade. Although smallholder agricultural production fed people at
the local level, the state, military, and political elite depended on the
profits generated from the direct sale of slaves into the slave trade as
well as from the taxes that were generated by that trade. Dahomey
also acquired weapons, textiles, and cowrie shells through the trade.
Slaving produced victims for human sacrifice, which occurred during
the Annual Customs, a major public ceremony that advertised the
power and legitimacy of the king and his role as head of state. This
was a state, then, geared to war and that valorized success in battle, as
Law felicitously stated: "[P]artly as a consequence of its long history
of participation in the slave trade – the principal source of slaves for
which was capture in warfare – Dahomey was a warrior state, with a
deep-seated military ethos which involved disdain for agriculture."[35]

Over the course of the eighteenth century, hundreds of thousands
of slaves – who were again mostly women – were retained in Dahomey.
Many retained slaves must have worked in agricultural production.
Although there is some evidence that this labor was organized in a
plantation-style system, it is far from overwhelming or complete. It is
most likely that over the course of the century slaves began to work
on agricultural estates to produce goods for the rulers of the state,
but we simply do not know how those estates were organized. The
broader pattern we see in Dahomey: local warfare, state consolidation, expansion southward to the coast, and an economic reliance on
the slave trade became common throughout the coastal region during
the eighteenth century. Oyo, a state to the east, also exported slaves
through the ports along the coast and became a major slave trader.
Like Dahomey, there is little evidence that the many slaves retained
were used as slave labor in a centralized plantation sector. It seems
likely that retained slaves were used to produce goods for rulers and
slave owners on the estates of rulers and aristocrats, but we cannot be
certain. To the east, in the interior of the Bight of Biafra (along the
coast of what is now Eastern Nigeria and parts of Cameroon), slaves
were exported in large numbers through a very decentralized trading
system. Here too, traders and big men increasingly came to depend
on the export trade for their economic well-being. Here too, we have
virtually no evidence that slaves were used as labor on plantations or

---

[35] Robin Law, "The Politics of Commercial Transition: Factional Conflict in Dahomey
in the Context of the Ending of the Slave Trade" in *The Journal of African History* **38**,
2 (1997), 215.

large-scale farms. Slaves were retained for a variety of purposes, of course, but most were used in the manner that they long had been: as labor within households, which involved agriculture, or as porters and household retainers.

What was different about this region versus the Savanna and Sahel zone was the degree to which states hitched their economic fortunes to the transatlantic slave trade. Slaves were economically important because they financed the growth and consolidation of states like Dahomey and Oyo. European commerce and trade stimulated economic growth and led to the consolidation of high-density slavery. But this did not occur everywhere. Indeed, local demand and economic change were more important in some places, especially the Gold Coast and Asante. In all places, Africans used slaves to overcome long-standing internal constraints on labor and productivity; the transatlantic slave trade encouraged Africans to acquire and retain more slaves for local use. These changes picked up speed over time. By 1800, most states in this region traded and used slaves. Slaves were used more widely in production than ever before. Slavery was increasingly a central and economically important institution. Although some slaves produced agricultural commodities, we do not have enough evidence to know whether that production occurred on centrally managed plantations before 1800, nor can we fully assess the level of agricultural intensification in this period. But we do know that the external slave trade was strongly connected to the increased slave use in Africa.

The Political Economy of Slavery in South, East, and Central Africa before 1800

Although West Africa was the center of high-density slavery before 1800, economic and political change also led to the economic use of slaves elsewhere. High-density slavery developed in centers of economic growth or political consolidation that also faced shortages of available labor, or that had difficulty in extracting labor from free people. These changes were focused in parts of South Africa (especially the western Cape), parts of Central Africa (especially the Kingdom of Kongo and the Luba and Lunda Empires), and parts of Eastern Africa (especially Buganda). In each region, slaves continued to be used for a wide-variety of purposes within household units, but, at the same time, more slaves were used in productive capacities.

In the seventeenth century, Holland was at the center of a success-ful global commercial empire. As part of Dutch expansion, in 1652, the Dutch East India Company landed ships at Table Bay and estab-lished a small way station in what would soon become Cape Town, South Africa. The way station was supposed to resupply passing com-pany ships through the labor of company farmers and trade with local African communities. It became apparent very quickly, however, that neither company employees nor local African trade could generate the necessary supplies, especially of food. The solution to this problem was to release a small number of company employees from their con-tracts to become free burghers or free farmers who worked available land to provide those supplies. What appeared to be a minor decision would eventually unleash new economic and political forces that cre-ated a colony of settlement (the Cape Colony) governed by the Dutch East India Company, as well as a system of slave production that dominated the region until the nineteenth century. Comparatively, it might appear that the Dutch factor sets South Africa apart from the rest of the continent. But on closer examination, environmental constraints, the lack of available free labor, and the consolidation of a commercial economy led to the development of high-density slavery. Although better developed and capitalized, slavery in South Africa shared may of the features of high-density slavery throughout the rest of the African continent.

After 1657, company officials hoped that free burghers would intensively farm the region around what became Cape Town and offer food for sale at fixed prices to the company. But many farmers soon found that they did not have the labor or the capital to make inten-sive farming successful. Some simply gave up and made a living in Cape Town, others left the immediate vicinity and migrated farther into the interior, where they began extensive farming, focused mostly on stock raising (especially cattle, sheep). Some stayed close to the Cape, where they established productive farms that produced grain and grapes. Eventually, a tripartite settlement pattern emerged: the urban core focused on Cape Town, the close settled and more densely populated arable farming zone that received reasonable amounts of rainfall, and finally the vast, ever-expanding frontier zone of extensive (often subsistence) farms and stock raising that was very lightly popu-lated, received little rainfall, and was often beyond the control of the Company. This expansion was not without cost for Africans. Local populations of the pastoralist Khoikhoi and hunting-and-gathering

San were displaced (and killed) through war and disease, especially smallpox. The survivors and the children of survivors became "servants" to white farmers.

Thus, Cape settlement patterns were shaped by environmental constraints, which necessitated different forms of agricultural production, and by the fact that everywhere labor was in short supply. In each of the three settlement zones the solution to the labor question became slave labor, although slaves were used for different reasons and in different ways. As early as 1655, Jan van Riebeeck, the Commander of the Cape, noted that "a good many slaves would be necessary for them which could ... be easily fetched from Madagascar or even India and given out on credit."[36] Well before the end of the eighteenth century, the Cape Colony had become a slave society. In 1793, the census tells us that there were 13,830 free burghers compared to 14,747 slaves, although scholars suggest that the number of slaves was underestimated. By 1723, 97.2 percent of farmers in Cape District – those arable farms close to Cape Town that grew grapes and grain – held at least one slave. Slavery spread outward from the core into surrounding districts, including Stellenbosch (ranging over the eighteenth century between roughly 48 percent and 75 percent), Drakenstein (39–81 percent), and Swellendam (46–51 percent). Slaves came from a wide variety of places, including from continental Africa, Madagascar, the Indian subcontinent, and the Indonesian archipelago. The slave population was, therefore, remarkably diverse both culturally and linguistically.

What did slaves do? Everything! However, the economic use of slaves varied by region. In Cape Town, private individuals and the company itself owned slaves. Company slaves lived together in the slave lodge and performed numerous and important tasks, especially the maintenance and construction of public works, working the docks, portage, and fetching firewood. Privately held slaves in Cape Town might work as domestic laborers, artisans, or fishermen. A large number – probably the majority – of slaves were used as agricultural laborers on the arable farms in districts closest to Cape Town. In 1730, one visitor to the Cape noted: "[T]he expansion of the colony demands an ever increasing number of slaves. Every farmer requires many more slaves than members of his own household to grow his crops and develop

[36] Nigel Worden, *Slavery in Dutch South Africa* (Cambridge: Cambridge University Press, 1985), 6.

his land."[37] These slaves worked hardest during sowing and harvesting times (including crops of grapes, wheat, and barley), but, because most farms were mixed, they performed a variety of tasks, especially the management of livestock. For slaves, work on arable farms was hard, often beginning – at peak periods – before dawn and lasting until 10:00 PM. To maintain a sufficient labor force, farmers hired out their slaves during non-peak periods, but many also tried to make the nature of mixed-farming work for them by using slaves at a variety of seasonal tasks over the entire year. Finally, slaves were economically important in the pastoralist districts farthest from Cape Town. However, many of these farmers had less capital and fewer slaves than did the mixed farmers closer to the Cape. These farmers relied almost completely on stockbreeding. They tended to use local Khoikhoi labor (whom they called servants) rather than the imported slave labor used in the arable farming districts. Over time, these so-called servants looked increasingly like slaves; they and their children were indentured for long periods and were subject to severe punishments should they disobey their masters, although, before the law, most were not technically slaves. Nonetheless, some of these Khoikhoi "servants" were indeed slaves. There was an active slaving frontier in the eastern parts of the Cape Colony, which only got larger in the nineteenth century. Free burgher households often formed commandos and raided for slaves. Thousands of slaves were captured, traded, and held as property in this region, most of whom were children. These young slaves were forced to work in free burgher households as herders, domestics, and even as farmers in some cases.

Thus, by the eighteenth century, the Cape Colony depended heavily on slave labor and developed legal and coercive structures to keep a large slave population in check. As Nigel Worden noted: "[B]y the beginning of the eighteenth century slavery had become the basis of the economic and social position of a large proportion of the settler community."[38] Slaves were a vital part of nearly every economic activity in the Colony. In 1804, Governor Jan Willem Janssens stated that any thought of abolishing slavery would in the end "destroy all property and plunge the colony into misery ... the whole industry of the country is based on the existence of slaves."[39] Slavery was profitable

---

[37] Worden, *Slavery in Dutch South Africa*, 10.
[38] Worden, *Slavery in Dutch South Africa*, 18.
[39] Worden, *Slavery in Dutch South Africa*, 64.

and productive, especially for larger landowners. Like high-density slavery elsewhere in Africa, the economic importance of slavery meant that manumission occurred much less often than it did in low-density settings. This was especially true for the slaves who worked as agricultural producers. Urban slaves in Cape Town managed their way to freedom more often.

Until the nineteenth century, only pockets of high-density slavery emerged outside West and South Africa. West-Central Africa was a major supplier of slaves into the transatlantic slave trade, but did not use slaves in economic roles as much. According to Lovejoy, roughly 800,000 slaves were exported in the seventeenth century and 2.3 million were shipped from the same region in the eighteenth century. The states doing the trading depended on this trade and, in the words of Lovejoy, "The supply mechanism thereby limited the expansion of a slave mode of production. Far too many slaves were exported in comparison with the domestic slave-population" for slaves to be central to agriculture, commerce, or other economic sectors.[40] Given the long time period and size of the area involved, there were a number of exceptions, however. Mariana Candido demonstrates, for example, that even at the center of slave exports in Benguela, many slaves were retained for economic purposes. Slaves worked on the docks and in construction, transported goods, mined salt, farmed, and became concubines.[41]

> During the eighteenth and nineteenth centuries, slavery and the slave trade became vital to life in Benguela. The town's central economic function was the slave trade. Slave labor was also employed locally, performing different kinds of economic activities. As soon as vessels docked in Benguela, slaves unloaded the ships and carried passengers to the decks. Porters also transported luggage and other belongings of administrators and priests around town and in expeditions to the interior. Slaves worked in the ... farms of local residents, and in the salt mines.... Slavery was the dominant labor system and influenced every social relationship in town.[42]

Likewise, the kings and nobles of the Kingdom of Kongo used slaves on large agricultural estates that surrounded the cities of São Salvador

---

[40] Lovejoy, *Transformations in Slavery*, 127.
[41] Mariana P. Candido, *An African Slaving Port and the Atlantic World: Benguela and its Hinterland* (Cambridge: Cambridge University Press, 2013), 113–122.
[42] Candido, *An African Slaving Port and the Atlantic World*, 113–114.

and Mbanza Sonyo. Slavery had existed in the kingdom almost from its beginning, but increased in scope as the state expanded geographically, consolidated politically, and became increasingly involved in the transatlantic slave trade. Until the late seventeenth century, the Kongo kings managed their participation in the trade quite effectively. They pursued their own policies that increased the kingdom's participation in the trade and their internal use of slaves. Most Kongo slaves were acquired in war and originated from places outside the kingdom itself. Kongo citizens were as a rule not enslaved. By the end of the seventeenth century, however, slaving increased and was less centrally controlled. This change was driven especially by civil war and internal conflict within the Kongo itself. As the political compact that held the Kingdom of Kongo together dissolved, many more Kongo citizens were caught up in the cycle of war and slaving.

What do we know about the nature of slavery and slaveholding in the Kongo? By 1648 roughly 60,000–70,000 slaves worked on agricultural estates, mostly to provide foodstuffs for the political elite and the population of the São Salvador and Mbanza Sonyo. Giovanni Francesco da Roma noted that the nobility often had problems managing the large number of slaves. Antonio Cavazzi, who lived in the region between 1654 and 1668, noted that "the number of slaves is almost equal to the number of freepersons" and that the main source of material wealth was in the form of "slaves."[43] In all likelihood, then, the slave population of the Kongo by the end of the seventeenth century equaled around 100,000, only slightly less than the total free population of the kingdom. Household production dominated most of the Kongo economy. These households were integrated also into broader kinship groups. Although they were subject to the Kongo king, they produced largely for themselves or for sale in local and regional markets. The Kongo kings and nobility, on the other hand, came to rely on slave labor to feed and clothe their households. In this case, the unwillingness and inability of the elite to coerce free people into producing what they needed – and their desire not to enslave their own subjects – led to the expansion of slave production within the Kongo. As early as 1657, Cavazzi noted that slaves worked very hard: "[T]hey are exhausted by all manner of tasks; their lives are always very trying; the only payment they can hope for is a slight improvement in the treatment they receive."[44]

[43] Heywood, "Slavery and Its Transformation in the Kingdom of Kongo," 20.
[44] Cited by Lovejoy, *Transformations in Slavery*, 128.

Initially, as the capital of the Kongo, São Salvador contained the largest number of productive slaves. However, after the capital was sacked in the Kongo civil wars (1665–1709), the largest number were located in Mbanza Sonyo. Lovejoy notes that the population of this city doubled in the late seventeenth century. Many members of the political elite opened new lands for farming in its hinterland, using slave labor. As the entire region of the Kingdom of Kongo fractured, more slaves also came to be used to the south of the Kongo, especially in the states of Kasanje and Matamba. In the main, slaves in these regions were used in both agriculture and portage; indeed, by the second half of the eighteenth century, many retained female slaves were used as agricultural workers and as raffia cloth weavers.

By the eighteenth century, slavery became less a result of the elite's inability to extract wealth from local households and much more a result of the destruction of centralized kingship and emergence of warlordism. By this period, conditions of life for almost all Kongolese people – free and slave – were very precarious. Slavery was common, and many free people faced risk of enslavement. The warlords who replaced the centralized authority of the kingdom owned large numbers of slaves whom they used as retainers, soldiers, and workers. They also sold large numbers of slaves into the transatlantic slave trade. Slavery, then, helped drive and maintain the cycle of warfare that divided the region, and also was a central economic resource via trade and production for the elite. Given the continual political violence and the expanding use of slaves in economic and agricultural capacities, the conditions of slave life in this period were increasingly difficult and harsh.

High-density slavery also developed in small parts of Central and Eastern Africa. The kings of both the Luba and Lunda Kingdoms settled slaves on extensive agricultural estates in their capital districts between the seventeenth and eighteenth centuries. This was as much a result of the difficulty in controlling newly incorporated free persons in the context of political expansion as it was about the links these states may have had with the transatlantic slave trade on the West-Central African coast. The Luba royal court and capital was a center of "resource control and allocation."[45] Slaves produced grain, maize, beans, and manioc near the capital. Thomas Reefe notes

[45] Thomas Q. Reefe, *The Rainbow and the Kings: A History of the Luba Empire to* 1891 (Berkeley: University of California Press, 1981), 156.

that although agricultural production did not replicate new world-style plantations, it was nonetheless

> not particularly pleasant to be a slave and to have the lowest status in a hierarchical society like that of the Luba. Slaves were mutilated to mark their status, and they were easy targets when victims for ritual execution were sought. The dilemma of the slave in Luba society was expressed in the lament *Bantuka, ndya; le kalale ngende kwepi mashinda a kwetu kadi le onkayuka* ["They insult me, I eat; If I am angry and leave, I will not be able to find the paths to return (to my home, to my kin)"]. Only the slaves offspring could expect complete integration into a kin group, and even then, memory of former slave status of an individual's ancestors would last for generations.[46]

Finally, in eighteenth-century Buganda, slavery became one means kings used to consolidate royal power and increase available labor power. Buganda was a highly centralized kingdom located mainly in what is now Uganda. Initially the powers of kings were significantly limited by powerful clan heads, who controlled (and sometimes competed for control of) followers. These followers performed labor for both themselves and their clans and clan chiefs. The clan heads were also responsible for allocating land to their followers. As Buganda and the kingship itself consolidated, numerous kings waged successful wars of expansion, especially in the eighteenth century. These wars produced a large number of captives and added substantial new territory to the state. As a result of this expansion, Holly Hanson has argued, eighteenth-century Bugandan kings began to allocate land in the same manner as clan heads. How? A series of kings created new chiefships and provided them with land for cultivation and control. These new chiefships were called *ebitongole* chiefships. Kings also settled captives – slaves – on these lands to do the necessary labor. Thus, new chiefs, at least initially loyal to the king who appointed them, could work their lands with slave followers rather than being forced to provide incentives and rewards demanded by local and free populations, many of whom had preexisting political allegiances. To signify their economic role, *ebitongole* chiefships were named after the productive task assigned to them. Some were simply settled to help integrate new territories into Buganda, whereas others were described as being concerned with producing food, others with clearing the forests of elephants and buffalos, and still others were named so as to

[46] Reefe, *The Rainbow and the King*, 154.

signify their role in providing supplies for the king's servants or to the makers of the king's drums. Hanson describes the broader impact of these changes thusly: "Since non-free people diminished the value of free followers to their chiefs, *ebitongole* ... undermined the status of ordinary people in Buganda. Chiefs who had ... slave workers had less of a need to prove by their behavior that they were more generous and just than neighboring chiefs in order to retain followers," which led to increasing coercion over all people, but especially nonelites, in the kingdom.[47] Thus, *internal* and particular human choices, as well as political change and military success, led to the increasing use of slaves *internally*, without any connection to a broader international slave trade. The kings and new chiefs of Buganda understood that slave labor could meet their economic demands more easily and completely than could free labor, which in turn impacted the social history of kingdom, as all people became subject to an increasingly rapacious elite.

High-Density Slavery in the Nineteenth Century

The nineteenth century was a revolutionary period in African history. In the interior of West Africa, a series of Islamic revolutions swept through the Savanna, which resulted in the creation of new and transformative Islamic states. On the coast, beginning in 1807, the slave trade across the Atlantic gradually declined, as Britain, later followed by the other European slave-trading nations, abolished the trade. Africans and Europeans increasingly came to trade so-called legitimate commodities, including palm oil, groundnuts, and gum arabic. At the same time, the Omani gained commercial and political control over the Swahili coast of Eastern Africa, which led to substantial economic growth on the coast and increased violence in the interior. Slavery was deeply enmeshed in all of these changes. Although by 1800 high-density slavery had become common in many places, nowhere did it completely displace household production, which remained an important component of African economies. But the nineteenth century initiated, accelerated, and further consolidated transitions to

---

[47] See Holly Hanson, "Stolen People and Autonomous Chiefs in Nineteenth-Century Buganda" in Médard and Doyle (eds.), *Slavery in the Great Lakes Region of East Africa*, 168–169.

higher-density slavery in Africa. More than ever before, many African economies came to depend on slave-based production in a variety of economic sectors. There was no single factor that explains this transformation. In some places, like the West African Savanna, where high-density slavery was already common, religious revolutions helped produce new states and new economies that entrenched and expanded preexisting slave production. In East Africa, political change brought tremendous commercial and economic change, which produced high-density, slave-based production where low-density, household-based slavery had existed before. Whatever the reason, production became more deeply tied to slavery. In the regions where these changes were most pronounced, by the end of the nineteenth century, between 20 percent and 50 percent of the population were slaves.

We must, however, be cautious about the nature of these labor and productivity changes. Even in the areas most impacted by nineteenth-century transformations, large- and small-scale slave production coexisted. Slave populations certainly increased, but in many cases slaves continued to be used almost as independent producers. Although they were concentrated together in larger numbers, they worked essentially in the same way as small-scale producers did, with a lot of time provided for their own cultivation and trade. This occurred even on large agricultural estates. In other cases, this period did result in new systems of production: slaves were grouped in large units on plantations. Their labor was pooled together to work on tasks, with owners appropriating everything they produced. We will now turn directly to the emergence of high-density slavery by focusing on three major examples: the Sokoto Caliphate in the West African Savanna, Dahomey and Asante in coastal West Africa, and the Swahili Coast of Eastern Africa.

The Sokoto Caliphate and the Islamic Savanna

We have already observed that Islam had a long history in West Africa. Over time, more rulers adopted Islam and, increasingly, so did regular people. For centuries, Muslims were in the minority. They did not impose Islam on surrounding populations. Muslim rulers were usually in no position to require that non-Muslim subjects – often in the majority – practice Islam. To do so would have placed their authority at risk. On the other hand, because Muslims were in the minority in some societies, they often had to accommodate. David Robinson calls this the Suwarian tradition: "In this understanding Muslims must nurture their own learning and piety and thereby furnish good examples to the non-Muslims who lived around them. They could accept the jurisdiction of non-Muslim authorities, as long as they had the protection and conditions to practice the faith."[48]

By the end of the eighteenth century, Muslim reformers changed their approach. They came to believe that to remain "good Muslims" they must work to build societies where Islamic law and governance were fully practiced. They turned their backs on accommodation and looked to create new states that would preserve and expand Islam. Often these Muslims had been shut out from power by rulers who claimed to be Muslim but who were, in the opinion of the reformers, virtually infidels. Because Islam was practiced more widely by this time, reformers drew on Islam as a force to mobilize common people by claiming that proper Islamic governance would eliminate the exploitation and corruption the latter experienced. Thus, social and economic grievances, tied to a revolutionary Islamic ideology, led to a series of holy wars that toppled the existing states and created new Islamic states in their place. This remade the map of West Africa, created substantial economic growth, and led to the expansion of high-density slavery.

This process began as early as the eighteenth century. Futa Jallon was established in the 1720s after a jihad, although the state was not successful until the 1750s and 1760s, after years of warfare. Soon, the captives acquired in war, which continued after the foundation of the state, were allocated to agricultural estates throughout the state. Lovejoy argues that tens of thousands of slaves were used on these estates, which were mainly owned by the political and merchant elite of Futa Jallon. The Denyanke, who had been enslaved collectively after their military defeat, made up the core group of slaves. A brisk trade with both the coast and the interior further developed, partially fed by the slave-based production. One of these estates, located close to the capital of Timbo, contained 140 slaves, herds of cows and horses, and large amounts of cotton and rice, which were exchanged with European coastal merchants. In the nineteenth century, this pattern became even more common and more transformative. For example,

---

[48] David Robinson, *Muslim Societies in African History* (Cambridge: Cambridge University Press, 2004), 56.

slave production increased in another Islamic state – Futa Toro – and slaves accounted for at least 20 percent of the population (which is likely to underestimate the actual total). The Middle Niger Valley was likewise an important center of slavery, with slave populations in some locations reaching 40–50 percent of the total population.

But perhaps the best-documented example of the creation of slave-based agricultural sector occurred in the Sokoto Caliphate. Usman dan Fodio's holy war led to the consolidation of the Sokoto Caliphate beginning in 1804. Dan Fodio's representatives conquered virtually every Hausa city-state in the region. The Sokoto Caliphate was territorially vast, sophisticated, and effective. The unification of the formerly independent Hausa states created a productive regional economy that was linked to markets outside the Caliphate via the trans-Saharan trade, as well as by extensive trade routes into the forest zone. At the core of the Caliphate, the population grew and industrial production expanded in the form of textile manufacturing, leather production, and ironworking. The economy was monetized and highly specialized. Most important, that economy was dependent on slave-based production. In essence, Africans used slave labor to intensify agricultural production. By accumulating slaves, more hands could be put to work to hoe the soil and more land could be put into production.

Large-scale slave use occurred in the heart of the Caliphate, in the central emirates including Kano, Katsina, and Zazzau, as well as the capital districts of Gwandu and Sokoto. By the 1810s and 1820s, warfare continued on the borders of the Caliphate, which produced a continual supply of slaves (Figure 13). These slaves were generally transferred to the central emirates, where they were claimed or purchased by government officials and wealthy merchants. Slaveholders then used the slaves on holdings of land, where they produced a variety of goods. Emirs, for example, used thousands of slaves on large agricultural estates to produce the food they consumed in their palaces, as well as other commodities, such as cotton and indigo. Merchants used slaves to produce commodities, which were then sold both within and beyond the Caliphate. The internal market for slave-produced goods increased because the population and wealth of the Caliphate grew over time. In 1820, one agricultural estate was described as being mostly "inhabited by the slaves of the great in [Sokoto], who all have houses here, and their slaves, who are employed in raising grain, and tending

FIGURE 13. Slave raid to the South of Bornu in Hermann Wagner, *Schilderung der Reisen und Entdeckungen des Dr. Eduard Vogel in Central-Afrika* (Leipzig, 1860), facing page 218. Courtesy of UVM Bailey-Howe Library.

the cattle."[49] The slave-based agricultural economy gradually expanded from the heartland of the Caliphate into the frontier regions, where slavery became more common and economically important.

Over time, both large and small estates were founded, ranging from smallish farms with dozens of slaves to massive estates where slaves numbered into the thousands. In Zazzau Emirate, for example, 3,000 slaves worked on one estate that was owned by the emir. I want to be clear: these estates did not simply provide the elite with food and fodder, but provided massive amounts of cotton and indigo – as cash crops – on which the textile and indigo dying industry depended; in the nineteenth century, in Kano Emirate alone there were perhaps 50,000 dyers working between 15,000 and 20,000 dye pits. Tobacco was also an important crop, which was exported north into areas dominated by Tuareg. Given the nature of Islamic inheritance laws, the estates owned by private merchants tended to fragment into smaller units, whereas those owned by the state actors – the emirs and their

[49] Cited by Paul E. Lovejoy, "Plantations in the Economy of the Sokoto Caliphate," in *Journal of African History* 19, 3 (1978), 352.

officials – remained consolidated in larger units. By end of century, the slave population of the core region was in the range of 50 percent.

What was life like for slaves on these estates? Slaves grew a wide variety of crops, from shea nuts, tobacco, cotton, indigo, and millet to sorghum, locust beans, kola nuts, cowpeas, sugar cane, rice, and groundnuts. On larger estates slaves lived together in separate slave villages or, sometimes, on smaller estates, in separate quarters away from their owner. *Gandu* slaves were supervised by slave overseers, who were responsible to the owner of the estate. Slaves divided their time between cultivating fields owned by their masters and cultivating their own gardens, which provided them with food. At peak periods, slaves awoke early and worked on their master's fields until around 2 PM, and then used the remainder of the day to work their own small plots or gardens. Some slaves were given one or two full days off to work their gardens as well. Other work included firewood collection, house repair, construction, grass cutting, digging wells, carrying crops to market or storage, as well as moving manure to the farms. Slaves had numerous opportunities to acquire skills. Many loyal male slaves were given slave wives. If they had children, they too would be slaves. Although slaves were freed less often in this kind of high-density setting, some slaves purchased their own freedom. Their masters also freed them in accord with the ideals of Islam. Slaves fought to guarantee these rights and sought to renegotiate the term of their servitude. Given the scale of the Caliphate, there were always plenty of new slaves available to replace those who had gained their freedom; even those freed were bound tightly to their masters as clients. Indeed, many first-generation slaves spoke little or poor Hausa and were viewed as non-Muslims – as they were often acquired from areas outside the direct control of the Caliphate – which limited their ability to integrate into the dominant society.

The Atlantic World and West African Coast

The movement toward using large numbers of slaves on agricultural estates was not limited to the Savanna and desert-side zone of West Africa. On the coast, the gradual end of the transatlantic slave trade helped increase the economic use of slaves. Why? Many states in this region were built to supply slaves. After abolition, these states could not export as many slaves into a declining trade, but they could expand their use of slaves internally, to help produce the goods Europeans were buying, namely so-called legitimate commodities such as palm oil and palm kernels, as well as to transport those goods to coastal markets. Slaves continued to be used to produce food locally, and many slaves worked on smallholdings of land and within households. But it was in this period that slaves were widely used by merchants and rulers on what some have called plantations to produce commodities for the coastal and European markets.

Scholars have argued over the extent to which the actual productive process changed. Austen, for example, notes that in coastal West Africa, the use of slaves in export-oriented commercial agriculture was not unique, innovative, or new; instead, slaves were largely used, according to Austen, within preexisting household units and worked alongside their masters; in short, according to Austen, there is no evidence that in the nineteenth century export-oriented agriculture led to more intensive cultivation using slaves. Nor was labor discipline or organization of slaves transformed in any major way. While Austen is correct to argue that household production was vitally important (and often assisted by slaves), there really can be no doubt that slaves were used in larger numbers, and in larger units, to produce goods throughout the coastal zone. Indeed, the acquisition of slaves became an even more important way to accumulate capital. But on the other hand, nineteenth-century slavery did not completely break with the past. Well before this period, slaves had become perhaps *the* central means for Africans to amass labor power, which maximized their ability to extract wealth from dependents and subjects. It really should be of no surprise that the slave owners in this period looked to use their slaves in production in lieu of the external slave trade. The agricultural estates of the coast, like those of the interior, were substantially different than New World plantations: the work regimes of slaves were looser and less rigid, an ideology/veneer of assimilation remained something slaves could use to contest their subjugation, and commercialization, capital formation, and markets were all less well developed. There was nonetheless a truly massive increase in the number and use of slaves in this period.

In both Asante and Dahomey, slaves were widely used in commodity production. We have already seen that by the eighteenth century, the Asante capital district became more dependent on slave production to feed itself. The use of slaves in this capacity only increased in the nineteenth century; indeed, after 1810, numerous slaves were distributed broadly into rural areas where they farmed or served as porters for goods. This both increased production and limited the potential dangers of a slave revolt by reducing the slave population at the core of the state. Most important, after abolition, the kings of Asante diverted slaves into the production of kola nuts, which were then shipped into the interior, especially the Sokoto Caliphate. This production gave Asante access to important products from the interior, including textiles, livestock, salt, and leather goods. Numerous slaves were employed in gold mining, which increased substantially in the nineteenth century as well.

In addition to the growth of Asante's overall slave population, the number of commoners who owned slaves also increased in the nineteenth century. Although the political elite acquired many slaves – and used them in production – tens of thousands were also acquired by individuals or lineages, where they were used in productive and nonproductive capacities. Finally, a number of slaves were sold to the Fante states on the coast, which used slave labor to produce palm oil for export. On the coast, then, intensive palm oil production increased through slave labor. In one case, Ologu Pato – the paramount chief of Yilo Krobo – owned a huge number of slaves whom he used to cultivate palm oil on large farms and to process it year round. By the 1860s, Krobo merchants of the region used their slaves to cultivate palm oil on centrally managed agricultural estates. In the 1850s, Benjamin Pine, governor of the Gold Coast, noted: "Slaves have been shown to comprise the bulk of the property, the staple currency of the country. Our courts could not decide a case in which property is concerned without taking cognizance of slavery. Slavery meets us at every point."[50]

In Dahomey, slaves produced palm oil on agricultural estates, which was shipped to the coast for export. Although slave agricultural production existed in the 1700s, it really took off in the nineteenth century. Initially, the production of palm oil was focused on the coast, in the hands of Afro-Brazilians, small Dahomean producers, and freed slaves. King Gezo (reigned 1818–1858) encouraged the transition to palm oil production, although he continued to export slaves whenever he could. By the 1850s, the monarchy moved into palm

[50] Cited by Gerald M. McSheffrey, "Slavery, Indentured Servitude, Legitimate Trade and the Impact of Abolition in the Gold Coast, 1874–1901: A Reappraisal" in *Journal of African History* **24**, 3 (1983), 353.

oil production in a big way. Centers of slave palm oil production surrounded Abomey, the capital, as well as the important cities of Whydah and Porto Novo. Many of agricultural slaves were Yoruba, captured in a series of wars against Oyo. Although their labor was valuable, they were also a threat that needed to be controlled because they spoke the same language and worked together in large units. F. E. Forbes, who visited Dahomey in 1851, made special note of the "plantations" that produced a wide variety of crops in addition to palm oil. Dahomean officials supervised each plantation. Forbes believed that the total slave population of the capital was 10,000 (out of a total population of 30,000). Slaves were used in such numbers because it took a large amount of labor to produce palm oil. Laborers first climbed the trees to pick clusters of fruit. Then palm nuts were separated from the core of the fruit. The nuts were then cooked until oil could be extracted. Manning estimated that it took 315 workdays to produce a single ton of palm oil from 17 tons of palm oil bunches. One ton of kernels – produced by "cracking open" the nuts after the oil had been extracted – required another 167 workdays. To say that the processing, collection of palm oil fruit in bunches, and transport was labor intensive is an understatement.[51]

The growth in slavery in the nineteenth century can partially be explained by placing the economic use of slaves in historical context. The slave trade and its abolition certainly created opportunities for increasing and intensifying the use of slaves, but this process was not so much a transformation in how slaves were used as it was a continuation of earlier labor practices designed to overcome factors that historically reduced output, productivity, and economic growth. In other words, slavery was a highly efficient form of labor mobilization. In this context, the most effective way to extract labor and increase productivity was to use coerced labor in the form of slavery. Most important, with the gradual decline of the export sector, there were many more slaves available for work, trade, and sale. Thus, the real transformation after the abolition of slavery was that many societies were faced with the necessity of reducing their slave exports and expanding production to make up the difference. In most cases, slavery was the only way to make that transition possible.

---

[51] Edna Bay provides an excellent summary; see Edna G. Bay, *Wives of the Leopard: Gender, Politics, and Culture in the Kingdom of Dahomey* (Charlottesville: University of Virginia Press, 1998), 195.

Agriculture and Slavery in East Africa

Movement toward large-scale slave production also emerged along the Swahili Coast of East Africa. The various city-states along the Swahili coast had long been centers of production and international trade via the Indian Ocean. By the early 1700s, the Omani had imposed themselves on the region. In the second half of the 1700s, the governing Omani dynasty – the Busaids – encouraged migration from Oman to East Africa. In 1839, they moved their entire capital to Zanzibar and presided over a loosely knit commercial empire along the coast and into parts of the interior, through locally appointed governors. The Omani and Swahili were extensively involved in slave trading from the interior into Indian Ocean networks. Zanzibar was a commercial and trading center as early as the eighteenth century, but – and most important for our purposes – the Swahili and Omani political elite began to invest in clove production on the islands in the nineteenth century, first on Zanzibar and then on Pemba. Clove production was labor intensive. Land had to be cleared, trees planted, and the surrounding land continually weeded. Twice per year trees needed to be harvested. Rich merchant and political families also invested in large-scale farming of grains (mostly on the mainland), coconut, and sugar (that failed to fully develop as a cash crop). Slave labor made this new kind of production possible. Although slaves had long been used as domestic servants, concubines, and farmers, in the nineteenth century more slaves were acquired than ever before. They were used in a new way: as agricultural slaves producing commodities for local, regional, and international markets. By 1857, there were, conservatively, 200,000 slaves on Zanzibar Island alone, out of a total population of roughly 300,000. As international demand for these products grew, more slaves were transported from the interior to the coast, often along with ivory, which was sold into world markets. While this demand helped consolidate a dynamic commercial system along the coast, it brought violence and disorder to the interior regions that supplied the slaves and ivory. In some interior locations high-density slavery developed as well. As part of a flourishing slave and ivory trade along the Zambezi Valley, many women were retained and used for agricultural labor. In Shire Valley many slaves were likewise used to produce crops for big men and warlords. Thus, the emergence of plantation agriculture stimulated the rapid expansion of a very brutal slave trade that spread extensively into the interior. Interior peoples were hard-pressed to respond to this trade, and were subject to increased disorder and violence throughout the century.

How did this agricultural system work in practice? According to Cooper, on Zanzibar Island, there were a number of very large estates, but many more were medium or small-sized, often backed by credit from Indian merchants. Although Islamic inheritance patterns made large estates difficult to maintain, the richest and most powerful of the planters held together large estates throughout the nineteenth century. In the 1890s, for example, Sultan Seyyid Bargash owned numerous estates and 6,000 slaves.[52] Others owned as many as 1,000–2,000 slaves. Some of these large estates contained as many as 10,000 clove trees. The smaller estates averaged thirty to forty slaves, although some were small indeed, with only one or two slaves. As the century progressed, more plantation owners lived immediately on their estates for at least a period of time so that they could directly supervise their operations, instead of leaving the supervision in the hands of their trusted slaves. Estates also produced food crops to ensure subsistence even in bad years (when clove prices declined). On the mainland, estates produced mainly grain and coconuts. By the 1820s they had displaced small-scale family-organized labor with large-scale slave labor in places. The expansion of Indian Ocean commerce and the clove economy drove some of these changes. Slaves on the mainland supplied millet and sesame, for example, to Zanzibar Island as well as to states located throughout the Indian Ocean via dhows. When visiting Malindi, a central grain-producing region on the mainland, Fredric Holmwood observed "fine farms well stocked with slaves extending for miles in every direction."[53] These estates were more profitable than Zanzibar was, which by the middle of the nineteenth century suffered economic reversals when the price of cloves declined. Cooper suggests that in Malindi and Mambrui alone there were up to 10,000 slaves. There were a few large estates (1,000 acres or more) with large concentrations of slaves (200–300) and many more smaller estates (1–999 acres) with fewer slaves. The average size of an estate was nonetheless reasonably large, roughly 61 acres, but many slave owners owned more than one estate.

[52] See Frederick Cooper, *Plantation Slavery on the East Coast of Africa* (Portsmouth, NH: Heinemann, 1997), 68.
[53] Cited by Cooper, *Plantation Slavery*, 84.

By the nineteenth century, slaves were valued for their productive rather than domestic and social roles. Slaves worked longer and harder on estates throughout the year. The highest labor demands were often at harvest, and were subject to reasonably close supervision by other slaves and often their masters. Some crops required more work than others, but in all cases labor was more regimented and more closely supervised on estates compared to small household farms. This represented a dramatic shift for slave laborers. It is important, however, not to overstate the impact of these changes. Ideas about patron-client ties and Islam – and the social struggles of slaves themselves – encouraged integration and protected slaves from becoming nothing more than faceless units of production, as Cooper noted: "Slaves were still part of their master's following, and their presence was valued even when the income they generated fell."[54] The skills required for successfully harvesting cloves provided slaves with room to make demands about their work and personal lives. Slaves generally worked until midday, and often tilled their own plots of land where they produced food crops. Some slaves worked on their own and gave their masters a share of what they produced, although this only occurred in areas with the least well-developed estates. Masters did not simply accede to the demands of slaves because they were altruistic. Slaves struggled, fought, and resisted. Slaves drew on patron-client ideologies – which offered opportunities to negotiate terms of work or status – and demanded that masters acknowledge those values or face resistance. Thus, slaves fought for social inclusion using preexisting ideas about slavery and clientage. Masters often found it in their best interests to recognize those ideas in order to placate their slaves, which made their exploitation more efficient by making it more palatable. One European observer characterized the master-slave relationship as fundamentally paternalistic. Although nineteenth-century masters regularly punished their slaves and demanded production, they also acknowledged the limitations of their own coercive power:

> The masters, knowing the latent power they have to control, manage their slaves with great prudence and tact, and never have the least to fear of a servile revolt. The slave knows very well that there are certain orders that he must obey, and that he must do a certain amount of work for his master, but he knows equally well that the master dare not

[54] Cooper, *Plantation Slavery*, 149.

and would not transgress the understood privileges and acknowledged rights of their slaves.[55]

Even this kind of master-slave relationship was defined as much by conflict as it was by cooperation: slaves often ran away when faced with extreme situations. They also rebelled. These struggles were a central part of the history of the East African coast in the nineteenth century. Glassman has demonstrated that slave resistance and rebellion increased as the productive use of slaves increased. Why? Masters clearly demanded more labor from their slaves and were less willing to accede to their demands. Slaves who were faced with coercive masters and new labor regimes sometimes chose flight or outright rebellion. Clearly masters used the carrot as well as the stick, but overall, the nineteenth century was a bad time to be a slave in many parts of East Africa.

Although we have focused on three select regions during the nineteenth century, these were not the only places where the large-scale use of slaves in production emerged. In Central Africa, Lozi, Lunda, and Kazembe all used slaves in production, mostly as agricultural laborers. In West Africa, Yoruba warlords built towns and used slaves in agriculture throughout the nineteenth century. The Imerina on the island of Madagascar used slaves as labor on the vast irrigation projects that surrounded the capital. Although free people tended to do most of the actual rice farming, over time more slaves worked the fields to make up for the fact that free men performed military service. By the middle of the nineteenth century in Imerina, slaves made up almost half the population and were central to nearly every productive activity, from mining and smelting, to collecting firewood, to public works projects. In general, slaves were regularly used for economic purposes unrelated to agricultural production. The use of slaves as porters had long been common. In the nineteenth century, portage became even more economically important. In centers of slave production, slaves hauled many tons of commodities along trade routes to be eventually bought by merchants. Portage took a variety of forms, from hauling by foot to paddling canoes. The Bobangi, for example, developed a loose collection of competing commercial firms that came to dominate trade along the Zaire River. They used slave women as farmers and slave men as canoemen and traders. Slaves were collected in huge numbers and vastly outnumbered free persons. In this context, slave men had

[55] Cited by Cooper, *Plantation Slavery*, 169.

many opportunities for social mobility, and some even established their own trading firms independent of their master's control.

Conclusion: Free and Slave Labor in African Economies

By the end of the nineteenth century much had changed. Although states rose and fell, high-density slavery became increasingly widespread. Many states relied on the *economic* contributions of slaves, especially in agriculture, but also as weavers, salt and gold miners, and porters. Millions of Africans were held in bondage. In some places easily 35 percent of the population were enslaved. Many worked in the fields producing millet, sorghum, palm oil, cotton, or indigo for their owners, who might be merchants, rulers, or aristocrats. This transformed slavery. The way slaves worked changed; many more slaves worked in gangs and were closely supervised. Fewer slaves were freed. Integration and manumission still occurred, but it often took longer, and former slaves bore that stigma longer. Yet, slavery was complex. Slaves struggled and negotiated with their masters for rights, better work hours, protection from punishment, and families. In many places, slavery remained small-scale, less directly productive, and more open than closed. Even high-density slavery was variable. Agricultural slavery absorbed a significant number of slaves in some areas in some times, but in most places slaves were bound to their masters in smaller numbers. They lived in slave settlements rather than working on centrally managed plantations. These slaves might owe a portion of labor to their masters – sometimes as much as two-thirds – but were free of direct supervision and performed other nonagricultural tasks during the dry season. Indeed, broader paternalistic ideas about dependents, clients, and slaves were common throughout Africa and persisted over time. Slavery was exploitative, of course, but the views of masters were varied, and they often balanced absolute exploitation and coercion with subtler and less coercive means of extraction; indeed, the struggle of slaves against their own exploitation helped influence how high-density slavery operated. Thus, at one end of the continuum there were small numbers of slaves employed in a wide variety of tasks, living alongside their masters, producing enough for basic reproduction. At the other end of the continuum, there were large slave populations organized in concentrated productive units farming cereals, cotton, or other goods that were consumed internally and traded externally.

This chapter has tried to answer the question: how and why were slaves used in economically essential roles in Africa? The danger in the way I have approached the subject is that it might appear as if a singular "high-density" slave "system" replaced a singular "low-density" slave "system." Rather, my intention was to demonstrate that Africans often faced similar challenges: building states and economies in situations where labor was difficult to mobilize. Local and regional variations were substantial. This was a process. At some point human beings made the decisions. Sometimes, those decisions worked and sometimes they did not. Economic growth certainly occurred in precolonial Africa without the existence of slavery. The needs of local populations everywhere were met by their own labor. Slavery was but an option – one possible route – to mobilize labor. Yet slavery became an essential and productive institution throughout the continent. Relative land abundance compared to overall population was a key variable that led to the choice to use slaves. But politics mattered too. As states consolidated and developed hierarchies, prisoners of war – who were the by-products of state building – were made into slaves. Eventually they were used to produce commodities for exchange and to meet the consumptive needs of the elite. Merchants associated with these states likewise acquired slaves as workers. High-density slavery, in all of its manifestations, provided opportunities to rationalize labor, increase production, and accumulate private capital, which were otherwise difficult goals to accomplish in most African political economies.

Manning has argued that the reliance on slave labor was a "historical dead end" because it was "doomed to fail" from external pressures and internal resistance.[56] However much twenty-first-century historians and students might abhor slavery, what becomes clear after looking at the African evidence is that by the mid-nineteenth century, some Africans had created dynamic and profoundly exploitative economies based on slave labor. Nothing about their end was preordained. Slavery successfully intensified agricultural production in ways that would have been impossible for small-scale household farms. Yet, by 1936, slavery was mostly a memory. Given the scale and diversity of slavery across the continent, why did such an economically successful system come to an end? The next chapter addresses this fundamental social and economic transformation.

[56] Manning, *Slavery and African Life*, 146.

CHAPTER 6

The End of Slavery in Africa

Introduction

During 1903 and 1904, Salemi fled from the interior to the coast of Italian Somalia after a number of laws were passed by the colonial government that – at least in theory – abolished the institution of slavery. Salemi had, twenty years previously, been captured as a slave on the Mrima coast. He was then taken by traders to Merka, where he was sold to Sherif Omar, who kept him until 1896, when he was sent to Abiker bin Mire to pay off a debt. His new master worked him very hard in the fields, and even put him in leg irons. Salemi eventually escaped and fled to the coast.[1] Many other slaves also fled the plantation. Of Abiker bin Mire's original twenty working slaves, only eight remained by 1904.

★ ★ ★

> We never paid a *zakat*, partly because there were no cereals, but primarily because we did not own anything, we could not give anything because we had no ownership over anything at all. We could not even marry. After the arrival of the French, if we wanted to become independent we could try to pay a sum [*fansa*] to the master, and the master would have to free us. Money was rare, back then, so one would give animals. But

---

[1] See Lee V. Cassanelli, "The Ending of Slavery in Italian Somalia: Liberty and the Control of Labor" in Suzanne Miers and Richard Roberts (eds.), *The End of Slavery in Africa* (Madison: University of Wisconsin Press, 1988), 316–317.

176

before the French, ransom was not possible because we had nothing, we could not earn anything either.... Life was different, and a slave had no independence. A slave was like one of the animals of his master. He could not move without his master's agreement.... Now many old masters are not powerful anymore. The sources of their wealth were animals and milk, which allowed them to support their dependents. But now it's the time of money and *tuwo*. Now, the old masters are our younger brothers. We may even send each other reciprocal gifts to commemorate our past relation. Our old masters can remember about us and send us clothes or sugar. There is no more slavery. Thanks to the [whites], we have entered the market.... I have two arms. Give me one job, any job that I can do, and I will not look for the former masters again. And even if an old woman cannot work, she can still go to her relatives, rather than her masters, if they have a job and can support her.[2]

★ ★ ★

Slavery ended when the English arrived. The English were stronger than the slaves' masters; the masters had nothing to say against them.... But the fields were the property of the masters and the masters retained them; the slaves had nothing. The masters still reaped crops, but not as before, because now their own slaves had been let go and they had to hire workers.... The local people could get plots, but only with difficulty, as European-run plantations took up many hectares. For us individual cultivators the available land was just small plots, as you see it is until today. The fields had been taken by the Europeans for sisal planting, as for Europeans sisal was wealth.... The workers for these sisal fields came from the mainland: from Tunduru, Songea, and the Wamavia from Mozambique.[3]

★ ★ ★

In late 1913 – long after slavery had supposedly been abolished – Amadou Diop bought a boy for 400 francs. The boy (whose brother had also been sold) was forced to work for Diop, who when brought

---

[2] From an interview in Ader, Niger, with a descendant of slaves. Interview conducted by Benedetta Rossi; see Benedetta Rossi, "Without History? Interrogating 'Slave' Memories in Ader (Niger)" in Bellagamba, Greene, and Klein (eds.), *African Voices on Slavery and the Slave Trade*, 536–554.

[3] From an interview with Mzee Sefu in Mingoyo, Tanzania. Interview conducted by Felicitas Becker, "Common Themes, Individual Voices: Memories of Slavery around a Former Slave Plantation in Mingoyo, Tanzania" in Bellagamba, Greene, and Klein (eds.), *African Voices on Slavery*, 71–87.

to court admitted that he had enslaved the boy, but noted that this was
still common practice:

> Yes. I bought him from a Mauritanian during the winter of 1913. I paid
> 400 francs for him. The Mauritanian found me in Diadj. He spent a
> day in my concession and once we agreed on the price, I accompanied
> him to Same where he gave me the child. I bought that child to replace
> my son, who is a soldier. I know very well that I have done wrong and
> that the purchase of people is prohibited, but like everybody else does in
> Gandiolais, it did not bother me [to purchase the child].[4]

The demand for children as slaves was strong during this period: they
were easier to control and exchange. Eventually, a district tribunal
investigated the case, and the two boys were returned to their mother.
Diop, on the other hand, was sentenced to five years in prison.

★ ★ ★

By the end of the nineteenth century, millions of Africans were slaves.
Slavery was deeply embedded in African political, economic, and
social structures; indeed, Africans – more than ever before – depended
on slave labor. No one seriously questioned the legitimacy of slavery
as an institution. Yet, by the middle of the twentieth century, slavery
had largely disappeared. The legacies of slavery remained potent, and
individual slaves continued to work in some places, but slavery as an
institution, for the most part, ceased to exist. To understand this transformation, we must turn to the European conquest and occupation of
Africa. Colonial rule transformed how Africans governed themselves,
the kinds of economies they could develop, and the ways in which
they viewed labor, all of which led to the decline and end of slavery
in Africa.

The process was (yet again!) complex and contradictory, as this
chapter's introductory stories illustrate. Lovejoy has aptly called the
transition a "slow death" of slavery.[5] In most of Africa, slavery persisted for decades after the conquest. Colonialism introduced new
possibilities and problems for Africans. Masters and slaves often
looked to preserve or remake slavery in a time that was dominated

---

[4] Cited by Richard Roberts, "A Case of Kidnapping and Child Trafficking in Senegal,
1916" in Bellagamba, Greene, and Klein (eds.), *African Voices on Slavery*, 404–414.
[5] Paul E. Lovejoy and Jan S. Hogendorn, *Slow Death for Slavery: The Course of Abolition
in Northern Nigeria, 1897–1936* (Cambridge: Cambridge University Press, 1993).

by uncertainty. African slave owners, in particular, sought to preserve control over current and former slaves. Colonial governments
usually wanted to end the slave trade within Africa but hoped to
perpetuate unfree labor in their colonies when possible. But colonial
regimes also depended on European parliaments for their budgets.
In all countries – except maybe Portugal – abolitionist sentiment
constrained the colonial regimes' policy options. Thus, colonial officials on the ground often had to satisfy abolitionist sentiment at
home, while also (sometimes secretly) pursuing policies that allowed
slavery to persist or that sought to replace slavery with less coercive forms of labor mobilization. Many colonial states played what
W. G. Clarence-Smith has called a "double game": they created a
"facade of abolition" by passing laws that technically abolished slavery without, in practice, actually ending it.[6] In general, then, both
European officials and African slave owners perpetuated the structures of dependence. Yet, slavery gradually faded away. Why? In the
short term, the broader decline of the internal African slave trade
made the reproduction of indigenous slavery difficult. Over the long
term, the political economy of Africa changed. By the 1930s and
1940s, colonial legislation, new forms of labor mobilization, currencies, tax and land use policies, and the rapid growth of an export-
oriented, cash-crop sector led to the decline of slavery. Slaves and
ex-slaves increasingly moved into the wage labor sector. Colonial
policies and economic changes do not tell the whole story, however.
The end of slavery was also produced by slave resistance. Slaves fled
their masters or sought to renegotiate the terms of their bondage in
order to improve their living conditions and status. Such actions by
slaves demonstrate that, while many forms of African slavery theoretically encouraged the assimilation and incorporation of slaves, in
practice they largely failed to do so, or they set such profound limits
on slaves' rights that slaves took the opportunity brought by colonial
rule to successfully challenge and resist their exploitation in ways
that were often unexpected and surprising.

---

[6] See Kevin Grant, *A Civilised Savagery: Britain and the New Slaveries in Africa, 1884–
1926* (New York: Routledge, 2005), 114 and W. G. Clarence-Smith, *Slaves, Peasants,
and Capitalists in Southern Angola, 1840–1926* (Cambridge: Cambridge University
Press, 1979), 31.

The Colonial Conquest and African Slavery

Anti-slavery was one of the central justifications for European expansion in Africa. In 1890, as the occupation of Africa was under way, the major European governments signed the Brussels Conference Act, which committed them to ending the internal African slave trade and protecting fugitive and freed slaves. Although colonial governments never made a public commitment to end slavery as an institution, they tied their own expansion to anti-slavery ideology, expressed in a humanitarian language that garnered public approval and support. By 1903, the entire continent, with the exception of Liberia and Ethiopia, had been occupied. Despite the altruistic and paternalistic rhetoric, in the conquest period (peaking in the 1890s), Europeans relied on slavery to help make the colonial conquest possible. Colonial powers aimed to run their regimes as cheaply as possible, but they needed soldiers – labor – to fight and to occupy the parts of Africa they claimed. They often turned to African slaves, runaway slaves, or freed slaves. The use of former slaves and captured labor as soldiers, even if they were paid, was both cheap and effective.

Colonial powers used slaving strategies similar to those used in nineteenth-century African states: they sought to acquire dependent individuals on whose loyalty they could rely and who could help them build states – all in a context where labor (and loyalty) was hard to find. In most cases, African soldiers were used in areas that were very distant from their places of origin. In the minds of colonial officials, this practice ensured that the soldiers would feel no loyalty to those they were fighting, killing, raiding, or "policing." The use of slaves and ex-slaves in this way increased the violence inflicted on Africans. The soldiers of the Belgian colonial army or *Force Publique*, for example, had an especially well-deserved reputation for violence. They seized women, beat up civilians, and plundered homes with impunity. The Belgians were especially effective at making soldiers of the *Force Publique* – many of whom were slaves or ex-slaves – view themselves as fundamentally different from the population they terrorized; they were loyal only to each other. Although he was speaking about conditions in modern Zaire, Gen. Molongya Mayikusa's depiction of the nature of the *Force Publique* nicely describes the nature of the colonial army

> [that] used to resemble an army of mercenaries who lived removed from the population at large. This is reflected in the fact that the soldier

considered himself an elite, while viewing civilians as nothing but "savages." The soldier [was] a person without faith or soul, torturers of the civil population.... The antagonism was exploited to a point where the military and the civil populations, though united by blood, thoroughly and profoundly detested one another.[7]

The British, Germans, French, Belgians, and Portuguese relied on African soldiers to effect conquest. How were African soldiers acquired? Sometimes slaves were forced to join colonial armies. Some were simply bought on the open market or from their masters by Europeans and then made into soldiers. In many instances, slaves became colonial soldiers in the hope of improving their economic and social prospects. Indeed, they were generally freed after service. The success of colonial armies was partially a result of the decisions of former slaves, who looked to military service as a means to emancipate themselves; dependence was often a route to power in Africa. For slaves, joining colonial armies provided protections and opportunities otherwise unavailable. Thus, the use of acquired slaves as soldiers was widespread. When Frederick Lugard and the British East Africa Company invaded Buganda, for example, they used large numbers of slave soldiers who originated from the southern Sudan. Likewise, the British West African Frontier Force (WAFF) was composed of large numbers of slaves or former slaves, as were the French *tirailleurs* who conquered large parts of what became French West Africa. Similarly, what became the Congo Free State, King Leopold II's agents and officers "redeemed" slaves and conscripted them into the *Force Publique*. Although colonial officers claimed that they were in effect freeing slaves, redemption was simply a cloak used to hide the actual exchange of human beings. In practice, Belgian officials demanded that local chiefs send them conscripts. Chiefs often chose to offer up persons who were already slaves, although they provided free persons of especially low status as well. Finally, many *Force Publique* soldiers had simply been captured in the numerous colonial raids and warfare (in the Eastern Congo especially).

It was common practice to allow African soldiers to acquire slaves captured during military campaigns as a reward for their service and to maintain their loyalty. In other words, colonial armies lived off

---

[7] Mwelwa C. Musambachime, "Military Violence against Civilians: The Case of the Congolese and Zairean Military in the Pedicle 1890–1988" in *The International Journal of African Historical Studies* **23**, 4 (1990), 648–649.

plunder not much differently than precolonial armies did. Gaining access to female dependents as servants and wives was one of the central attractions of colonial military service for Africans. In Buganda, the slave soldiers who served the British controlled an average of eleven "followers," including female slaves and slave concubines.[8] During the conquest of Southern Nigeria, Hausa soldiers, many of whom were former slaves, did not just loot and seize property, but deliberately released Hausa slaves in the Yoruba towns they conquered or occupied. No doubt many retained female slaves for their own use as "wives." French military officers in West Africa regularly distributed female slaves to their soldiers, as well as to their African allies. In 1891, 3,000 such slaves were distributed to African soldiers by Colonel Louis Archinard. Likewise, in 1898–1899, a military expedition sent to occupy Chad spent most of its time enslaving women instead. Six hundred female slaves were then distributed to African soldiers, who only months before had been soldiers in the armies of African states, in order to "buy their loyalty."[9] The French often argued that they were doing these women a favor; in reality, they were making them into slave wives and domestic servants. For the women, such arrangements no doubt offered a degree of protection in a time of strife and violence. But they were not simply dependents. They were *slaves*, which reduced the rights, protections, and privileges they could claim in comparison to free wives. The use of female slaves by colonial armies was not limited to British and French Africa. African soldiers in the German colonial army, or *Schuztruppe*, in Tanganyika commonly possessed female slaves. Europeans everywhere also kept slaves themselves or simply sold them into the open market for profit. In 1894, *Commandant* F. Quiquandon, for example, owned 140 slaves he had captured in a raid. The scale of these slaving operations was large and involved considerable violence. During the capture of Sikasso in 1898, one witness noted that about 4,000 captives were first gathered, and then "[e]ach European received a woman of his choice.... All the *Tirailleurs* received at least three each."[10] In another case, also in French West Africa, an observer commented that African

---

[8] See Mark Leopold, "Legacies of Slavery in North-West Uganda: The Story of the 'One-Elevens' " in *Africa* **76**, 2 (2006), 186.

[9] J. Malcolm Thompson, "Colonial Policy and the Family Life of Black Troops in French West Africa, 1817–1904" in *The International Journal of African Historical Studies* **23**, 3 (1990), 439.

[10] Thompson, "Colonial Policy and the Family Life of Black Troops," 439.

soldiers returned "with their prisoners marching 40 kilometers a day. The children and those who are too tired are clubbed or bayonetted to death. One does not have time to concern one's self with whether they are free or not."[11]

Early Colonial Rule, Abolition, and Slave Labor

If colonial states relied on structures of slavery during conquest, their reliance on slave labor generally increased during the early colonial period, although the approaches taken by colonial powers differed. Colonial officials were a varied lot. In some cases – especially in parts of French West Africa – officials created the conditions for liberation via legislation, whereas the British, Portuguese, and Germans successfully squelched emancipationist impulses. Whatever the views of individual officials, most colonial governments soon passed legislation that affected slavery and the slave trade in Africa (for example: 1833 in South Africa, 1874 in the Gold Coast, 1897 in Zanzibar, 1900 in Uganda, 1901 in Nigeria, 1903–1905 in French West Africa, 1907 in coastal Kenya, and 1910 in Mozambique and the Congo). Most colonial powers focused on legislation that ended the internal slave trade, reduced the coercive power of the masters over their slaves, or abolished the "legal status" of slavery before the courts without immediately emancipating slaves. Initially, colonial states were weak. Colonial officials were faced with the reality of creating colonial administrative structures while having few resources at their disposal. Because no European governments wanted to expend substantial metropolitan capital in Africa, colonial officials needed to finance their administrations with whatever they could extract from Africans. Although they had access to the means of destruction, and a substantial technological advantage, they had too few colonial officers in the field and understood very little about the societies they had conquered. At conquest in 1903, for example, Lugard had 231 officers (few of whom spoke Hausa, the local language) to "administer" roughly 10 million Africans in Northern Nigeria alone. As a result, in the early phases of colonial rule, Europeans were dependent on African intermediaries (as clerks or interpreters, for example), African soldiers and police,

---

[11] Thompson, "Colonial Policy and the Family Life of Black Troops," 439.

and, most important, local ruling elites. All colonial states needed to work through Africans, although their methods differed.

The precarious nature of early colonial rule dramatically impacted slavery and abolition. Although every colonial power claimed to have abolished the internal African slave trade – and often claimed to have abolished slavery itself – colonial officials almost uniformly sought to maintain slavery or, at the very least, to limit the impact of abolition. As Jan-Georg Deutsch notes, "local administrative officers ignored the practices they were supposed to suppress, circumvented them, or neglected to inform slaves of their legal rights."[12] Most officials believed that slavery was necessary to maintain a ready supply of workers and to boost local productivity on which colonial states depended. Because colonial states generally needed cooperative relationships with African elites, many of whom owned substantial numbers of slaves, colonial officials hoped that by keeping slaves in place they would maintain important local alliances, which would have been at risk had African slave owners lost all their slaves. Until World War I (1914–1918), African slave owners and colonial officials essentially collaborated to maintain the institution of slavery in one form or another; in short, slavery was simply too essential to be immediately abolished in practice. When one French visitor to Dar al-Kuti suggested that emancipation be pursued, he was met with this response from al-Hajj Tukur, an important advisor to the sultan:

> What would you have us do without slaves? Where would you want the sultan to obtain porters necessary for your travels? Who would cultivate the fields? Look at our arms (and he showed me the thin arms of a Fulbe). Do you think they are strong enough to turn over the earth? Where would you have us find the cattle that your government requests if we had no slaves to give to the northern Arabs in exchange for their herds?[13]

Until World War I (and sometimes later), colonial governments were also unable to eradicate slave raiding and dealing. Men, but especially women and children, were bought and sold under the noses of

---

[12] Jan-Georg Deutsch, *Emancipation without Abolition in German East Africa, c.* 1884–1914 (Athens: Ohio University Press, 2006), 2.

[13] Cited by Dennis D. Cordell, "The Delicate Balance of Force and Flight: The End of Slavery in Eastern Ubangi-Shari" in Roberts and Miers (eds.), *The End of Slavery in Africa*, 160.

every colonial power. In short, the exchange of slaves often continued for a period of time, which further undermined early abolitionist policies. In Nigeria, for example, Hamman Yaji, Emir of Madagali, raided, killed, and enslaved thousands of people, which he carefully documented in his diaries, until he was arrested and deported in 1927. Thus, to reiterate, early colonial states were economically dependent on slavery in ways similar to precolonial African states. They sometimes used African labor directly. In other cases, they allowed Africans to use slave labor. In all cases, slave labor was an essential component in the development of many early colonial cash crops. Eventually, most colonial states sought to replace slave labor with other forms of usually coerced labor, although the extent to which that occurred varied over time and place.

In 1833–1834, the British abolished slavery in the Cape Colony of South Africa. However, abolition produced problems, not the least being that tens of thousands of free burgher settlers in the frontier regions of the Eastern Cape depended on slavery and resented any British intrusion into their management of labor. This resentment led to the migration of settler households out of Cape Colony and into the interior in what became known as the Great Trek. These *voortrekkers* did not just take their slaves and servants with them into the interior; they sought to acquire more slaves in the process. In the three central areas of the *voortrekker* settlement – Transvaal, Transorangia, and Natal – the *voortrekkers* raided surrounding African societies for slaves. Many slaves thus acquired were children whose parents had been killed by *voortrekker* guns. Although these slaves were often called "apprentices" – or sometimes *voortrekker* households claimed that they were simply caring for "orphans" – there was both an active slave trade and a substantial slave population in the region; indeed, these supposed "apprentices" were captured through violence and could be bought and sold like slaves. For example, in 1851, after the capture of two children, their mother

> came to Voussie, and begged for the children, and was refused them. She then begged to be allowed to serve along with them, and was permitted to do so. She soon afterwards ran away with them. After a time, Mr. Voussie met one of them in possession of a Boer in Albert district, and asked where he got it [her]. He said he had bought it [her] from Baillie. Voussie produced his title-deed [to the child], and recovered possession, and upon asking "Sara," how she came there, she stated that

she had been recaptured, and that her sister had been sold to a Boer in Aliwal.[14]

Although Afrikaners agreed to prohibit slavery and slave trading north of the Vaal River after the 1852 Sand River Convention, little changed. Like elsewhere in Africa, *voortrekkers* (by mid-century they were called Afrikaners) and the British recognized that the abolition of slavery in the interior was essentially unenforceable and in practice meaningless. As a result, thousands of slaves were captured and put to work. But what did these slaves do? The vast majority of enslaved children and women worked as domestics in Afrikaner households or as farmers and herders. Cash cropping in sugar cane, coffee, maize, wheat, tobacco, and cotton emerged in this period (especially in Western and Central Transvaal), so labor was in high demand. Although children were technically only in service (as "apprentices") until adulthood, very few were ever manumitted and were, in practice, treated like property, as one contemporary noted in 1859: "They will tell you that they are ... apprenticed till the period of manhood, when they are freed. Don't believe it. Unless they make a run for it ... they are slaves for life."[15]

In the British-controlled Cape, ex-slaves likewise had few options or economic resources. Many would soon, in the words of R. L. Watson, resume "their role as an exploited labor force."[16] Between 1834 and 1838, freed slaves worked as so-called apprentices and received no wages in a system that was virtually indistinguishable from the slave labor regime that dominated the region before abolition. Apprentices in the Cape could not leave their masters and could even be subject to sale via the sale of their contracts. Although former slaves challenged their masters when they broke laws that were supposed to protect them as apprentices, they were often ignored; indeed, the laws that protected ex-slaves were not normally enforced. After full emancipation in 1838, many slaves/apprentices left their former masters, especially in frontier regions, but few had the economic resources to sustain long-term independence. Cape farmers feared that the end

---

[14] Cited by Elizabeth A. Eldredge, "Slave Raiding across the Cape Frontier" in Elizabeth A. Eldredge and Fred Morton (eds.), *Slavery in South Africa: Captive Labor on the Dutch Frontier* (Boulder, CO: Westview, 1994), 120.

[15] Cited by Fred Morton, "Captive Labor in the Western Transvaal after the Sand River Convention" in Eldredge and Morton (eds.), *Slavery in South Africa*, 174.

[16] R. L. Watson, *Slave Emancipation and Racial Attitudes in Nineteenth-Century South Africa* (Cambridge: Cambridge University Press, 2012), 1.

of slavery would create a labor shortage. In response to fears about the danger of ex-slaves and the lack of labor, two master-and-servant ordinances were passed in the Cape. The 1841 ordinance effectively enhanced white control over black labor. The law levied criminal penalties for worker "misconduct" that included "refusals or neglect to perform work, negligent work, damage to master's property through negligence, violence, insolence, scandalous immorality, drunkenness, gross misconduct."[17] The punishments included periods of forced labor, imprisonment, or the docking of wages. The 1856 ordinance sought to control and discipline ex-slave labor by levying similar penalties. In the Cape, then, even after abolition, ex-slaves remained in highly coercive and dependent relationships with their masters, former masters, and employers.

Although the legal status of slavery was abolished in the Gold Coast in 1874, it took until 1908 for that policy to be extended to the Asante region of the interior. Colonial officials on the spot recognized that slavery was central to elite power and wealth in Asante. These officials were concerned that immediate emancipation would alienate the political elite and destroy local production and prosperity. Slave labor was, for example, more important than free labor in the planting of cocoa trees. Slave labor helped initiate the cash-crop revolution in the region between 1900 and 1916. Early pioneers of cocoa production used slave labor, the labor of pawns, and short-term free coerced labor. Kwame Dei, an early producer of cocoa, used slaves on his cocoa farm, for example. Austin notes that "it is reasonable to conclude that the speed and scale of the early growth of cocoa cultivation owed much to the inputs of coerced (slave, pawn, *corveé*) labour, supplementing self and free family labour."[18] Wage labor was not common in the period before World War I. The only way to expand production beyond the family was to use coerced labor, although over time the acquisition of slave labor became increasingly difficult.

French West Africa was more complicated. The French used slave labor as early as the 1880s. During the French invasion of the Western Sudan, Joseph Gallieni established so-called liberty villages that housed runaway slaves who seized the opportunity brought by

[17] Roberts Ross, "Emancipations and the Economy of the Cape Colony" in Michael Twaddle (ed.), *The Wages of Slavery: From Chattel Slavery to Wage Labour in Africa, the Caribbean and England* (London: Frank Cass, 1993), 142.

[18] Austin, *Land, Labour and Capital in Ghana*, 241.

French intervention to flee from their masters. A major goal of the French was not to provide succor to slaves, but to address the labor shortage they faced (and to encourage slave flight from their enemies). The "freed" slaves who inhabited these villages were used as a captive labor force. As soon as the French no longer needed their labor, they were returned to their masters. Throughout the 1890s French officials aimed to keep slaves in place to preserve craft and agricultural production. Many slaves continued to work producing cotton, sorghum, millet, or salt, among other things. But after 1900, when civilians took over much of the administration of the region, real attempts were made to reduce the sale and traffic of slaves, and fugitive slaves were no longer *supposed* to be returned to their masters, although the regulations were unevenly followed. Thus, civilian French officials – including Ernest Roume and William Merlaud-Ponty – sought to reduce the importance of slave labor in favor of other forms of labor mobilization, which undermined slavery between 1901 and 1914 (although their orders were often ignored by those who favored slavery on the ground). By 1908, wage labor and forced labor were much more common as a result. Yet, in places, the French still relied heavily on slaves as porters and to build railways into the interior, and slave labor remained essential to the production of groundnuts in parts of French West Africa until 1905.

Despite numerous anti-slavery decrees in German Cameroon, slavery remained an important productive institution during the first decades of colonial rule. Among the Douala, for example, commercial cocoa farming was initially dependent on slave labor, and slave prices rose as a result. Slaves were also used in palm oil cultivation. At the beginning of twentieth century, German colonial officials estimated that more than 400,000 slaves worked in German East Africa (Tanganyika). Slavery was not even legally abolished until 1922, when it was no longer German East Africa. German officials actually facilitated the buying and selling of slaves, and taxed many of the transactions to the benefit of colonial coffers. German officials believed that the best approach to sustain the colony was to allow slaves to continue working in the fields and thereby avoid a disruption in African agricultural production, focused especially on rice, sugar, and coconut. They were also concerned that the abolition of slavery would both wipe out the wealth of slave owners and reduce their own access to labor. A German colonial officer wrote: "[N]ow all major government projects are being carried out at the same time by slaves on the order of the *majumbe* (chief) and slave owners" because local chiefs had no power to compel free people to work.[19] Overtime, the growth of the colonial economy – especially wage labor – led by 1914 to a decline in the actual numbers of slaves from 400,000 to roughly 165,000 (using the numbers generated by colonial officials).

In Northern Nigeria, British officials – like the French – followed the path of "legal status" abolition. But the British officials were much more intent on limiting slave liberation. In 1901, the British issued a proclamation that ended the legal status of slavery. This abolition did not, however, free persons who were currently slaves; in short, all persons held in slavery before 1901 remained slaves. Slavery persisted in some regions until 1936, when it was finally and officially abolished. Certainly the *public* goal was to *eventually* eliminate slavery, but Lugard and his officials recognized that slavery needed to continue in one form or another for a long transitional period in order to ensure stability, the continued production of food and other commodities, as well as good relations with the elite. Otherwise, Lugard believed that the colony would be overwhelmed by social and economic disruptions:

> The wholesale repudiation of their obligation, to labour by the entire slave class would in the case of men, obviously produce in every great town a mass of unemployed vagrants and increase the criminal classes: in the case of women it would tend to increase prostitution: while both classes would beyond doubt bring upon themselves unforeseen misery by cancelling the obligation under which their masters lie of providing for them in sickness, or caring for their wives and children during absence from their homes.... The upper classes would be reduced to misery and starvation, and as a consequence to hostility against the Europeans who had brought this chaos about. The result would probably be a rising throughout the Protectorate, with which we do not have the Force to deal. Our ill-advised action would therefore possibly result in both ourselves and our supposed philanthropy being swept away.[20]

Slaves therefore continued to work throughout Northern Nigeria. Slave labor was central to the groundnut boom of 1912 and 1913–14. Although many free farmers produced groundnuts, the emir of Kano and other slave owners used slaves extensively on large landholdings to produce groundnuts for the external market. Emir Abbas, for

---

[19] Cited by Deutsch, *Emancipation without Abolition*, 151.
[20] Cited by Lovejoy and Hogendorn, *Slow Death for Slavery*, 81–82.

example, used a large number of slaves in groundnut production at his agricultural estates in Fanisau.[21] How did the British and slave owners keep slaves in place? The colonial state passed a vagrancy law to force slaves back to their masters and denied runaway slaves access to land through the codification of land tenure policies. Slaves who stayed in place had to pay their masters in kind, cash, or labor to even work on land owned by their masters. The British also encouraged a system of self-redemption that required slaves to pay their masters a fee before they were given their freedom. This effectively compensated masters for the loss of their capital investment and ensured that slaves remained in place for a substantial period. These British policies were nicely summed up by Charles Orr, who in 1911 argued that it was essential to deny slaves access to land until the slave "had contracted to purchase his freedom from his former master ... in order to prevent vagabondage and occupation of the land by hordes of masterless runaway slaves."[22] Many slaves were either returned to their masters when they fled or the British simply looked the other way when masters recaptured them.

Slavery remained the dominant mode of labor mobilization in Portuguese Africa until at least 1911 (and sometimes much later). The Portuguese either wanted slaves to remain working for their masters or to work for the colonial state. In theory, the 1899 labor code committed Portugal to suppressing slavery and advocated that Africans be "taught" how to benefit from free labor, which essentially served to benefit the colonial state. Slavery was not "legally" abolished until 1910. The reality of the transition from slave to free labor was considerably more complex. Over the colonial period, the Portuguese (and nearly every other colonial power) used forced labor extensively. We cannot always call this forced labor slavery. However, in the early colonial period, forced labor depended on persons of slave status. It was, in effect, an attempt to continue slavery by simply calling it something different: "contract labor." In Angola and Mozambique, Africans were required to sign labor contracts. Many so-called emancipated slaves were forced to sign five-year labor contracts with their "redeemers," which effectively bound "former" slaves directly to their "former" masters under the guise of a labor "contract." At expiration, the contracts were commonly and automatically "renewed" for another five years, without the knowledge or consent of the laborer. Slaves were

---

[21] See Mohammed Bashir Salau, *The West African Slave Plantation: A Case Study* (New York: Palgrave, 2011).

[22] Cited by Lovejoy and Hogendorn, *Slow Death for Slavery*, 87.

even exchanged (sold) via this system of redemption. Thus, slavery and the slave trade were perpetuated under the guise of free labor. In a report published in 1925 – long after slavery was supposedly abolished – Edward Ross recorded the comments of a group of villagers put to work by the Portuguese:

> They say that in the time of the [Portuguese] monarchy (before 1910), although they were slaves, they were better off and got more for their work. Their lot is getting harder. Things got abruptly worse for them in 1917–1918. The Government makes them work but gives them nothing. They return to find their fields neglected, no crops growing. They would rather be slaves than what they are now.... This Government serfdom is more heartless than the old domestic slavery, which was cruel only when the master was of cruel character. Now they are in the iron grasp of a system which makes no allowance for the circumstances of the individuals and ignores the fate of the families of the labor recruits.[23]

In the parts of Portuguese Africa where slavery was widespread, the precolonial slave labor system was the basis for the emergent forced labor system of the Portuguese. Dependents and former slaves became the backbone of Angola's colonial labor force, for example, to the benefit of both the colonial state and Ovimbundu big men. Africans in this region continued to use slaves as well. Local Ovimbundu leaders in the highlands of Angola deliberately sent their slaves to meet the quota of laborers that the Portuguese required of them. They continued to use slaves in agriculture to produce cash crops for the market. In 1913, one Ovimbundu leader possessed roughly 100 slaves who worked for him producing commodities. The high labor demands of both the Portuguese and Ovimbundu elite led some to outfit caravans to purchase slaves in the interior. In 1926, Willem Jaspert ran across a caravan that was still buying and selling slaves.[24] The Portuguese also sought to acquire slaves directly. Colonial officials traveled throughout (and sometimes beyond) their colonies to purchase slaves, who were then forced to sign labor contracts. For example, roughly 70,000 slaves were purchased in Angola and sent to São Tomé and Principe mainly to work on cocoa plantations. Although these contract laborers were *supposed* to be paid, they seldom were. Masters found ways to

---

[23] Eric Allina, *Slavery by Any Other Name: African Life under Company Rule in Colonial Mozambique* (Charlottesville: University of Virginia Press, 2012), 76.
[24] See Linda Heywood, *Contested Power in Angola, 1840's to Present* (Rochester, NY: University of Rochester Press, 2000), 44.

deny paying salaries. Sometimes masters imposed fines for bad behavior, or deducted money for periods of sickness. One observer noted that contract labor in São Tomé and Principe looked to him like slavery: "If this is not slavery, I know of no word in the English language which correctly characterizes it."[25]

Abolitionist Policies and African Slave Flight

Colonial officials and African slave owners ensured that slavery persisted well into the colonial period. There were major continuities between the precolonial and colonial periods. Slaves were widely used as workers and as soldiers throughout the continent during and after the colonial conquest. But slavery was also in flux. Colonial policies often had unintended consequences. Masters, slaves, peasants, settlers, artisans, and colonial officials themselves were faced with new *colonial* worlds that were filled with uncertainties and contradictions. Moreover, although many colonial policies served to reinforce slavery and dependency, others undermined slavery. Slave raiding and trading were increasingly restricted by colonial powers, as was the ability of African states to wage war. The reproduction of slavery *as an institution* became increasingly difficult. Many colonial powers also abolished the legal status of slavery. Although this was often window dressing – and many colonial powers sought to avoid implementing these policies in practice – legal status abolition meant that colonial states nonetheless intervened to reshape the relationship between master and slave. How? New colonial laws restricted the legal and coercive power that masters had over their slaves. In addition, legal status abolition meant that slavery did not exist before the law in courts, which undermined the power of masters. Although some colonial governments hoped that these policies would reshape slavery for the better, without fully destroying the institution, they sometimes led to the end of slavery. Other colonial officials hoped that their policies would lead to transformation of slavery into a different – although still coercive form – of labor, including contract labor. But most important, African slaves themselves took action against slavery. Slaves used the opportunities brought by the colonial conquest and legal status abolition to leave their masters. The decisions and actions of millions of African slaves

[25] Cited by Kevin Grant, *A Civilised Savagery*, 126.

mattered. In some times and places, the pressure placed on colonial powers and masters by slaves led to the end of slavery more completely and quickly than anyone had envisioned.

Scholars have debated the extent to which slave flight occurred in the context of colonial rule. Although we have observed how colonial powers delayed abolition and accepted slavery, they all eventually issued proclamations that impacted the legal status of the institution. How did slaves respond to these colonial policies? Some argue that most slaves stayed in place. For them, the colonial period was not terribly disruptive and slaves had few reasons to leave their masters. Slaves preferred to remain within dependent relationship that offered opportunities for assimilation. These scholars take at face value the erroneous colonial assessment that African slavery was benign and that African slaves were invariably well treated. Other scholars argue that the majority of slaves left their masters, which led to tremendous disruption. As Getz noted, by framing the question as a choice between two extremes, scholars have oversimplified the options available to slaves.[26] Certainly there was much to keep slaves in place. Sometimes homes were distant memories or far away (or both). Some slaves were loyal to their masters and hoped for rewards. Some slaves succumbed to social and community pressure to stay, or they judged that the risks of staying outweighed the risks (and unknowns) of leaving. Women often had a harder time than men did because it was harder for women to gain access to land and labor and because they were concerned about the fate of any children they might leave behind. But most important, while it is clear that in many places slaves stayed in place, in other places the reactions of slaves led to profound disruptions. Hundreds of thousands of slaves fled from slavery to make new homes and worlds for themselves, despite the obstacles they faced. Slaves fled throughout parts of British and French West Africa. In German East Africa many slaves had left their masters by 1914. Slaves fled in places as diverse as Sierra Leone, Italian Somalia, Sudan, Tanganyika, Kenya, and Zanzibar. Even the slaves who stayed seized on opportunities brought by colonial rule to renegotiate the terms of their bondage. The choice was not simply whether to stay or go; rather, the slaves who stayed did so *not* because African slavery was automatically assimilative and benign, but because this specific historical period provided slaves with many more opportunities to expand

---

[26] See Trevor Getz, *Slavery and Reform in West Africa*, 121–125.

their rights and to force masters to ameliorate slavery. Most slaves in Africa, then, experienced some kind of change in their status or position as a result of colonial policies.

Although slaves left everywhere, the scale of those departures varied quite substantially; there were regional differences in the scale of flight. In some places slavery was only gradually transformed. In others – often those with the most slave resistance – slavery ended more quickly and abruptly than could have ever been imagined by colonial officials or slave masters. Slaves had many reasons for leaving. But large-scale slave flight occurred most often in regions dominated by high-density slavery. First-generation slaves probably fled more often that those born into slavery. Slaves had the most to gain from flight when faced with highly commercialized slave systems that limited assimilation and that were highly exploitative. French West Africa is perhaps the best example of this unexpected movement from a gradualist to an immediate approach to abolition. French abolitionist policies led to widespread economic disruption and slave migration throughout their West African colonies. How? The *legal status* of slavery was officially abolished by the French on November 10, 1903. These instructions did not immediately end slavery; rather, slavery was no longer to be recognized before any court or tribunal. Other reforms followed that further limited the exchange of slaves and the practice of returning escaped slaves to their masters. In practice, the decree dramatically reduced the coercive power of masters over their slaves. They could no longer reclaim slaves, nor were their claims to slaves as property recognized in law. As Lovejoy and A.S. Kanya-Forstner note: "Henceforth, masters would be able to or reclaim their slaves only with the latters' consent or by force – and the use of force would leave the masters themselves liable to legal action."[27]

French officials were concerned that these policies – and any further moves toward abolition – risked leading to social and economic disruptions. They were correct. Many slaves began to leave their masters. Much of this slave flight was initially focused in the Banamba region of the Middle Niger, where slavery was a central economic institution, although slave flight had been a broader problem since the conquest in the 1890s. The slave population was concentrated in settlements

---

[27] Paul E. Lovejoy and A.S. Kanya-Forstner (eds.), *Slavery and Its Abolition in French West Africa: The Official Reports of G. Poulet, E. Roume, and G. Deherme* (Madison, WI: African Studies Program, 1994), 9.

that surrounded cities, where they produced goods for export. In the spring of 1905 thousands of slaves began to leave their masters. The French initially intervened to broker an agreement that promised to improve the living conditions of slaves in exchange for their return to their masters; the French did not want this exodus to gain momentum. For example, promises were made to allow slaves two days to cultivate their own farms, and masters proclaimed that they would not break up slave families. This agreement lasted less than one year. Masters continued to treat slaves quite poorly; indeed, before the exodus in 1904, one French official noted that

> slaves are poorly fed, mistreated, and poorly clothed. Masters rarely give them their two free days [which is theirs] by custom. They prefer to feed them poorly and to be assured of their labour all the time ... Moko Tala, a slave of Touba, belongs to a master who "generously" gives three *moules* of millet [about six kilograms] for the rations of twenty-five slaves. The *services administratifs* estimated that a daily ration is one kilogram [of cereal] per person per day. Another slave called Hinebahalafé Konati, also of Touba, told us that twenty slaves of his master were given four kilograms per day.[28]

The problem masters faced was that slaves had more options given the economic and political changes more or less accidently brought by the French. Thus, in 1906, the exodus of slaves began again. The French were basically powerless to stop slave migration. The exodus at Banamba soon spread throughout the Middle Niger and Western Sudan. According to French reports, by 1908, some 200,000 slaves had left. By 1911, that number climbed to 500,000. Klein estimates that one in every three slaves had left their masters.[29] For French West Africa as a whole, perhaps 1 million slaves left their masters in this period. Eventually, the French were left with no other option than to support the slave exodus and look for ways to minimize the disruption. In this case, it was the slaves themselves who made a more radical French abolitionist policy inevitable. To what did these slaves flee? Some returned to their places of origin and farmed. But many more took up positions in the new colonial economy – as construction or railway workers, for example. Still others entered the cash-cropping

---

[28] Cited by Richard Roberts and Martin A. Klein, "The Banamba Slave Exodus of 1905 and the Decline of Slavery in the Western Sudan" in *The Journal of African History* 21, 3 (1980), 390.

[29] Klein, *Slavery and Colonial Rule in French West Africa*, 173.

economy and produced peanuts as labor for others or on their own acquired land. Some took up weaving. Regardless, the importance of wide-scale slave labor in production for African slave owners was on the way out (in some places sooner than others): slaves could no longer be acquired, nor could slaves be subject to the necessary coercion. Yet, ex-slaves became a vital part of the new colonial economy, especially as workers and as farmers.

Although French West Africa probably experienced the largest number of slave departures, slaves everywhere sought to renegotiate the terms of their bondage in this period, which often involved some amount of slave flight. Slave labor gradually disappeared in German and British East Africa, for example. In some places colonial states managed to control the situation better. In Northern Nigeria, for example, the British were faced with problems similar to those the French faced. They too proclaimed that the legal status of slavery had been abolished, but nonetheless hoped to maintain slavery as an institution for as long as possible. Slaves still took advantages of the uncertainties of the conquest – and of British legal status abolition. In the early days of colonial rule, tens of thousands of slaves left their masters. Lovejoy estimates that 10 percent of the slave population fled – perhaps 200,000 slaves in all. Although the British desperately sought to keep slaves in place (and returned many fugitive slaves to their masters), they were, initially, unable to stem the tide. Large numbers of slaves (who had been central to the agricultural production of the Sokoto Caliphate) abandoned their master's farms. As late as 1907, British official Featherstone Cargill could comment: "The slaves are becoming more self-assertive and less willing to work for their masters. There is now practically nothing to prevent slaves asserting their freedom by the simple process of walking away from their masters."[30] Lugard outlined what the British faced, and their methods, in a 1902 report, which deserves to be quoted at length:

> On leaving Sokoto I had a very disagreeable task to perform. Hundreds of slaves had secretly crowded into our camp, hundreds more clambered over the walls to follow us, and no prohibition would stop them. Turned out of the line of march, they ran parallel to us through the fields, or ran on ahead. I had promised not to interfere with existing domestic slaves; I had no food for these crowds, and in front of us was a desert untraversed and unmapped, in which the infrequent wells were far apart, and

---

[30] Cited by Lovejoy and Hogendorn, *Slow Death for Slavery*, 47.

could only supply a vey limited amount of water. Moreover, this exodus of slaves would leave Sokoto ruined, and its social fabric a chaos. There was nothing to be done but send these poor wretches back, and instruct the Resident to enquire into all deserving cases. We did so, and presently found that the King of Gober [Gobir], who was following me with an army of 300 or 400 wild horsemen of the desert, had appropriated all he could catch. We made him disgorge them, and set them at liberty to return. Doubtless very many bolted to neighboring towns, but I considered my obligations of honour and of necessity were satisfied when I turned them out of my own following, and I did not enquire too curiously what became of them.[31]

Where did the 200,000 slaves go? Regions that had lost population in the precolonial period – often as a result of slave raiding, the British conquest, or famine – were repopulated by these fugitive slaves. Slaves sought to return home, where they established new farm and villages. In later periods ex-slaves took advantage of economic opportunities, especially in wage labor, that were brought by the British colonial state. In sum, although the British kept slaves in place through law, regulation, and force until 1936, the decisions slaves made nonetheless had a major impact on the formulation and exercise of British abolitionist policies.

Finally, we turn to three examples beyond West Africa: Italian Somalia, the Sudan, and British East Africa. In Italian Somalia, many ex-slaves joined agricultural settlements operated by Islamic orders to secure their freedom. In this region, 15,000–30,000 slaves sought to reduce their dependency on their masters or former masters. They did not want to work for European wages, but instead farmed on land provided by Islamic religious orders. So many slaves found alternatives that slave-based agriculture rapidly declined throughout the region. Flight to the protection of Islam (especially Sufi orders) was not unique to Italian Somalia. In the Senegambian region, for example, Amadu Bamba's Mourides attracted thousands of ex-slaves. They worked in agricultural settlements for the order – usually for eight or so years – and then were allowed to marry. Ex-slaves thereby acquired land, wives, and children. In the colonial Sudan, British officials believed that the immediate emancipation of slaves would lead to the creation of a population of landless, dangerous, criminal, and lazy ex-slaves whose freedom would lead to economic collapse. As

---

[31] Cited by Lovejoy and Hogendorn, *Slow Death for Slavery*, 45–46.

a result, British officials did their best to avoid the question of slavery whenever possible. Colonial land tenure and agricultural policies ensured that tens of thousands of slaves remained working for their masters, who produced cash crops for export (cotton) or consumption (sorghum, dates) that were in high demand. As they did in Northern Nigeria, colonial officials returned runaway slaves and passed vagrancy laws to keep slaves in place. Still, slaves continued to run away. Although Ahmad Sikainga is no doubt correct that most slaves stayed with their masters, the main path to freedom in the Sudan during the early colonial period was flight. The case of the Sudan demonstrates that even when a colonial state was quite successful at keeping slaves with their masters, flight became perhaps the best option for slaves seeking freedom or autonomy. In the areas of the Sudan where there was available land and potential for cultivation, many thousands of slaves ran away and established new villages and farms. Some also left for urban centers or to become soldiers. Slave flight also affected large parts of the East African coast. Here too scholars disagree about the numbers of slaves who fled. Regardless, evidence demonstrates that slave flight was a common response along the East African coast in the early colonial period. Fred Morton argues that this flight was not a new phenomenon; slaves had been fleeing to form their own communities throughout the nineteenth century.[32] In the 1890s, thousands left to work on the railroads or in urban areas and thus abandoned slave-based plantations and estates. Thousands more took advantage of colonial rule to run from their masters, despite the efforts of many British officials, both before and after slavery was legally abolished in 1907.

Abolition and Renegotiating Dependency

Although slave flight occurred regularly, many slaves stayed in place during the early colonial period. Slaves born into slavery, who often had more protections and opportunities than first-generation slaves, were the most likely to stay, whereas those first-generation slaves subject to the most direct and complete economic exploitation were the likeliest to flee. Fleeing meant risk. For many, old homes were too far

[32] Fred Morton, *Children of Ham: Freed Slaves and Fugitive Slaves on the Kenya Coast*, 1873–1907 (Boulder, CO: Westview Press, 1990).

away and economic opportunities too unlikely to make flight worth-while. Dependence and attachment via clientage and even slavery were, moreover, routes to power throughout the precolonial period. Remaining attached – and protected – as a dependent was often a bet-ter long-term option for slaves, as long as their rights and protections were acknowledged or expanded. Slaves who remained affiliated with their masters did not simply submit to the status quo. They sought to refashion the relationship between masters and slaves. In short, as with flight, the early colonial period offered slaves opportunities to reduce their exploitation, which in some cases led to the end of slavery as an institution. As legal status abolition took hold in many places – and as the internal slave trade declined – slaves who stayed often found themselves in better positions to negotiate with their masters than ever before. This was especially the case in places that experienced sub-stantial slave flight, because the slaves who remained were even more valuable to their masters.

What did negotiation look like in practice? Slaves normally sought protections for their marriages and families as well as more control over when and how they worked. In the Gold Coast Protectorate, legal status abolition occurred in 1874, which was so early that slaves had few opportunities in urban areas or in the wage labor sector. Although some slaves certainly fled, a significant number stayed in place and sought to renegotiate the terms of their dependency. In some cases, slaves cleared unoccupied land that they then worked for themselves on their own time and controlled what they produced. But it was much more common for slaves to retain ties to their masters. In the latter case, slaves were given land in close proximity to their master's holdings. In return they gave their masters service in the form of labor (or in later periods a portion of their crops) in a sharecropping-style arrangement.[33] The success of slaves varied over time and place, but in all cases the master-slave relationship was being reworked. Slaves had more control over their time, their farms, and their produce. But they were still dependents. Getz notes, for example, that slaves regularly gave gifts to their masters to confirm their lower and still dependent status.

[33] See Getz, *Slavery and Reform in West Africa*, 133–134 and Raymond Dumett and Marion Johnson, "Britain and the Suppression of Slavery in the Gold Coast Colony, Ashanti and the Northern Territories" in Roberts and Miers (eds.), *The End of Slavery in Africa*, 88–89.

In other cases, masters came out on top in the negotiation. In Northern Nigeria, for example, many of the slaves who stayed in place paid a sum known as *fansar kai* to their masters. These slaves worked for themselves for a portion of each week. Over time they accumulated cash through the sale of crops or via wage labor, and gave some of those proceeds to their masters. Once they paid the full *fansar kai* amount or price, they were freed, which was otherwise known as self-redemption. Colonial officials ruled that all slaves should have the option to redeem themselves whether or not their master agreed. These practices sometimes reduced the direct supervisory control of masters over slaves, and slaves gained more control over what they produced. But in the case of Northern Nigeria, the room for slave negotiation should not be overestimated. Self-redemption benefited masters (who were compensated for the loss of their capital assets by the slaves themselves) and the colonial state (which managed to keep many slaves in dependent relationships with their masters for a long period) more than it did the slaves. In cases when a slave refused to work for his or her master, they could lose their access to land, food, and clothing, for example. Masters retained substantial control over the work lives of their slaves. The colonial government and masters, for example, imposed the payment of *murgu* on slaves. In order to work on their own account – a necessity if slaves were to pay the redemption fee – slaves had to pay an annual fee in cash – *murgu* – to their masters for the right to do so. In other words, slaves had to pay for the right to pay for their own redemption. Thus, tens of thousands of slaves continued to farm for their masters during the wet season. During the dry season they sought work to meet the cash payments required by their masters, but were otherwise closely connected to their masters' farms and the agricultural cycle. Many slaves did not seek self-redemption but instead worked portions of their masters' farms in exchange for paying rent, often in kind.

Renegotiating dependency occurred outside West Africa as well. Along the Swahili Coast of East Africa, for example, British colonial officials abolished the legal status of slavery in Zanzibar in 1897 and in Kenya on the coast in 1907. On the islands especially, British officials sought to preserve as much of the power of slave and plantation owners as possible while keeping slaves in place. Although this process favored the interests of the colonial state and the masters, slaves used the changes brought by colonial rule to gain control over their work and family lives. On the islands of Zanzibar and Pemba, and on the Kenyan mainland, slaves successfully redefined their positions. Many sought inclusion and control by acquiring property, participating in social, religious, and community rituals from which they had been previously barred because of their slave status, or appropriating the dress of free people for themselves.[34] Slaves also renegotiated the terms of their work. In Zanzibar, some slaves reduced the number of days they worked for their masters from five to three and managed to reduce their labor requirements on the days that they did work for their masters. The results of these struggles varied: some slaves negotiated payments in kind or cash to their masters in lieu of labor; they farmed more or less for themselves. In 1902, for example, ex-slaves on Suliman bin Mbarak's estate made agreements to work three days per week for their ex-master in exchange for access to land and the right to work outside the plantation for wages on their off days. They were even paid for the cloves that they picked during harvest.[35] In other circumstances slaves became independent smallholders by clearing new and previously unused land for themselves. Cooper argues that slaves resisted the labor demands of plantation owners *and* the attempts of the colonial state to make them into landless wage laborers: "Ex-slaves did not merely resist two conceptions of labor which they regarded as oppressive. They used elements of each against the other: new kinds of jobs created by the colonial economy enabled ex-slaves to escape the plantation, while access to plantation land kept ex-slaves from becoming too dependent on those jobs."[36] Indeed, slaves often tried to work for more than one landholder or engaged in casual urban wage labor in an effort to reduce their dependence on a single person.

Slaves fought for these changes. Nonetheless, slaves faced persistent economic and social barriers. Access to land and control over work could be difficult to achieve, especially in the early colonial period. Many remained in dependent relationships with their former masters. Although slaves and ex-slaves farmed on their own accord, and often left if masters were stingy or cruel, masters retained the rights to the land they occupied and the crops they produced. The 1907 abolition of slavery in Kenya allowed masters to go to court to claim compensation if slaves left their estates or refused to work. Indeed, at

---

[34] See Laura Fair, "Dressing Up: Clothing, Class and Gender in Post-Abolition Zanzibar" in *The Journal of African History* **39**, 1 (1998), 63–94.

[35] Frederick Cooper, *From Slaves to Squatters: Plantation Labor and Agriculture in Zanzibar and Coastal Kenya, 1890–1925* (New Haven, CT: Yale University Press, 1980), 77.

[36] Cooper, *From Slaves to Squatters*, 4.

the beginning of the twentieth century, a number of ex-slaves cleared and farmed land north of Malindi. Thirteen years later a rich land-holder from the city arrived and demanded the slaves pay rent for the land they occupied. After the slaves refused, the landowner took the case to court and gained title to land and to the rent he demanded.[37] In Zanzibar, masters retained their rights to clove trees, which made it difficult for slaves to establish clove farms and enter the market them-selves. The East African plantation economy came under increasing stress and eventually disintegrated, first on the mainland and then on the islands, but struggles over access to land – as well as between mas-ter and slave – remained central and contentious issues well into the colonial period, which indicates just how intensely slaves and former slaves pursued their freedom and autonomy. We know less about what happened beyond the coast in the immediate East African interior. Nonetheless, it is clear that slaves were not used in production exten-sively and were fewer in number than on the coast. Miers argues that here the British essentially ignored the institution. It took at least a decade for slaves to learn that the British no longer returned runaway slaves to their masters.[38]

Slavery, Labor, and the Maturing Colonial Economy

If half-hearted abolitionist policies and the actions of slaves themselves helped transform and end slavery in Africa, so too did colonial eco-nomic change. Initially, it suited many European colonial officials to use African dependent labor. Slavery kept Africans working within a new colonial system and ensured collaborating African slave-owning elites remained loyal. New markets opened for cash crops (such as ground-nuts, cocoa, cotton, and rubber), which led to new opportunities for African workers. As colonial governments became more established, knowledgeable, and competent, they sometimes nudged the abolition of slavery along in the hopes of creating (in the minds of colonial offi-cials) a more disciplined and hardworking labor force that produced what the colonial officials wanted (although until World War II they did not want to make Africans into *workers* but simply wanted them

---

[37] Cooper, *From Slaves to Squatters*, 183.
[38] Suzanne Miers, "Slavery to Freedom in Sub-Saharan Africa: Expectations and Reality" in *Slavery and Abolition* 21, 2 (2000), 251.

to work more efficiently while retaining their rural homes, livelihoods, and identities). Coupled with the general decline of slave raiding and the end of warfare between African states, both of which produced the majority of slaves before conquest, wage labor, increasing urbanization, effective taxation, the introduction of new currencies, and the growth of cash cropping helped erode more completely the institution of slavery in the years between the two world wars. These changes shaped the end of slavery in Africa in three ways: they further transformed the relationship between master and slave, they undermined the basic economic structure of slavery, and they helped change colonial abolitionist and labor policies.

Wage labor and cash cropping provided slaves with more opportunities outside slavery. Fugitive slaves more easily found alternative means of economic support, while those slaves who stayed enhanced both independence from, and negotiating power with, their masters. How? Some ex-slaves acquired land themselves, where they farmed the cash crops demanded by the colonial economy. Thus, European demand for groundnuts, cocoa, and palm products offered some slaves economic alternatives. In the Yoruba region of Nigeria, for example, some ex-slaves eventually became cocoa farmers, as they did in parts of the Gold Coast and Asante, although this process did not really take off in the 1930s and remained tied to slave labor and sharecropping in many places. Slaves more commonly used the colonial demand for a variety of cash crops to gain access to cash. The rubber boom in Upper Guinée, for example, offered fugitive slaves a chance to sell rubber. By collecting and selling rubber between 1890 and 1913, slaves financed their mobility and resettlement; indeed, Emily Osborn argues that "the rubber market should be considered seriously as a force in changing the labor and social relations of the Soudan in the first decade of the twentieth century."[39] Likewise, Searing demonstrates that in the Wolof-dominated regions of what is now Senegal, cash cropping took off between 1890 to 1914, although it is also important to recognize that cash cropping began earlier. As free peasant household units increasingly became involved in the production of groundnuts, they sought access to labor beyond the family. Peasant farmers turned to runaways and ex-slaves (as well as to free migrants) as wage laborers to fill the increasing seasonal labor

---

[39] Emily Lynn Osborn, "'Rubber Fever', Commerce and French Colonial Rule in Upper Guinée, 1890–1913" in *The Journal of African History*, **45**, 3 (2004), 451–452.

demand, which helped propel the growth of cash cropping and at the same time facilitated the decline of slavery by providing economic opportunities to fleeing slaves and by undermining (and outperforming) production on large-scale slave-based estates. Former slaves held by the Soninke of the West African Savanna likewise traveled widely in search of land and labor opportunities in this region, although until World War I they often worked only temporarily before they returned home to live beside their former masters until the next growing season. One French officer observed that "the former slaves of the Sahel go down in groups into Senegal where they covered the surrounding of the new railway line ... with cultivated fields; once the growing season was over they regained their villages announcing their intention to return more numerous next year."[40]

The expansion of commodity production and the broader colonial economy did not just increase the demand for agricultural labor; it also led to new options in the service sector, including porters, canoemen, cooks, construction workers, and dock workers, among others, all of which provided new wage labor opportunities for slaves and ex-slaves. Slaves and ex-slaves rapidly moved into new economic niches brought by colonialism. Many supplied key commodities to Europeans, while others acted as interpreters, domestic help, or guards. Still others tried to acquire wealth through petty trade. Some ex-slaves joined Christian mission stations or churches, acquired an education, and moved into the skilled colonial wage labor sector. These migrations had an impact on the rural sector. In the Mauritanian Adrar, for example, nobles complained to the French in 1922 that slave women were leaving in large numbers for the city of Atar. Disputes over this issue continued well into the 1940s. Men too fled for the city. Agricultural production suffered as a result.[41] Likewise, by the 1920s in the vast region of Equatorial Africa, recently acquired slaves had moved out from under their masters' control into positions provided by the colonial government and economy.

Not all slaves benefited from colonial economic change, however. Although urban migration was quite common, some of these economic options were quite grim. Many slaves who could not acquire

[40] Quoted by François Manchuelle, "Slavery, Emancipation and Labour Migration in West Africa" in *The Journal of African History* **30**, 1 (1989), 99–100.

[41] See E. Ann McDougall, "A Topsy-Turvey World: Slaves and Freed Slaves in the Mauritanian Adrar, 1910–1950" in Miers and Roberts (eds.), *The End of Slavery in Africa*, 372–373.

land or farms became what Murray and Nwokeji call "rural refugees," who migrated to cities in search of a living.[42] Ex-slave migrants who became wage laborers in colonial cities often performed the most menial jobs. Some ex-slaves, for example, worked as prostitutes. In addition, slaves in some areas were far removed from centers of colonial economic growth and migration routes. They had no or little access to wage labor or cash cropping, which limited their ability to acquire enough economic or social capital to change their lives. These transformations – and access to opportunities – were not always about choice. Environmental changes – such as drought or famine – might push more ex-slaves into labor migration whether they wanted to or not. This in turn tightened the overall availability of wage labor for both free and ex-slave laborers and no doubt drove some ex-slaves into undesirable occupations. Likewise, economic busts, especially during the Great Depression of the 1930s, made life even harder for ex-slaves, many of whom were already living close to the margins, as wages and crop prices declined. In really bad times, even the masters who still owned slaves were sometimes forced by their tightened economic circumstances to let them go. For a long period of time, forced labor, wage labor, and even slave labor coexisted; economic change was not immediate, nor did it affect slavery everywhere. Nonetheless, by the interwar period, the major economic transformations brought by colonialism contributed to the gradual but continual decline of slavery, as well as to the reorientation of the dominant forms of labor mobilization in Africa.

Gender and Abolition

Gender played an important role in the abolition of slavery in Africa. Gender affected opportunities available to female slaves during the colonial period. They faced what scholars have labeled a "double burden": they were subordinated as women and as slaves.[43] Women slaves generally had less access than men did to the colonial economy. While male slaves might acquire land, profit from the sale of cash

[42] The phrase is Murray's, see C. Murray, "Struggle from the Margins: Rural Slums in the Orange Free State" in Fred Cooper (ed.), *Struggle for the City: Migrant Labour, Capital, and the State in Urban Africa* (Beverly Hills, CA: Sage, 1983), 227.

[43] See Miers and Roberts (eds.), *The End of Slavery in Africa*, 39 and Wright, *Strategies of Slaves and Women*, 1–45.

crops, and work for wages as porters, farmhands, or railway workers, women were generally shut out of these sectors. To be sure, women worked in fields, and were active in beer brewing and petty trade, and in places gained access to wage labor, but men tended to control land, highly paid wage labor, and the cash crops themselves. Although many women fled with men in groups, which gave them access to colonial economic opportunities, female slaves generally faced more difficulties leaving their masters independently and in becoming economically secure afterward. Of course, many women nonetheless fled. But in so doing they faced the reality that their families might be punished. They had to weigh the decision to flee against the possibility that their children might be sold or beaten as a result. In 1883, for example, one female slave in Senegal who had indeed fled her master stated: "I was a slave of Abdou Sarr, a farmer at N'Diebene. I escaped and received my freedom at Saint Louis. As soon as my flight was known my master in Kajoor sold my son ... in order to take revenge on me."[44]

The departure of male and female slaves further burdened free and slave women who stayed behind. The loss of so much labor meant that women took on larger labor responsibilities to make up the difference, which led to household instability. Free women sought divorces to protest their changed circumstances as slaves left in the face of their own rising workloads. Many colonial officials preferred to look the other way in cases involving female, household slaves. They usually considered female slaves to be part of the domestic unit – often as concubines – which colonial officials regarded as something akin to marriage. Female slaves continued to be exchanged and used as concubines for a substantial period of time. In Northern Nigeria there was a large clandestine trade in both women and children (often girls who were on their way to becoming concubines) until World War II. Indeed, even female children who were born after legal status abolition (1901) faced substantial risk in being forced into concubinage by free men. Free people considered these girls to have inherited their parent's servile status despite British proclamations otherwise.

On the other hand, some women stayed in place because they believed that their best opportunity to improve their position was by remaining within their masters' households. It is vital we do not ignore the sexual exploitation that occurred within these households. Slave women were regularly forced into sex and subjected to violence.

---

[44] James Searing, *"God Alone is King": Islam and Emancipation in Senegal: the Wolof Kingdoms of Kajour and Bawol, 1859–1914* (Portsmouth, NH: Heinemann, 2002), 177.

Many slave women, furthermore, worked in the fields, far away from their masters and had little ability to attach themselves to kinship and household units. Still, female slaves embedded in some households developed opportunities to use their positions as slave wives or concubines – and as mothers of their masters' (or their masters' sons or uncles, for example) children – to belong more fully to not just the household but to the dominant, free society as well. In many Islamic settings, the children of concubines and free men were free themselves. These children gained access to all the rights of free people, including inheritance. Slave mothers of free children were also afforded more security and were regarded as something closer to full members of the household. In Zanzibar, for example, Laura Fair notes that "it appears as though the power of women's fecundity to effect social mobility was widely recognized throughout Zanzibar society."[45] In non-Islamic settings, female slaves could also be integrated into households, and had significant opportunities to move toward the center of belonging, most especially via marriage and motherhood; female slaves were, in short, able to manipulate their masters' dependence on them as wives, nannies, wet-nurses, and domestics. Women in these positions no doubt saw their options in the colonial world differently than did men, boys, or unattached women and girls.

Freedom?

At the beginning of this book I argued that Africans understood and valued freedom. Africans sought membership in meaningful economic, family, religious, and political units. Membership offered protection, more autonomy, and control over work and family life. Slaves understood what freedom meant. In the words of Klein, "Some writers have questioned whether slaves understood the concept of Freedom. For the vast majority, freedom in whatever language they used meant in very concrete terms the right to work for themselves and control their family life."[46] Slaves also sought the honor that had been denied under slavery. Slaves sought honor to challenge their masters' social and ideological dominance. Slavery was fundamentally exploitative, but was also subject to continual negotiation between

---

[45] Fair, "Dressing Up," 89.
[46] Klein, *Slavery and Colonial Rule in French West Africa*, 177.

master and slaves. Long before the colonial period, slaves sought to expand their autonomy and to gain protection. This continued in the colonial period. Some slaves resisted their bondage by running away or rebelling. Others changed their names or bought and wore clothing that signified free status; indeed, some ex-slaves in Zanzibar even placed their deed of freedom in a small box hung around their necks like a necklace. Still others sought to better belong to the dominant society via marriage or service, or sought to enhance or protect their right to families (as husbands and wives, fathers and mothers, or sons and daughters), or better control over their time and labor as slaves. In the words of Jeremy Prestholdt, "What enslaved and freed people seemed to desire ... was to define their own place in the social order, to represent their own political and social interests, sometimes in contradiction and sometimes in accordance with the interests of their (ex-) owners."[47] Colonial rule offered slaves a broader range of opportunities than ever before: some chose to stay with their masters under adjusted work regimes, others fled to new farms, mission stations, or Islamic orders, and still others left to gain access to the new colonial economy as laborers or traders. Slaves knew what they were doing. Immediately after conquest in Kano, Nigeria, slaves clamored to touch the British flag because they believed it would set them free – and they sang the following song:

> A flag touching dance.
> Is performed by freeborns alone.
> Anybody who touches the flag,
> Becomes free.
> He and his father [master],
> Become equals.[48]

But it is important not to overstate the extent of slave mobility and autonomy in the colonial period. In the words of Miers, "[T]he expectations of the humanitarians and the general public in the mother countries that slavery would disappear with colonial rule had not been met in some areas as late as the 1930's and sometimes even later."[49] Moving out of slavery was seldom uncomplicated. Inequality persisted. Sometimes slaves accepted their master's hegemony and

[47] Jeremy Prestholdt, *Domesticating the World: African Consumerism and the Genealogies of Globalization* (Berkeley, CA: University of California Press, 2008), 135.
[48] Quoted by Lovejoy and Hogendorn, *Slow Death for Slavery*, 53.
[49] Miers, "Slavery to Freedom in Sub-Saharan Africa," 253.

acceded to their servile status. Everywhere both masters and colonial governments put up legal, administrative, and/or economic roadblocks to make the movement out of slavery difficult. Slaves often had to pay for their freedom. Many ex-slaves remained dependents for a generation or more; indeed, they were still embedded in power and economic relationships dominated by their former masters. Slaves of the Fulbe of the Savanna and Sahel zones of West Africa extracted rent from their (supposedly) ex-slaves until the end of the colonial rule, for example.

Ex-slaves likewise faced barriers that marginalized them. Access to land or high-wage occupations was difficult in places. In the case of Igboland, Nwokeji noted that "[e]ven after it abolished slavery, the colonial state ... could not alter the rural land tenure system that privileged certain groups with access to land on the basis of their charter status and continues to bind slave descendants as tenants, tributaries, or contract labourers of the freeborn."[50] Likewise, in Lasta (Northern Ethiopia), ex-slaves (who were only officially freed in 1935) remained in marginal economic and social positions. Until 1975, their inability to hold land – or gain access to capital – meant that ex-slaves became part of a poor rural population that depended on temporary wage labor to make ends meet, and lacked the security and self-sufficiency that came with land ownership.[51] In 1948, ex-slaves of the Tuareg of the Ahaggar (in the Sahara) earned two-fifths of the income of their former masters, and in Mauritania masters earned 60 percent more than their ex-slaves did and maintained control over land as well.[52] In other cases, slaves out-earned their masters but were still inhibited by the stigma of slave origins. Even in the case of low-density slavery – when most slaves sought to be absorbed into dominant kinship units – the stigma of servile origins lasted for generations and prevented many ex-slaves from acquiring the powers, obligations, and protections that came along with full membership and insider status.

More broadly, as they lost control over some of their slaves, masters became even more concerned about differentiating between

---

[50] G. Ugo Nwokeji, "The Slave Emancipation Problematic: Igbo Society and the Colonial Equation," 341.

[51] See James McCann, "'Children of the House': Slavery and Its Suppression in Lasta, Northern Ethiopia, 1916–1935" in Miers and Roberts (eds.), *The End of Slavery in Africa*, 354–355.

[52] John Iliffe, *The African Poor: A History* (Cambridge: Cambridge University Press, 1987), 144–145.

themselves and other freeborn (the honored) and slaves and ex-slaves (the dishonored), even if the economic bonds between master and slave had been broken. In the 1950s in a village in Gambia, David Ames recorded that

> Jam [slaves] are still expected to show deference in the presence of the free born. How-ever, some of them have taken advantage of the freedom given them by the British and as one elderly freeborn man put it, they throw their hats as far as they can. Jam still take off their shoes when greeting their masters and respectfully greet them as 'grandfathers'. Not all jam, of course, follow these patterns; some of them avoid such behaviour to the extent that they are permitted to do so by society.[53]

Some ex-slaves maintained deferential relations with former masters so in times of trouble they would at least have other economic options should their crops or wages not be enough. Roberts recorded an interview with a descendant of slave owners in the French Soudan, in which the master's paternalism cannot disguise the persistence of an unequal power relationship grounded in the necessity for the ex-slave to both honor and serve his former master:

> [A] type of kinship was substituted for slavery. But masters retained a certain superiority. The former slave, however, had the right to work for himself, but continued to render services to his former master. The former master remained his protector and the head of the family. He presided over marriages, baptisms and circumcisions of the children of former slaves. He called him his "son" and the former slave called him "father." Former slaves would never agree to their former masters carrying even the smallest load in their presence. Age meant nothing.[54]

Although colonialism brought some slaves opportunities, colonial rule was itself fundamentally exploitative. Early on, fugitive slaves were regularly returned to their masters; Lugard himself said: "[It was] lucky that nothing gets into the papers" because he was "up to all sorts of dodges ... for avoiding the slavery proclamations."[55] As time passed, colonial roadblocks to freedom became subtler. Ex-slaves not only faced increased taxation; they often had access to only the most difficult and menial jobs, which paid low wages. Many ex-slaves had

---

[53] Quoted by Martin Klein, "The Concept of Honour and the Persistence of Servility in the Western Soudan" in *Cahiers d'Études Africaines* **45**, 179/180 (2005), 835.

[54] Richard Roberts, "The End of Slavery in the French Soudan, 1905–1914" in Miers and Roberts (eds.), *The End of Slavery in Africa*, 295–296.

[55] Miers, Slavery to Freedom in Sub-Saharan Africa," 252.

little (or nothing) in the way of capital, and were especially vulnerable to fluctuations in the price of food and other essential commodities. Even ex-slaves who chose to farm cash crops made ends meet by
engaging in dry-season and temporary migrant labor (or by driving a
taxi in Dakar, for example). Some masters, on the other hand, became
more exploitative and cruel and used slave labor as best they could to
profit from the colonial economy. In short, for many the struggle out
of slavery took place over generations and, in general, did not put an
end to economic inequality.[56] Although by the end of World War II
slavery had largely died out, colonial governments had replaced slavery with other coercive measures and policies designed to mobilize
labor, ranging from land alienation, to forced labor, to compulsory
crop production in addition to wage labor. By 1945, colonial governments generally avoided using direct and violent coercion to acquire
labor, but they did not become overnight humanitarians. The end of
slavery in Africa is not the story of colonial progress; rather, colonial
governments continued to seek control over African bodies and labor
for their own purposes.

Did slavery end everywhere? No. Often, in lieu of slaves, masters and
others in need of labor turned to pawns and pawning, which increased
quite dramatically during periods of the twentieth century (and which
was sometimes simply a cloak that covered the actual exchange of
slaves) when access to currency or labor or was scarce, or when the
economy was in crisis. Although slavery was basically dead, in some
parts of the continent a clandestine trade in slaves persisted. Women
and children especially continued to be traded (even after World War
II, in parts of the continent). Likewise, servile status did not disappear completely. At the very least, slave descent continued to carry a
stigma. For some the stigma of slave descent affected their choice of a
potential marriage partner or their ability to inherit land and wealth.
In more extreme cases slavery simply continued; indeed, the fight for
liberation from slavery is a continuing one. It was only in July 1980, for
example, that Mauritania officially abolished slavery (and it was only
criminalized in 2007), which effectively demonstrates that servility in
some parts of Africa continued to persist long after colonial rule and
continues to be a political issue in Mauritania itself. The problems
associated with contemporary slavery in Africa are not restricted to
Mauritania. Forms of slavery continue to exist throughout the Sahara

---

[56] This is Martin Klein's phrase.

and Sahel. In Niger, for example, girls of slave descent are transferred via sale to men who use them as slave concubines and domestic labor. In Sudan, years of war led to the enslavement of Dinka women in large numbers. Anti-Slavery International managed to interview Ahok Ahok, for example, who explained how she had been enslaved:

> Our family was captured about six years ago [i.e., about 1994] when we were already fleeing north and had crossed into the North into Kordofan. I was captured with my son, Akai, and my two daughters, this one called Abuk ... who was about eight at the time, and a younger one, about two. We were taken by a tribe called Humr [i.e., Misseriya Humr], who split the three of us up. The man who took me subsequently sold me on to some other nomads to look after cattle, for about 130 Sudanese Pounds. I had to look after their cows and spent about six years with them before I managed to escape to Makaringa village.... Meanwhile, my three children had been taken away by others. For six years, until I reached Makaringa village, I had no news of them. When I reached the village, my son Akai heard where I was and joined me there. He is with us at this CEAWC centre. We then contacted the Dinka Committee and they were able to find my daughter Abuk, who had been renamed Khadija. She had initially been put to work looking after livestock, but had got into trouble when some animals had escaped – she was too little to look after them. After that, she was employed as a domestic servant. She hardly speaks any Dinka language now, only Arabic.... I still have no news of my youngest daughter and am still hoping to find her.[57]

Anti-slavery organizations have emerged in countries of the Sahel and Savanna to advocate for slaves and ex-slaves. *Timidria* in Niger and the Dinka Committee in Sudan both continue to fight against slavery. In the 1970s, former Mauritanian slaves created *El Hor* (Free Man) to fight against the oppression of slaves and former slaves in that nation. In the 1980s, *El Hor* brought cases to the courts on behalf of slaves in order to demonstrate that despite the abolition in 1980, discrimination remained all too common. A similar organization, *SOS-Esclaves*, emerged in 1995. It focused on assisting rural slaves and on developing international linkages.[58] *El Hor* and *SOS-Esclaves* – and those labeled slaves or of slave descent – continue to face many obstacles:

---

[57] Anti-Slavery International Report, *Is There Slavery in Sudan?* March 2001, 11.
[58] The local politics and history is too complicated to fully recount here; see E. Ann McDougall, "Living the Legacy of Slavery: Between Discourse and Reality" in *Cahiers d'Études Africaines* 45, 179/180 (2005), 957–986.

It is uphill work.... Some of their members have been imprisoned. Seeking help through the courts is usually useless. Shari'a courts maintain that slavery is legal. Since no laws have been passed, laying down penalties for enslavement or detailing the rights of slaves, other courts and local officials maintain that they have no jurisdiction if slaves bring cases for custody of their children or try to establish their right to remain on the land they farm. Former owners may also claim the property even of freed slaves when they die.[59]

Conclusion

Slavery as an institution disappeared only gradually throughout Africa. At the beginning of the nineteenth century, slavery was too important and widespread to be simply and neatly abolished. Many colonial states aimed to perpetuate slavery as long as possible; colonial officials continued to use slaves as soldiers, workers, or concubines, for example. Eventually, colonial policies gradually chipped away at the institution. By World War II, slavery in most parts of the continent had hit a reproductive dead end. Because new slaves could no longer be acquired through war, raids, or sale, slaves who had been manumitted, fled, or died could not be replaced. This, coupled with political and economic changes – as well as the decisions and actions of slaves themselves – led to the end of slavery in West, East, and Central Africa. Many slaves fled or sought to renegotiate the terms of their bondage. All sought the respectability and honor that had largely been denied them. The end of slavery in South Africa paralleled these broader processes. In the South African case, abolition did not end exploitative relationships between master and slave but recast them in ways that appeared more palatable to humanitarian interests while still securing the overall interests of masters. Eventually, the transition to paid farm and mining labor in the nineteenth century reduced the scale of slavery, but at the cost of the imposition of a harsh and relentless system of labor migrancy. What also changed were broader African ideas about labor. Ideas about wealth in people still mattered to a degree, but many more people were integrated into wage labor markets. Although slaves used the market to gain freedom and independence, wage labor

[59] Suzanne Miers, "Contemporary Forms of Slavery" in *Canadian Journal of African Studies* **34**, 3 (2000), 723.

and colonial capitalism ensured that the path out of slavery was difficult. Many ex-slaves moved into tenuous positions for low wages.
More broadly, abolition and emancipation opened the door for the
even more intensive exploitation of African workers by other means,
as Cooper notes: "Ultimately ... free labor implied the submission of
workers to a uniform code of laws, to the rigors of the market, and to
internalized discipline, in contrast to the person control and coercion
of the slavemaster."[60]

[60] Cooper, *Slaves to Squatters*, 2.

Conclusion

The struggles that slaves and the descendants of slaves continue to face in parts of contemporary Africa should serve as a reminder of just how common those struggles were in the African past. This book has examined different societies across what was – and is – a large and diverse continent. There were multiple African slaveries; indeed, I have repeatedly emphasized that forms of exploitation varied and that the opportunities for integration differed. But exploitation was always at the center of slavery. Masters and slaves repeatedly struggled – and sometimes came to negotiated agreements – about the way(s) slavery operated. More broadly, the consolidation of slavery was ultimately tied to specific political and economic strategies pursued by Africans. Attaching outsiders via slavery gave African slave owners access to the exploitable political, reproductive, social, and/or economic labor of *slave* dependents. How they were attached was dependent on the social structures of the societies using the slaves. At key moments in the African past, then, insiders built new forms of power, innovative states, or more productive economies by using outsiders as slaves. That is, some Africans used slavery to access and control fully exploitable dependents outside the normal ways (i.e., birth, marriage) dependents were acquired. This proved to be a huge advantage in local political struggles over belonging, power, and resources. As high-density slavery coalesced in parts of the continent, the integrative ideal sometimes present in low-density settings was transformed. Although emancipation and amelioration were always possible, the more commercialized and central the institution of slavery became, the more masters resisted the requests of slaves for protection, their claims to belong, and their desire for autonomy from slavery. The exploitation and exclusion of slaves were not static, nor were they endless, but slavery made possible some of the most important events in African history, from the emergence of big men in Central Africa and the consolidation of the Sokoto Caliphate to the expansion of ivory and clove production along the Swahili Coast and the construction of early colonial infrastructure across the continent, to provide but four examples. Indeed, the legacies of slavery and the various slave trades are many – and extend far beyond the African continent – but that is the subject for another book.

Index

Printed in the United States
By Bookmasters